MRS. THATCHER'S REVOLUTION

MRS. THATCHER'S REVOLUTION

The Ending of the Socialist Era

PETER JENKINS

HARVARD UNIVERSITY PRESS
Cambridge, Massachusetts

Excerpt from "Annus Mirabilis" from HIGH WINDOWS by Philip Larkin.
Copyright © 1974 by Philip Larkin. Reprinted by permission of
Farrar, Straus and Giroux, Inc.

Library of Congress Cataloging-in-Publication Data

Jenkins, Peter.
    Mrs. Thatcher's revolution : the ending of the socialist era /
    Peter Jenkins.
        p.   cm.
    Bibliography: p.
    Includes indexes.
    ISBN 0-674-58832-0 (alk. paper) (cloth)
    ISBN 0-674-58833-9 (paper)
    1. Thatcher, Margaret.   2. Great Britain—Politics and
    government—1979-   3. Socialism—Great Britain—History—20th
    century.   4. Conservatism—Great Britain—History—20th century.
    I. Title.
DA591.T47J46 1988   88-7231
941.085'8'0924—dc19   CIP

*To Polly, Amy,
Milly, Flora and
Nathaniel*

Contents

Illustrations

The author and publishers would like to thank the following for permission to reproduce photographs: Agence France Presse (no. 22); Associated Press (nos 28 and 30); Camera Press (nos 7, 10, 11, 18, 20 and 26); The *Independent* (no. 9, nos 19 (Brian Harris) and 31 (Jeremy Nicholl)); Popperfoto (nos 8, 14, 15, 16, 17, 24, 25, 27, 29, 32 and 33); The Press Association (nos 6, 12 and 21); and Syndication International (nos 1, 2, 3, 4, 5, 13 and 23).

Introduction to
the American Edition

Seldom has the leader of another nation been as widely acclaimed in the United States as Margaret Thatcher. Not that she is without honour in her own country – far from it – but although respected, and twice re-elected, she has not been the best loved of British prime ministers. Her popularity among her own people does not compare with Ronald Reagan's popularity with Americans, even after the failures and disgraces of his second term. No one since Winston Churchill between the wars has aroused such strong passions as Thatcher. Adored by some sections of the population, she is detested by others, who spit with hatred the very name 'Thatcher'. These strong feelings cut somewhat across conventional party lines: through patriotic and populist appeals she has won the support, even the adulation, of many working people, while on the aristocratic wing of her own party, within what used to be the Establishment, she is widely regarded with misgiving or snobbish disdain. As for the liberal intelligentsia, they loathe her.

Americans took to Mrs Thatcher before the British did. Shortly after she replaced Edward Heath as leader of the Conservative Party in 1975, she visited the United States, stopping in New York, Chicago – for her the Mecca of monetarism – and Washington. On that trip she made her debut as a star of the early morning network shows, and in Washington she captivated the National Press Club. Partly this was because of her novelty value as a woman, the first ever to aspire to be Britain's Prime Minister, although she brusquely rejected all feminist blandishments. Also her anti-socialism was music to the ears of most Americans, although it got her into trouble at home, where a Labour government was in power. The custom was to refrain from partisan politics when overseas. Eric Sevareid told CBS viewers that Harold Wilson, then Prime Minister, was 'the passing figure and she the arriving one'. He proved to be correct, but that was not how she was generally seen in Britain at the time. The columnist George Will was closer to the mark when, after her election in 1979, he compared the bewilderment and shock of many of the British to the reaction of Americans to Barry Goldwater's capture of the Republican nomination at San Francisco in 1964.[1]

In the period between May 1979, when she became Prime Minister, and January 1981, when Ronald Reagan was inaugurated, the tide in the United States was flowing towards the Conservative right. Britain was of special interest to American commentators as a laboratory for a monetarist experiment. Thatcherism was seen as a rehearsal for Reaganism. But already in 1981 some of the New Right commentators, who earlier had held her up as an example, were presenting her as a cautionary tale. According to George Gilder, for example, she had 'failed to combine her reduction in basic monetary growth rates with a reduction in government taxing and spending'.[2]

The truth was that she had never been a supply-sider, and it is this more than anything else that sets Thatcherism apart from Reaganomics. She remained an old-fashioned fiscal conservative. A tax-cutter, yes, for cutting taxes was a way to sharpen the incentives to enterprise, but she never came to believe, with the supply-siders around Ronald Reagan, that tax cuts themselves would increase revenue to cover borrowing. Reaganomics was a magic formula by which inflation would be conquered, taxes cut, and the defence budget massively increased all at the same time. For her, monetarism was closer to good housekeeping, or storekeeping; for governments it meant not printing more money, in exactly the same way that a housewife should spend no more money than is coming in. 'We don't have to choose between inflation and unemployment – they go hand in hand', declared Reagan in 1981. In her seminal budget of that year Margaret Thatcher chose fiscal rectitude, and throughout her first term rising unemployment was one of the hallmarks of Thatcherism.

There are other differences too between the style we call Thatcherism and the politics of Ronald Reagan. The Moral Majority, that unappetising brew of ultra-patriotism and social puritanism, fermented by religious fundamentalism, does not exist in Britain. Margaret Thatcher seldom mentions God and has no political need to do so. She supported the legalisation of abortion in 1967 and has not bowed since to the anti-abortion lobby. Ronald Reagan may have kept the Moral Majority at bay, but it was a part of his constituency nonetheless. The first non-governmental group to receive an audience in the Reagan White House in 1981 was the March for Life.[3]

All the same, there are striking similarities between Thatcherism and Reaganism, and between Ronald Reagan and Margaret Thatcher. Both are of humble origin, almost mandatory for an American president but rare in the case of the leader of the British Conservative Party. Both were born above a small-town store, although her father owned his store. As politicians, both played the outsider role, he not belonging to the Eastern Establishment which mostly dominated Washington and she not belonging to the charmed upper crust which dominated the Conservative Party. Each came to office possessed of a vision, he of a golden age restored and she of an American Dream come true in Britain. Each, by the same token, believed it their mission to arrest and reverse a process of national decline. The Reaganites spoke of a 'Reagan Revolution', or, as their opponents saw it – a counter-revolution, an attempt to repeal the New Deal.[4] She was no less explicit in her ambition to roll back the tide of socialism and put an end to what she called 'consensus politics', which, she claimed, had governed Britain since the election of a Labour government in 1945. She shared with Reagan a belief in the efficacy of market economics, scarcely remarkable in an American politician and certainly not in a Republican, but somewhat more novel in a British leader, even a Conservative. For in Britain the neo-Keynesian consensus has been far more pervasive. Both leaders were pledged to cut government expenditure, but not on defence. She vied with him as a gut anti-Communist and earned herself in Moscow the soubriquet 'Iron Lady' – in which she reveled – before Reagan inveighed against the 'evil empire'. Both were novices in foreign affairs, and both were gut nationalists. They were also populists, mixing patriotism and pocket-book economics to appeal to blue-collar workers. Both won election by making major inroads into the traditional coalitions of their opponents.

A theme of this book is that the Thatcher Revolution was as much the product of her times as the shaper of them. I describe how and why the collapse of the old political order brought her to power and enabled her to practice her brand of right-wing 'conviction politics'. In this she also resembles Ronald Reagan, the twice-rejected conservative (1968 and 1976) and belated heir to the Goldwater coup of 1964. For at first Reagan, like Thatcher, was seen as something of an aberration, brought to power through the default of opponents. Neither his sweeping victory in 1980 nor hers the previous year was

immediately seen as a 'watershed', or critical elections like those of
1932 in the United States and 1945 in Britain, events which resulted
in profound and lasting changes in the political landscape. The
subsequent course of British politics seems to confirm that in Britain
1979 was such a watershed year. Whether the same is true of 1980 in
the United States remains to be seen. The most general opinion
seems to be that there has been dealignment rather than realignment, and this could turn out to be true in Britain also, although after
three elections the defection to the Conservatives of a substantial
part of the working-class vote looks to be hardening into a habit.

In Britain the decline of the Labour Party as an electoral force
invites comparison with the plight of the Democratic Party. They
are, of course, very different political creatures inhabiting quite
different cultures. Nevertheless, almost everywhere – West Germany is another striking case – parties of the left appear to be
increasingly unable to reconcile the wishes of the special interests to
which they are prey and those of their own activists with the preferences of the electorate at large. This causes them to alienate even
many of their own traditional supporters.

In the case of both the Democrats and Labour, this drawing apart
of party and people was exacerbated by changes in rules and procedures. In the American case the McGovern reforms of 1972 had the
effect of enfranchising party activists at the expense of the party
bosses and their proverbial smoke-filled rooms. In Britain the so-
called democratisation of the Labour Party took the form of remov-
ing power from the parliamentarians and conferring it upon the party
in the country. Members of Parliament were made liable to mandatory re-selection by party activists in their constituencies. The
leader (who is, in effect, the candidate for Prime Minister), instead
of being elected exclusively by MPs, henceforth was to be chosen in
an Electoral College in which the trade unions held 40 per cent of the
votes, constituency activists 30 per cent, and MPs only 30 per cent.

As the party became more responsive to its activists, for example
adopting policies such as unilateral nuclear disarmament, it made
itself more repulsive to the electorate. The consequence was comparable to that of the excesses of anti-war politics in the McGovern
period. In the United States the proliferation of primaries, and the
rules concerning delegates to the Democratic Party convention, has
meant that the credentials of a candidate for nomination are likely to
be in inverse proportion to his qualifications for winning a presidential election and for governing thereafter. In Britain the Labour
Party is similarly tugged between the vested interests of the trade

unions and the middle-class radicalism of party activists; the preferences of these groups not only conflict but are unattractive to the electorate in equal degree.

The Mondale campaign of 1984 has been described as 'interest-group liberalism in its worst possible incarnation – serving the lobbies without rousing the voters'.[5] The words would do as well for the Labour Party. At Britain's 1979 election, law and order and educational standards had become more salient issues. In much the same way as Richard Scammon and Ben Wattenberg's 'social issue',[6] these concerns helped to drive former Labour voters into the arms of Mrs Thatcher. When sections of the Labour Party later took up sexual politics, championing gay and lesbian rights, traditional working-class supporters became still more alienated. The shrill anti-racism of the left in Britain has had the same effect in driving away blue-collar workers as black caucus policies have had in disaffecting white Democrats, especially in the South.

As the Democrats have suffered disproportionately from the decline of partisanship and the weakening of party, so has the Labour Party. Some of the reasons are similar. Media influence has contributed to more volatile, issue-oriented voting behaviour. However, candidates play a less important role in British campaigns, where party is still the crucial factor. Single issues also play a relatively small role. We have no PACs, and campaign finances and political broadcasting are strictly limited. Demographic and socio-economic factors have played a larger part in the erosion of party allegiances in Britain than seems to be the case in the United States.[7] In Britain there has been a marked decline in size of the working class and, more controversially, of class voting in a country where politics has been predominantly class-based. The disintegration of the old Roosevelt coalition is an important aspect of the decline of the Democrats as a presidential party. As William Schneider put it, contrasting the vote for Adlai Stevenson in 1956 and for Walter Mondale in 1984: 'Both got about the same share of the popular vote . . . But the nature of their support was very different. Mondale did significantly better than Stevenson among black voters, college graduates, women and professionals. On the other hand, Stevenson's support was much stronger among whites, Southerners, blue collar workers, union members and Catholics.'[8] Mrs Thatcher's new majority – or, to be accurate, her new plurality – in 1979 was founded on an unprecedented level of support among blue-collar workers and trade union members.

The Labour Party and the Democrats today are both victims of political geography. Britain is increasingly polarised between north and south, city and suburb, town and country, with the weight of the population increasingly concentrated in the south and moving away from the cities. The result is that Labour piles up useless votes in its mostly northern class strongholds while the Conservatives hold sway across the bulk of the country. The arithmetic of the Electoral College is similarily hostile to the Democrats, especially as a result of the continuing defection of the white South.[9]

It is often said in Britain that we are moving towards a more presidential style of government. That may be true with regard to the imperiousness of the Prime Minister (not only Mrs Thatcher) and the use of modern media techniques for promoting party leaders. Moreover, there is more superficially American razzmatazz at election times than there used to be. But the purpose of a General Election in Britain is to elect a House of Commons; whoever leads the largest party becomes Prime Minister. As partisanship declines, voters may identify more with the party leader than with the party, but come election day, the voter has no choice but to make a party choice. There is no way to split a ticket, no way to elect one party to a majority in the legislature and the leader of another to head the government. The American voter can choose a president from one party while, ostensibly, maintaining his traditional allegiance to the other.

For all that, I am tempted by the theory that in spite of differences in political systems and traditions, voters in advanced democratic societies behave rather similarly. Inside the British voter there is a ticket-splitter trying to get out. The nearest equivalent phenomenon in Britain is the growth of electoral support for third-party politics. In 1951 the two major parties in Britain monopolised 96.8 per cent of the votes cast, by 1983 this monopoly was down to 72 per cent, and in 1987 it recovered only to 75 per cent.

Mrs Thatcher and Thatcherism, and the decline of Labour and the tendencies towards a realignment of party politics are two themes of my book; a third is Britain's decline. That too may have a topical resonance for American readers. Mrs Thatcher came to power pledged to arrest and reverse the long downward trend of the British economy relative to others, and by 1987 she could lay claim to having succeeded at least in arresting the trend, although how permanently is a question I discuss. For decline is a matter not simply of relative economic performance but also of the longer-term determinants of future performance. The literature on the British case, now voluminous, has increasingly discovered the roots of Britain's malperformance in cultural factors or structural deficiencies which have their origin in Victorian times. One of the chief culprits has been the neglect of education, especially technical education, from the mid-nineteenth century onwards.

In the present case of the United States, the resilience and adaptability of its vast continental economy has been so prodigious that it is difficult to take altogether seriously the latest cries of gloom and doom. However, Paul Kennedy in an influential book has shown how even the mightiest empires can fall when their economic resources prove inadequate to the military demands upon them.[10] Meanwhile, that most prolific of prophets, Felix Rohatyn, warns that the United States already has lost its independence, has become 'a first-rate military power and a second-rate economic power'.[11] Strategic overextension was an important cause of Britain's long decline, as it was of Rome's downfall. There is also, perhaps, some analogy between the industrial and technological challenge which Britain, then the predominant industrialised nation, faced towards the end of the nineteenth century from the United States and the nascent economies of Germany and France and the challenge which the United States faces today from Japan and the economies of the Pacific Basin. Moreover, some of the symptoms of the 'British sickness' are today part of the American condition: low investment, technological lag, educational neglect, and possibly some waning of the spirit of enterprise, all adding up to uncompetitiveness. But in Britain's case, remember, an economy utterly dependent upon international trade and with a small, though ravenous, domestic market was required to adapt over a short period to a major transformation in the global economy. In the process Britain disposed of an empire and saw her overseas assets wiped out by war. The task facing the United States in adjusting to a relative decline in power and wealth strikes me as in no way so severe.

The organisation of this book may require a word of explanation to readers not wholly familiar with the course of post-war history in Britain. My story ostensibly begins in 1979 with the advent of Margaret Thatcher as the first Prime Minister in the post-war period determined not merely to postpone the march of collectivism but to drive it into permanent retreat. However, in order to explore the roots of what I present as the end of the *ancien régime* in 1979, it is necessary to look back as far as 1945, when the first majority Labour government came to power and laid the foundations for the new age of Keynesian economic management and welfare. Indeed, when I come to the politics of decline (in Chapter 2) it is necessary, as I have already mentioned, to track back as far as the Industrial Revolution in the nineteenth century. In this way I have treated the narrative thread of my account of the Thatcher years rather in the manner of a clothesline on which to hang laundry as it comes to hand. For example, the moment of her election in 1979 seemed the appropriate point to discuss electoral trends over the previous decade and more (Chapter 5). And the moment of schism in the Labour Party in 1981, with the breakaway of the Social Democrats (Chapter 4), seemed the place to chart the capture of the Labour Party by its activists, which had begun as early as 1973, and (in Chapter 5) the rise of third-party politics during the 1970s. These chapters may help to clear up perplexities remaining from the earlier ones. Gradually, I hope, everything will fall into place.

There is scarcely a mention of foreign policy, of Anglo-American relations, or of Margaret Thatcher's 'personal relationship' with Ronald Reagan (or her remarkable empathy with Mikhail Gorbachev) until (in Chapter 12) I reach the point in 1986 at which the nuclear issue came to a head in British politics. Then it blew apart the alliance between the Liberals and the SDP and severely damaged any chance Labour might have had of winning the 1987 General Election, while Neil Kinnock adhered to his position of unilateral nuclear disarmament.

Some American readers may be puzzled at the omission of Ireland, apart from a passing mention. That is not because Ireland is unimportant or uninteresting, but because it is peripheral to the story of Mrs Thatcher's Revolution. It is part of the tragedy of the Irish Question to be of no relevance to anything happening anywhere else in the world save, possibly, the techniques of counter-terrorism. It throws no light on any of the themes of this book.

Since the publication of this book in Britain, nothing has happened to cause me to revise my assessments of the Thatcher era. If the world is sucked into recession as a result of the market crash of October 1987, the British economy will be sucked down with it. That would be bad luck and, depending on its severity and duration, a recession could affect the outcome of a General Election in 1991 or 1992. Nevertheless, since September 1986 the fundamentals of the British economy have, if anything, grown stronger. This supports my tentative view that Britain's decline has been temporarily arrested, although I doubt permanently reversed.

The further disintegration of the political centre has reinforced my conclusion that if anyone is the realigner of British party politics it is Mrs Thatcher. There are now two centre parties in the field, a merged party of Liberals and Social Democrats calling itself the Social and Liberal Democrat Party and a rump of the SDP loyal to Dr David Owen. Under the iron law of the British winner-take-all electoral system, this can only damage the prospects for a third party and further postpone any remaining possibility of a realignment on the centre-left. So far, the beneficiary has not been Labour, as the only credible alternative to Mrs Thatcher, but Mrs Thatcher herself.

Meanwhile, she has pressed ahead with the third phase of her revolution, meeting – as in her second term of office – a good deal of opposition from within her own party. The crisis in the National Health Service, which was an issue in the 1987 campaign, came quickly to the fore once more. As a result she was obliged to add the NHS, the last remaining pillar of the Post-War Settlement, to her agenda for radical reform, although how radical remains to be seen. The National Health Service remains a popular institution in Britain, supported by all classes. Behind her rhetoric Mrs Thatcher is a shrewd and, often, a cautious politician.

At the beginning of 1988 she became the longest-serving Prime Minister of this century. She shows not the slightest intention of retiring. She speaks as if she will run again for a fourth term of office in 1991 or 1992. No successor to her is in sight. In peering into the future, however, we should take heed of some wise words of George Orwell: 'Power-worship blurs political judgement because it leads, unavoidably, to the belief that present trends will continue. Whoever is winning at the moment will always seem to be invincible. If the Japanese have conquered South Asia, they will keep South Asia for ever; if the Germans have captured Tobruk, they will infallibly capture Cairo; if the Russians are in Berlin it is not long before they will be in London, and so on'.[12]

London
February 1988

Notes

1. Quoted in Allan J. Mayer, *Madam Prime Minister*, 1979, p.197.
2. Quoted in Peter Riddell, *The Thatcher Government*, 1983, p.14.
3. Lou Cannon, *Reagan*, 1982, p.316.
4. Ibid., p.321.
5. Robert Kuttner, *The Life of the Party*, 1987, p.25.

6. Richard M. Scammon and Ben J. Wattenberg, *The Real Majority*, 1970, p.21.
7. Martin P. Wattenberg, *The Decline of American Political Parties, 1952–1984*, 1986, pp.141–6.
8. Quoted ibid., pp.141–2.
9. Kuttner, op. cit., p.112; Martin P. Wattenberg, op. cit., pp.147–9.
10. Paul Kennedy, *The Rise and Fall of the Great Powers: Economic Change and Military Conflict from 1500 to 2000*, 1987.
11. *New York Review of Books*, February 18, 1988.
12. Quoted in C. A. R. Crosland, *The Conservative Enemy*, 1962, p.134.

Chronology

1945

July   General Election. Labour 393, Conservative 213, Liberal
          12, Others 22. Labour majority 146

          Prime Minister: Clement Attlee
          Foreign Secretary: Ernest Bevin
          Chancellor of the Exchequer: Hugh Dalton

October   Dalton's first Budget: income tax reduced, profits tax in-
          troduced

1946

April   Dalton's second Budget: purchase tax reduced, income tax
          allowances increased

1947

January   Fiercest winter in living memory, with acute fuel shortages

          Coal industry nationalized

April   Dalton's third Budget: profits tax, purchase tax, Stamp
          Duty, and tobacco duties all raised

August   Sterling made convertible into US dollars causing a run on
          the pound. Convertibility suspended

November Dalton's 'Austerity' Budget: profits tax, purchase tax, and
          alcohol duties raised

          Dalton resigns as Chancellor after leaking contents of the
          Budget to a newspaper, Stafford Cripps succeeds him

1948

January   Railways nationalized

March   Marshall Plan aid begins

April   Electricity supply industry nationalized

          Cripps's first Budget: capital levy, tobacco and alcohol
          duties raised, betting tax introduced

July   National Health Service inaugurated by Aneurin Bevan

1949

April   NATO treaty signed

            Cripps's second Budget: income tax relief reduced, alcohol
            duties cut, betting tax raised

September   Sterling devalued from $4.03 to $2.80

November   New agreement reached with Trades Union Congress
            (TUC) on wages freeze

1950

February   General Election. Labour 315, Conservative 298, Liberal 9,
            Others 3. Labour majority 5

April   Cripps's third Budget: income tax reduced, fuel and pur-
            chase tax increased

September   TUC votes against incomes policy

October   Cripps resigns as Chancellor, Hugh Gaitskell succeeds him

1951

February   Steel industry nationalized

March   Herbert Morrison appointed Foreign Secretary

April   Gaitskell's first Budget: income tax increased, purchase tax
            and petrol duties raised

            Aneurin Bevan resigns over the introduction of health ser-
            vice charges

October   General Election. Conservative 321, Labour 295, Liberal 6,
            Others 3. Conservative majority 17

            Prime Minister: Winston Churchill
            Foreign Secretary: Anthony Eden
            Chancellor of the Exchequer: R. A. Butler

1952

March   Butler's 'set-the-people-free' Budget: tax thresholds low-
            ered, fuel subsidies cut

May   London bus strike

July   France, Germany, Italy, Netherlands, Belgium, and Lux-
            embourg establish the European Steel and Coal Commu-
            nity. Britain plays no part

1953

April   Butler's second Budget: Excess Profits Levy abolished, in-
            come tax and purchase tax cut

May   Steel industry denationalized

October	Labour Party conference in Morecambe. The Bevanite left make important gains on the National Executive Committee

1954

April	Butler's third Budget: new 'investment allowance' scheme introduced
October	Rationing finally abolished
	Government reshuffle. Harold Macmillan becomes Minister of Defence
November	Nasser becomes President of Egypt

1955

April	Winston Churchill retires as Prime Minister, Anthony Eden succeeds him. Harold Macmillan becomes Foreign Secretary, Lord Home Commonwealth Secretary
	Butler's fourth Budget: income tax cut, personal allowances raised
May	Warsaw Pact signed
	General Election. Conservative 344, Labour 277, Liberal 6, Others 3. Conservative majority 58
October	Butler's fifth Budget: purchase and profits taxes raised, housing subsidies cut
December	Cabinet reshuffle. Selwyn Lloyd becomes Foreign Secretary, Harold Macmillan Chancellor of the Exchequer, R. A. Butler leader of the House of Commons
	Hugh Gaitskell succeeds Clement Attlee as leader of the Labour Party

1956

April	Macmillan's first Budget: income tax relief, profits tax increased, tobacco taxes raised, Premium Bonds established
	First protest march to the atomic weapons research establishment at Aldermaston
July	Nasser nationalizes the Suez Canal
November	Anglo-French invasion of Suez causes domestic and international furor
	Soviet forces enter Hungary
December	Anglo-French forces leave Suez under American pressure

1957

January	Anthony Eden resigns as Prime Minister, Harold Macmillan succeeds him. Peter Thorneycroft becomes Chancellor of the Exchequer, R. A. Butler Home Secretary

| March | Treaty of Rome signed establishing European Economic Community (EEC). Britain plays no part |
| April | Thorneycroft's first Budget: purchase tax reduced, company tax concessions increased |

1958

January	Thorneycroft resigns as Chancellor, Derek Heathcoat-Amory succeeds him
February	Campaign for Nuclear Disarmament founded by Bertrand Russell and Canon Collins
April	Heathcoat-Amory's first Budget: company tax concessions, purchase tax reduced

1959

April	Heathcoat-Amory's second Budget: income tax cut
July	Transport and General Workers Union supports unilateral nuclear disarmament
	Bad Godesburg conference of West Germany's Social Democrats rejects Marxism and accepts the role of markets
October	General Election. Conservative 365, Labour 258, Liberal 6, Others 1. Conservative majority 98
	Hugh Gaitskell unsuccessfully attempts repeal of Clause 4 of Labour Party constitution committing Party to wholesale public ownership
November	European Free Trade Area agreement signed as British response to EEC

1960

March	Sharpeville massacre in South Africa
April	Blue Streak missile cancelled, casting doubt on Britain's future as a nuclear power
July	Heathcoat-Amory resigns as Chancellor, Selwyn Lloyd succeeds him. Lord Home appointed Foreign Secretary, Edward Heath Lord Privy Seal
October	Labour Party conference adopts a policy of unilateral nuclear disarmament. Gaitskell vows to 'fight, fight and fight again'
November	Polaris submarine bases in Scotland announced
	John F. Kennedy elected American President

1961

| May | South Africa withdraws from the Commonwealth |
| July | Emergency Budget: pay pause and Government spending cuts |

August   TUC and employers join new National Economic Develop-
           ment Council established for the purpose of accelerating
           economic growth through indicative planning

1962

March   Liberals score sensational by-election victory at Orpington

July   In the 'night of the long knives' Macmillan replaces seven
           members of his Cabinet. Reginald Maudling becomes Chan-
           cellor, Peter Thorneycroft Minister of Defence

           Policy of economic expansion and income restraint
           launched

October   Labour Party conference votes against British membership
           in the Common Market

December   Macmillan and Kennedy meet at Nassau and reach historic
           agreement to provide Britain with US Polaris missiles

1963

January   Hugh Gaitskell dies

           General de Gaulle vetoes Britain's attempt to join the EEC

February   Harold Wilson becomes leader of the Labour Party, defeat-
           ing George Brown

June   John Profumo resigns as War Minister in scandal involving
           call girls

October   Harold Macmillan resigns as Prime Minister. Fierce contest
           for the premiership ensues, from which Lord Home
           emerges, renouncing his peerage to become Prime Minister
           as Sir Alec Douglas-Home. R. A. Butler, denied the suc-
           cession, becomes Foreign Secretary, Edward Heath Minis-
           ter for Trade, Selwyn Lloyd leader of the House of Com-
           mons, Henry Brooke Home Secretary

November   John F. Kennedy assassinated

1964

April   Maudling's Budget: tobacco and alcohol taxes increased

           Home postpones General Election until autumn

October   General Election. Labour 317, Conservative 304, Liberal 9.
           Labour majority of 4

           Prime Minister: Harold Wilson
           Chancellor of the Exchequer: James Callaghan
           Foreign Secretary: Patrick Gordon-Walker
           Home Secretary: Frank Soskice

November   Callaghan's first Budget: prescription charges abolished,
           pensions increased

1965

February   Prices and Incomes Board established

April   Callaghan's second Budget: corporation tax introduced

November   Unilateral Declaration of Independence for Rhodesia by Ian Smith

1966

March   Wilson calls General Election and wins handsome working majority. Labour 363, Conservative 253, Liberal 12, Others 2. Labour majority 96

May   Callaghan's third Budget: selective employment tax introduced

July   Seamen's strike deals a blow to the economy and to sterling

1967

March   Steel industry renationalized

July   New economic crisis forces emergency measures. Callaghan resigns as Chancellor, Roy Jenkins succeeds him

November   Sterling devalued

1968

March   George Brown resigns as Foreign Secretary, Michael Stewart succeeds him

May   Student riots in Paris set off wave of unrest in France

August   Soviet Union invades Czechoslovakia

1969

January   Government publishes White Paper 'In Place of Strife' proposing legal constraints on collective bargaining

April   Franchise extended to eighteen-year-olds

July   Wilson finally defeated in Cabinet over 'In Place of Strife'. Attempt to reform unions abandoned

August   British troops sent to Northern Ireland

1970

January   Selsdon Park Conference of Heath's Shadow Cabinet

May   Equal Pay Act passed

June   General Election. Conservatives score surprise victory. Conservative 330, Labour 287, Liberal 6, Others 7. Conservative majority 30

         Prime Minister: Edward Heath
         Chancellor of the Exchequer: Iain Macleod

	Foreign Secretary: Alec Douglas-Home
	Home Secretary: Reginald Maudling
	Education Secretary: Margaret Thatcher, the only woman Cabinet member
	Britain reapplies for membership in the EEC
July	Iain Macleod dies, replaced as Chancellor by Anthony Barber

1971

February	Decimal currency introduced
	First British soldier killed in Belfast
June	EEC negotiations completed
October	House of Commons votes for entry to the EEC, 356–244; Labour splits, 68 Labour MPs following Roy Jenkins into pro-Europe lobby

1972

January	'Bloody Sunday', 13 killed in Ulster
February	Government capitulates to striking miners
April	Roy Jenkins resigns as deputy leader of the Labour Party protesting the plan to submit EEC membership to a referendum
July	Maudling resigns as Home Secretary, replaced by Robert Carr
October	New Liberal revival marked by victory in the Rochdale by-election
November	Cabinet declares three-month wages and prices standstill
December	Liberals win Sutton and Cheam by-election

1973

January	Britain accedes to membership in the EEC
July	Liberals win Isle of Ely and Ripon by-elections
October	Labour Party conference accepts radical socialist programme
November	Miners begin overtime ban
	Yom Kippur war. The price of crude oil doubled by OPEC, heralding energy crisis
December	Three-day week imposed on industry in response to miners' action and to save energy
	Cuts in public expenditure announced

1974

February   Miners vote to strike

             Edward Heath calls General Election asking 'Who rules
             Britain?' Labour 301, Conservative 297, Liberal 14, Others
             23. No overall majority

March   Heath resigns as Prime Minister after negotiations with
             Liberals break down, Harold Wilson succeeds him. Denis
             Healey becomes Chancellor of the Exchequer, Roy Jenkins
             Home Secretary, James Callaghan Foreign Secretary

             Miners' demands met in full

October   Harold Wilson calls a new General Election seeking a Par-
             liamentary majority. Labour 319, Conservative 277, Liberal
             13, Others 26. Labour majority 3

1975

February   Edward Heath deposed as leader of the Conservative
             Party, Margaret Thatcher the surprise successor

June   Referendum on continued membership in the EEC, 67%
             vote Yes

July   Government and TUC announce £6 voluntary pay policy

             Unemployment passes 1 million

1976

March   Harold Wilson resigns suddenly

April   James Callaghan becomes Prime Minister, Anthony Cros-
             land Foreign Secretary

             Denis Healey announces tax cuts conditional on 4% pay
             policy

May   Jeremy Thorpe resigns as Liberal Party leader

July   David Steel elected Liberal Party leader

September   Roy Jenkins resigns as Home Secretary to become presi-
             dent of the EEC commission, Merlyn Rees succeeds him

             Sterling crisis obliges Denis Healey to call in the Interna-
             tional Monetary Fund (IMF)

December   Cabinet agrees to package of expenditure cuts in order to
             obtain further IMF credit

1977

February   Anthony Crosland dies, David Owen becomes Foreign Sec-
             retary at age 38, the youngest since William Pitt

March   Liberals enter into parliamentary pact with Labour to keep
             the Government in power

| July | Denis Healey outlines Phase III of the incomes policy |

1978

January	Special Liberal Assembly endorses Lib-Lab Pact conditionally
May	Notice given that the Lib-Lab Pact will end in November
June	5% decreed as limit for Phase IV of pay policy
September	Callaghan cancels expected election
October	Labour Party conference rejects 5% pay policy
December	House of Commons votes down sanctions against companies breaching the 5% pay policy

1979

January	Seven-nation summit in Guadaloupe discusses deployment of Cruise and Pershing missiles in Europe
	'Day of Action' in the public sector, followed by six weeks of strikes, the so-called 'Winter of Discontent'
March	Referendum rejects devolution in Wales. In Scotland it fails to result in 40% positive vote necessary. Leads to new parliamentary crisis
	Government defeated on confidence vote, 311–310
	Election called for May 3rd
May	General Election. Conservative 339, Labour 269, Liberal 11, Others 16. Conservative majority 43

Prime Minister: Margaret Thatcher
Chancellor of the Exchequer: Sir Geoffrey Howe
Foreign Secretary: Lord Carrington
Home Secretary: William Whitelaw

	Edward Heath rejects post of Ambassador to US
July	House of Commons decisively rejects death penalty
August	Soviet Union invades Afghanistan
November	Mrs Thatcher calls for £1000 million cut in Britain's EEC contributions
December	NATO agrees to deploy Cruise and Pershing missiles in Europe

1980

October	Unemployment passes 2 million
November	Ronald Reagan elected American President
	James Callaghan resigns as leader of the Labour Party. Michael Foot defeats Denis Healey on the third ballot to become, surprisingly, the new leader

1981

March	Budget: road, alcohol, tobacco, and petrol taxes raised
	The Social Democratic Party (SDP) launched by four former Labour Cabinet Ministers
April	Riots in Brixton, South London. 191 arrests
May	Local elections. Ken Livingstone defeats the leader of the newly elected majority Labour group on the Greater London Council to become Labour leader of the GLC
July	Riots in the Toxteth area of Liverpool. The police use CS gas for the first time
	Roy Jenkins standing as a 'Social Democrat with Liberal support' cuts the Labour majority from 10,274 to 1,759 in the Warrington by-election
September	First major purge of Mrs Thatcher's Cabinet. Three of her sternest critics replaced
	Liberal Party conference in Llandudno approves alliance with the SDP
October	Liberal wins the Croydon North-West by-election from the Conservatives
November	Shirley Williams becomes the first SDP candidate elected to Parliament in the Crosby by-election
December	Arthur Scargill elected president of the National Union of Mineworkers (NUM)

1982

March	Budget: road, tobacco, and petrol taxes raised
	Roy Jenkins becomes second elected SDP MP in the Glasgow Hillhead by-election
April	Argentine forces capture Port Stanley, capital of the Falkland Islands
	First Saturday sitting of the House of Commons since Suez
	Foreign Secretary Lord Carrington and Lord Privy Seal Humphrey Atkins resign. Francis Pym becomes Foreign Secretary. Naval task force sails for the Falklands
May	Argentine ship the *General Belgrano* sunk. Argentine navy withdraws from the Falklands conflict
June	Port Stanley recaptured by British task force
July	Roy Jenkins elected first leader of the SDP, defeating David Owen 26,000 to 20,000
	Rail strike defeated

1983

January	John Nott replaced by Michael Heseltine as Defence Secretary, Tom King becomes Environment Secretary
February	Liberal Simon Hughes wins the Bermondsey by-election from Labour after a bitter campaign and the largest-ever by-election swing
March	Budget: alcohol, tobacco, and petrol taxes raised
	President Reagan launches his strategic defence initiative with his 'Star Wars' speech
May	Mrs Thatcher calls a General Election
June	General Election. Labour receives 28% of the vote, lowest since 1918. SDP/Liberal Alliance is close behind at 26%. Conservative share of the vote goes down but their majority goes up. Conservative 397, Labour 209, Liberal/Alliance 17, SDP/Alliance 6, Others 21
	Cabinet reshuffle. Francis Pym replaced by Geoffrey Howe as Foreign Secretary, Nigel Lawson becomes Chancellor, Leon Brittan becomes Home Secretary, replacing William Whitelaw who receives a hereditary peerage
September	Unemployment falls for the first time since 1979
October	Neil Kinnock elected Labour leader. Roy Hattersley, defeated for the leadership, is elected deputy leader
	Cecil Parkinson resigns as Secretary of State for Trade and Industry in scandal over affair with his secretary
November	First Cruise missiles arrive at Greenham Common air base, Berkshire
December	30,000 women demonstrate at Greenham Common

1984

January	Staff at General Communications (intelligence) Headquarters in Cheltenham are deprived of the right to union membership
March	NUM begins strike action in protest at the projected closure of 'uneconomic' pits with the loss of 20,000 jobs
April	Lawson's first Budget: tax reforms
	Minor Cabinet reshuffle. James Prior replaced as Northern Ireland Secretary
June	SDP gains Portsmouth South from the Conservatives in a by-election
July	Violent clashes at Orgreave coking plant in Yorkshire

November	Bill abolishing the Greater London Council and six metropolitan local authorities passed in the House of Commons
	Ronald Reagan reelected American President
December	Soviet heir apparent Mikhail Gorbachev visits London

1985

February	Gorbachev becomes General Secretary of the Soviet Union
March	Miners' delegate conference votes 98–91 to return to work. Strike ends in defeat after a year of action
May	County Council elections, big swings to the SDP/Liberal Alliance
July	Liberals win Brecon and Radnor by-election by 559 votes from Labour, forcing the Conservatives into third place
September	Cabinet reshuffle. Patrick Jenkin replaced by Kenneth Baker as Environment Secretary and John Selwyn Gummer replaced by Norman Tebbit as Conservative Party Chairman. Leon Brittan replaces Tebbit as Secretary of State for Trade and Industry. Douglas Hurd becomes Home Secretary, Tom King Northern Ireland Secretary. Lord Young and Kenneth Clarke, both in the Cabinet, replace King at Employment
	Riots in the Handsworth area of Birmingham. Two Asians are killed
October	Riots in Tottenham, north London. A policeman is murdered by rioters
	Nottinghamshire miners vote to form a breakaway Union of Democratic Mineworkers
November	Geneva summit between Ronald Reagan and Mikhail Gorbachev
December	Westland helicopters controversy erupts

1986

January	Heseltine resigns as Defence Secretary over Westland crisis, George Younger succeeds him
	Printworkers dispute at News International headquarters in Wapping, east London, begins
March	Lawson's third Budget: income tax cut by 1%, cigarette and petrol duties raised
April	Labour gains Fulham from the Conservatives in by-election
	The Shops Bill to introduce Sunday trading defeated despite a three-line Government whip
	America bombs Libya using UK bases

May	Conservatives lose one safe seat to Liberals in the Ryedale by-election and hold a second by only 100 votes in West Derbyshire
	Sir Keith Joseph resigns as Education Secretary, replaced by Kenneth Baker. John Moore enters the Cabinet as Transport Secretary
September	Liberal Party conference rejects SDP/Liberal Alliance defence policy
October	Conservative Party conference puts forward radical plans for a third term of office
	Labour Party conference advertises Labour's new look, symbolised by red rose
	Reagan and Gorbachev meet at Reykjavik. Summit breaks down but makes progress on INF treaty
November	Lawson announces £5 billion increase in public spending
December	British Gas privatised

1987

February	SDP easily wins the Greenwich by-election from Labour who have held the seat since 1945
April	The Prime Minister visits Moscow, spending 5 hours with Gorbachev
	Neil Kinnock visits Washington, spending 20 minutes with Ronald Reagan
May	Local elections show Labour weakness after Greenwich defeat
	General Election announced
June	General Election. Conservative 375, Labour 220, Liberal/Alliance 17, SDP/Alliance 5, Others 28. Conservative majority 102

Abbreviations

ABM	Anti-Ballistic Missile	DTI	Department of Trade and Industry
ACATT	Association of Cinematograph, Television and Allied Technicians	EEC	European Economic Community
ALC	Association of Liberal Councillors	EEPTU	Electrical Engineering and Plumbers Trades Union
ASLEF	Associated Society of Locomotive Engineers and Firemen	GCHQ	Government Communications Headquarters
ASTMS	Association of Scientific, Technical and Managerial Staffs	GDP	Gross Domestic Product
		GLC	Greater London Council
AUEW	Amalgamated Union of Engineering Workers	GMBATU	General, Municipal, Boilermakers and Allied Trades Unions
CAP	Common Agricultural Policy	ILEA	Inner London Education Authority
CND	Campaign for Nuclear Disarmament	IMF	International Monetary Fund
CBI	Confederation of British Industry	INF	Intermediate-Range Nuclear Forces
CLPD	Campaign for Labour Party Democracy	IRA	Irish Republican Army
		MOD	Ministry of Defence
COHSE	Confederation of Health Service Employees	MORI	Market and Opinion Research International
CPS	Centre for Policy Studies	MSC	Manpower Services Commission
DHSS	Department of Health and Social Security	NAAFI	Navy, Army and Air-Force Institute

NATO	North Atlantic Treaty Organisation	PSL	Private Sector Liquidity
NEB	National Enterprise Board	PUS	Permanent Under-Secretary
NEC	National Executive Committee (Labour Party)	SALT	Strategic Arms Limitation Treaty
		SDI	Strategic Defence Initiative
NHS	National Health Service	SDP	Social Democratic Party
NUPE	National Union of Public Employees	SERPS	State Earnings-Related Pension Scheme
NUR	National Union of Railwaymen	SPD	Sozialdemokratische Partei Deutschlands
OECD	Organisation for Economic Co-operation and Development	START	Strategic Arms Reduction Talks
		TGWU	Transport and General Workers' Union
OPEC	Organisation of Petroleum-Exporting Countries	TUC	Trades Union Congress
ORC	Opinion Research Centre	TVEI	Technical and Vocational Education Initiative
PAYE	Pay As You Earn		
PLP	Parliamentary Labour Party	VAT	Value-Added Tax
		WEA	Workers' Education Association
PPE	Philosophy, Politics and Economics	YTS	Youth Training Scheme
PSBR	Public Sector Borrowing Requirement		

Author's Note

Where possible I have tried to make attributions or give references either in the text or in the notes, but a good deal of the material for this book is drawn from the elaborate notebooks in which I record conversations and thoughts and make notes from television, the radio, newspapers and other reading. Some of this information has to remain unattributed in any case within the conventions of political journalism.

1
THE OLD ORDER
CRUMBLES

I

Post-war Discontents

'I am not a consensus politician . . .' Margaret Thatcher said, in what was to become her most remembered statement, 'I'm a *conviction* politician.' The self-designation stuck: 'conviction politics' became the brand mark of her style, as well known as Harold Wilson's belief that 'ten days is a long time in politics' or Harold Macmillan's nonchalant shrugging off of a Cabinet crisis as a 'little local difficulty'. In these ways do politicians type-cast themselves.

But what did she mean when she said that she was not a consensus politician? For it is there we must begin, with the foundations of the post-war order which were to crumble and fall with the rise of Margaret Thatcher. The consensus she imagined herself to be smashing was founded more in myth than in reality. Because myth is as powerful in politics as reality, however, I shall refer to the 'consensus' as if it had literally existed. The word implies that throughout the post-war period the parties had had more in common than the differences between them and that government, and especially the management of the economy, had proceeded according to a broad agreement. They did no such thing. Indeed Britain suffered unduly compared with some other, more successful, countries from sharp and usually ideologically-inspired changes in direction – enactments and repeals, nationalisations and denationalisations. It is true that in 1945 all three parties – Conservative, Labour and Liberal – went to the country committed to principles of economic reconstruction and social reform which they had jointly endorsed within the war-time Coalition. 'A massive new middle ground had arisen in politics.'[1] Some of the spirit of the war-time consensus – although even the extent of that can be exaggerated – had lasted into the immediate post-war years but not for long: the austerities of 1947 – food rations cut, no petrol for private motoring, no currency for foreign holidays – soon put paid to it and in 1950 and 1951 the middle class voters in the towns and suburbs of the south who had crossed class lines in the euphoria of 1945 returned, chastened, to the Tory fold.

After 1951 the Conservatives set about dismantling the panoply of war-time and post-war controls which Labour had relied upon to plan production and arrange fair shares in conditions of austerity. The Welfare State was not attacked but there was no agreement about how it was to be financed, and whether to introduce charging and means-testing or not became a running battle between the parties. For reasons of prudence, Churchill – no union lover – pursued a conciliatory policy towards organised labour which endured, more or less, until the great London bus strike of 1957. By 1964 the privileged position of the trade unions, with their immunities from the law,[2] had become a party issue and by the late 1960s the 'union question' had come to dominate party politics.

'There never *was* a consensus . . . The parties never came together in their policies. Even the idea of "Butskellism" was sloppy and inaccurate,' said Edward Heath in 1971.[3] The notion of 'Butskellism' owed more to the easy elision of the names Butler and Gaitskell than to the similarities of their economic policies. To be sure, both R. A. Butler and Hugh Gaitskell made some use of Keynesian techniques of demand management but so would have any Chancellor of the Exchequer, or the Finance Minister of any other country, attempting at that time to maintain full employment with reasonably stable prices. They differed quite sharply, as Philip Williams has shown, on monetary policy, the convertibility of sterling, state controls and the distribution of wealth.[4]

Certainly, nothing resembling the civility of 'Butskellism' extended to the shop floor of British industry, where the battle lines remained sullenly drawn between 'them' and 'us'. On foreign policy a broad consensus in support of the Atlantic Alliance operated between the front benches – until Eden shattered it at Suez – but did not reach down into the Labour Party which was consistently split between Bevinists and Bevanites. In the 1960s the parties divided, and split within themselves, over British membership of the European Common Market. In short, the post-war consensus had never been much of a consensus. It became a convenient scapegoat for the economic failures and social dislocations of the 1970s which, as we shall see, it suited the Thatcherites to blame on a Keynesian collusion between the parties. What did break down towards the end of the 1970s was not so much a consensus as the Post-war Settlement which had grown out of the brief war-time suspension of party politics.

Like the 1688 Act of Settlement which finally resolved the constitutional issues of the Civil War, the Attlee government's social legislation, much of it inspired by the forethought of the Coalition, was designed to call at least a truce in the class war which had disfigured the politics of the 1920s and 1930s. [Full employment and the maintenance of the Welfare State became the accepted goals of both parties, if for no other reason than that to depart from them would be to court electoral defeat.] They set not only the framework but the agenda for post-war politics, for neither full employment nor the Welfare State could be maintained without an expanding economy. How to achieve faster and sustainable growth was the unsolved but ever-pressing question of post-war economic policy. Growth was inhibited by a balance of payments constraint which became increasingly severe from around the end of the 1950s, and by the tendency of the economy to 'overheat' and generate price inflation which exacerbated the balance of payments difficulties. Harold Macmillan, always the performer, described the task of managing the post-war economy as requiring the skills of 'a new Cinquevalli', a juggler capable of keeping four balls in the air simultaneously – full employment, an expanding economy, stable prices and a strong pound.[5]

Of these full employment was the first imperative because of memories of the mass unemployment of the 1930s; in countries where inflation had been the greater scourge, Germany for example, the folk memory worked in the other direction. In Britain the pattern of post-war economic government became bouts of inflation brought to an end by balance of payments crises. This was the depressing but seemingly inescapable 'stop-go syndrome' which defeated each and every government until the 'long boom' came to its end in 1973 and stop-go gave way to 'stagflation' – all stop and no go.

For Labour governments, growth was an even greater imperative than for Conservative governments living down their reputation of the 1930s. Growth was not only necessary for maintaining full employment, the cornerstone of the Post-war Settlement, but was indispensable if resources and wealth were to be redistributed in accordance with socialist priorities. This was the essence of Anthony Crosland's 'revisionist' insight: it was unnecessary, as well as undesirable, to engage in wholesale nationalisation; the mixed economy under Keynesian management had no need to approach socialism by means of a command economy; social justice and equality – the central values of the 'revisionists' – could be achieved by the re-allocation of resources and wealth, in other words by public spending. But all this was possible only if resources overall expanded at a sufficient pace. For redistributive justice would be acceptable enough if everyone was growing richer in absolute terms; the contrary strategy of soak-the-rich-to-feed-the-poor offered no way forward, for to redistribute wealth and income meant soaking not just the rich but also the mass of the better-off working class. That was a recipe both for inflation and electoral defeat.

Crosland later confessed that he had been too sanguine about growth. To all intents and purposes he had regarded the problem of production as solved, leaving all good socialists to get on with what more concerned them, and fell within their competence, the creation of a more just and equal society. It was a happy vision and one which by giving the State a lesser and more indirect role in the achievement of socialism seemed to remove the tension between equality and liberty. *Crosland*

In this he embodied the hopes of a generation. Not only in his thought, which was immensely influential, but also in the example of his lifestyle he combined social commitment and private freedom. With his seminal work published in 1956 he liberated socialists not only from the encumbrances of the Marxist tradition but also from the earnest worthiness of Sidney and Beatrice Webb, who had spent their honeymoon collecting information about trade unions in Dublin with no time to visit a theatre or a gallery. A famous passage towards the end of *The Future of Socialism* was headed, 'Liberty and Gaiety in Private Life; the Need for a Reaction against the Fabian Tradition', and it ended with the words: 'Total abstinence and a good filing-system are not now the right sign-posts to the socialist Utopia; or at least, if they are, some of us will fall by the wayside.'[6]

A figure of dazzling glamour and charm, Crosland had shaken off a stern religious upbringing by the Plymouth Brethren to become in the early part of his life a playboy intellectual, although the two roles were pursued in relentless parallel, the one not permitted to interfere with the other. The war had punctured his Oxford career and when he returned to complete his degree he stayed on for three years as a don, teaching economics. One of his pupils was Tony Benn. While still an undergraduate Crosland had been talent spotted by Hugh Dalton, then Chancellor of the Exchequer. Dalton, a roistering Old Etonian with a penchant for bright and beautiful young men (of whom Rupert Brook had been one) helped Crosland win a seat in Parliament as member for South Gloucestershire. That this in 1950 was a Labour seat (although no longer by 1955) is a measure of the times straddled by his career. At first he hated Parliament. It bored him and offended his fastidious intelligence. Perhaps this was as well for, when not drinking or womanising, Crosland settled down in his armchair and, with expensive fountain pen, wrote his great work. He was thirty-eight when it was published. At twenty-two he had declared in a letter: 'I am revising Marxism and will emerge as the modern Bernstein.'[7]

So he did. The book made him at once the *bête noire* of the Bevanites and fundamentalists but gave inspiration to a whole generation of socialist reformers. It provided new foundations for an ethical socialism centred on the pursuit of equality. It became the bible of so-called 'revisionist socialism' and, although never formally accepted by the Labour Party as its doctrine, in practice it coloured the approach of the Wilson and Callaghan governments.

The Future of Socialism provided an ideological basis for Hugh Gaitskell, who in the year before its publication had triumphed over Aneurin Bevan to succeed Attlee as Labour leader, and his supporters. Dalton had introduced Crosland to Gaitskell's circle – the 'Hampstead set' it was called by the Left – and it was Gaitskell who helped Crosland back into the Commons in 1959. Although the chief theorist of 'revisionism', he had not been in favour of Gaitskell's ill-fated attempt to revise the Labour Party's constitution to remove the commitment to wholesale nationalisation contained in Clause Four. Like many intellectuals he tended to make a cult of pragmatism. He liked to cite Max Weber's distinction between the 'ethic of ultimate ends and the ethic of responsibility', insisting that, 'he who follows the former has no interest in political power'. Rewriting the tablets, he thought, would prove more trouble than it was worth. He was right.

After Gaitskell's untimely death in 1963 he had gradually ceased to be a Gaitskellite. He did not change his views about socialism but he was not a man for faction. There was also a rivalry touching upon jealousy between himself and Roy Jenkins, who had been Gaitskell's other favourite protégé. Jenkins's view was that Gaitskell had preferred his company but Crosland's brain. The Jenkinsites became increasingly identified with the cause of 'Britain in Europe'. Crosland chose to regard this as a symptom of socialist atrophy. He remained in favour of Britain joining the European Common Market but insisted that this was not an overriding question. Those who believed it to be so did so because of their increasing inability to believe in the central values of socialism.

For these reasons he declined to join the pro-European Right, mostly former Gaitskellites, in the government lobbies in the historic division on 28 October 1971 which took Britain into Europe and prefigured the schism in the Labour Party ten years later. Crosland took to insisting that he was a democratic socialist, not a social democrat, claiming that the definition of the latter appeared to be somebody who was preparing to leave the Labour Party.

As time went on he donned a protective hide of populism, relegating a growing number of issues to a place so low on the list of the concerns of his Grimsby constituents as to be not worth the attention of serious people. 'Serious' was a favourite Crosland word, his anathema against all that was 'trivial' or 'fashionable' but also, increasingly, against what was uncongenial to his position. As a gilded youth he had become accustomed to being excused (or even loved) for bad behaviour and would sometimes use this to bolster the integrity of his convictions. For example in restaurants he was liable to complain loudly about the noise of 'frightful upper class voices'. He refused even when Foreign Secretary to wear evening dress (he would stoop to a dinner jacket) although on occasions (chiefly in his constituency) he affected to wear a flat cap. In *The Future of Socialism* he had advocated 'uninhibited mingling between the classes' – a phrase he had picked up from Dalton.[8] He remained to the end a fiercely egalitarian spirit.

But by the time of his sad and sudden death in 1977 his world, as we shall see, was collapsing around him. When the IMF foreclosed on Britain it foreclosed on Croslandism. The 1970s had confronted him with the implications of his theory in conditions of slow growth. As resources were withdrawn from personal consumption in order to finance the public expenditure needs of a Welfare State, the problem of inflation was exacerbated. That, combined with low productivity, 'sometimes makes the British economy seem unmanageable', he wrote; but he did not alter the primacy he attached to growth. 'We may take it as a certainty that rapid growth is an essential condition of any significant re-allocation of resources.'[9] In 1970 that was a pessimistic observation; after 1973, when the world was plunged into recession, it became tantamount to an admission that further redistribution had become impossible, or at least without the dire consequences which flowed from Crosland's own theory.

Not only that but, as he recognised, the problem had long since become not how to achieve a further re-allocation of resources but how to pay for what had already been created. With slow growth the financing of the Welfare State became increasingly problematical.

From the early 1960s Britain was trapped in a vicious circle as the rising costs of welfare resulted in higher taxation, resulting in accelerating wage inflation, resulting in higher welfare costs and more taxes, and so on. The cost of welfare increased partly for demographic reasons as proportionately more old and young became a charge on proportionately fewer wage earners and taxpayers but also because of a vast expansion in the numbers employed in the welfare bureaucracies. Moreover, many benefits were linked to inflation either directly or indirectly and in some years raced ahead of real earnings. In 1965 government expenditure, central and local, accounted for 37 per cent of Gross Domestic Product (GDP); by 1970 it had risen to 41 per cent, by 1975 to 50 per cent. In 1965 taxes financed four-fifths of the expenditure, by 1975 only three-quarters. The Welfare State was financed increasingly by borrowing.

The fast-rising cost of public spending, together with inflation, brought more and more wage-earners into the net of PAYE. In the 1950s the average wage-earner paid no income tax; in 1960 his tax and insurance contributions took some 8 per cent of his earnings; by 1970 they took nearly 20 per cent. In 1972 a married man with two children and with average industrial earnings paid 19 per cent of his gross earnings in taxes, direct and indirect; by 1976 he was paying 26 per cent.

This in itself represented a change scarcely less profound than that brought about by the Welfare State which had ensured universal access to medical care and social security. The working classes were not used to paying income tax. Now the great mass had for the first time become taxpayers. In the lowest income bracket the rate they paid was the highest in the world, according to Denis Healey in his 1976 Budget speech. The Welfare State had made us into a nation of taxpayers.

For Conservative governments too, growth was the means of keeping the people happy, of winning elections and of not putting too great a strain on the Post-war Settlement. Macmillan had never been able to forget the unemployment he had seen in Stockton in the 1930s and other Conservatives, with less developed or patrician social consciences, kept it in mind that memories of the 1930s had lost them the General Election of 1945, or so it was widely supposed. During the 1950s Britain boomed, although in fits and starts. Between 1952 and 1960 real earnings (that is, what money would buy after tax and National Insurance deductions) increased at an annual average of 2·8 per cent. When Gaitskell tried to make growth an election issue in 1959 Macmillan, although himself always at heart an expansionist, could brush the thought aside as a new-fangled craze to be compared with the twist, at that time the fashionable rage of the dance floors. But by 1961 he was himself dancing to another tune. The balance of payments constriction was now tightening, due to an overvalued pound and to Britain's over-extended post-imperial role. 'Stop' abruptly followed 'go', this time accompanied by a 'pay pause' – the first essay in pay restraint since the Cripps freeze in the austerity conditions of 1947. The 1960s had arrived.

The Post-war Settlement had placed another item on the political agenda – the collective bargaining system or what was to become the 'union question'. It dominated the politics of the 1960s and 1970s. Full employment had transformed the bargaining power of the unions. Slowly it became apparent that free collective bargaining, certainly on Britain's fragmented, competitive model, was not easily compatible with the maintenance of full employment with reasonably stable prices. From this realisation flowed two consequences, both of them profound. In order to defend full employment, promote economic expansion and avoid policies of crude wage restraint, trade unions were drawn into sharing responsibility for the management of the economy. To their members this appeared as a collusion with government and employers for the purpose of reducing real wages. The authority of national leadership was undermined, the power of shop stewards enhanced, and the fires of militancy fuelled. By the same process the government came to be held responsible for what people were paid, not only for the general level of wages but for the disparities between the pay of a nurse and a miner, a general and a policeman. Government soon found itself carrying a can of worms marked 'social justice'. The consequences were scarcely less disastrous than assuming responsibility for the English weather.

However, within the terms of the Post-war Settlement there was no alternative. There was no other way of keeping Harold Macmillan's four balls simultaneously in the air. When Harold Wilson came to power in 1964, on a growth ticket, he found himself obliged to query the traditional division of Labour whereby the political wing of the Movement concerned itself with governing the country while the industrial wing got on with its own business of collective bargaining. The then general secretary of the Trades Union Congress, George Woodcock, also saw that things could not go on as they were; if the unions themselves failed to come to grips with the 'wages problem', government would step in to do it for them, either by legislation or by abandoning full employment. Incomes policy was the chosen instrument for resolving these contradictions and for filling the lacuna left by Keynes in his theory of employment. If workers would restrain their demands for money wages, freeing themselves from the 'money illusion', prices would rise more slowly; this would permit sustained and faster growth, in consequence of which *real* wages would rise faster than would have been possible under conditions of free-for-all. That was the theory. It could never be put to proper test for the reason that the patience of the union members ran out before the completion of each experiment. Nevertheless, in order to obtain the co-operation of the unions, or, at least, as the TUC put it on one occasion, their 'reluctant acquiescence', governments were obliged, first, to intervene directly to obtain a commensurate restraint in prices, and, second, to endeavour to operate the policy fairly between one group and another and with some regard to economic efficiency. A Prices and Incomes Board was set up to study cases with regard to these criteria. The task which its chairman, Aubrey Jones, undertook with invincible confidence might have daunted Solomon with a computer. The Board pronounced on the marketing of soap powder, the productivity of baking and of brewing, the working practices of busmen employed by the Corporation of Dundee, the fees of solicitors and architects, the need for overtime in banks, and, altogether, 170 similarly arcane matters.

The Prices and Incomes Board was the archetypal institution of the Wilsonian era; it represented the apogee of the expert and of the belief in the powers of problem-solving social science. Aubrey Jones saw it as an opportunity to give institutional expression to Keynesian theory, no less. 'The Board's task was to prevent the opportunity for full employment opened up by Keynes from being defeated,' he wrote later.[10] But defeated it eventually was.

Incomes policy had begun as an instrument for achieving Labour's ambitious plans for faster economic growth. In no time it became part of the desperate deflationary defences of an over-valued pound and an over-extended frontier which, Wilson had claimed ludicrously, extended to the Himalayas. The use and misuse of incomes policy contributed to rising industrial unrest. In the two years 1963–4 some four million working days were lost through strikes. In the two years 1968–9 the total was 11·5 million. Wilson's answer to this problem was to try to reform the unions themselves. If incomes policy could not control the proceeds of collective bargaining the government would reform the processes of collective bargaining. The legislation proposed in the White Paper, 'In Place of Strife', resulted in the 'Battle of Downing Street'.[11] Wilson lost. The next year, in 1970, he lost the General Election.

In this way the attempts to sustain the Post-war Settlement had produced a crisis within the Labour Movement, its most severe since 1931 and the Ramsay MacDonald secession. The crisis was to continue through the 1970s and into the 1980s. Free collective bargaining, as practised or malpractised by British trade unions – 'free collective chaos', James Callaghan was to call it in 1978 – was simply incompatible with the preservation of full employment and the financing of the Welfare State, except at rates of inflation which would become intolerable. At the same time, the umbilical links between the Labour Party and the trade unions prevented a Labour government from effectively resolving this contradiction within the social democratic approach.

The Post-war Settlement now came under real strain. In the six years of Wilson government unemployment increased from 376,000 to 555,000. At about 2·5 per cent of the registered workforce this was scarcely a departure from 'full employment' but the upward trend was already a sign of what was to come. Then, about 1967, inflation really began to take off. This was not solely due to the contradictions now inherent in upholding the Post-war Settlement. The USA, at war in Vietnam, was running a huge balance of payments deficit, thereby swelling the world's money supply and exporting her own inflation to others. Pseudo-revolutionary events in France in 1968[12] triggered industrial and student unrest in other countries, including Britain. By the end of the decade inflation was running at an annual rate of over 8 per cent, compared with around 3 per cent at the beginning of it. Crosland, looking back on the 1964–70 Labour government, believed that no government could govern with 8 per cent annual inflation but by 1971 the annual rate was an alarming 13 per cent.

From 1964 the annual rise in living standards, an accustomed and expected feature of the post-war period, slowed almost to a standstill. Between 1964 and 1968 it averaged no more than 0·5 per cent a year. Then, in 1966 and 1967, real living standards on average actually declined for the first time ever in modern memory, apart from a few months during the Korean war when wages had temporarily failed to keep up with rising prices. Over the whole six years of Labour government real disposable income had increased on average by scarcely more than 1 per cent a year compared with 2·8 per cent in the 1950s. Increased taxation had bitten into real incomes. Indeed, taxes under Wilson had risen at twice the rate of average earnings. Yet little if any redistribution had been achieved in the direction of the working class. For the bulk of the population the Welfare State was probably largely self-financing: that is, people by and large paid for what they got.[13] By 1970 some five million people were living below a Labour Government's own declared poverty line. In that year *The Economist* commented: 'the failure to advance, or even maintain, the differential between the low-paid and pensioners on the one hand and the average wage earners on the other is a real increase in inequality which becomes more apparent as wages spiral.'

In 1970 it was the Tories' turn again. Edward Heath began by trying to govern the hard way. He came in pledging 'to change the course of history of this nation, nothing less.' He did not see it as his task to uphold 'consensus' which, as we have seen, he regarded as a fiction. The economy was to be set free again, as in 1951, but in contrast to then, the trade unions were to be put in their place within a framework of law similar to that envisaged in Labour's 'In Place of Strife'. Incomes policy, meanwhile, was discarded and pay claims were contested on a one by one basis; planning, brought into disrepute by the Labour government, was virtually discontinued; 'lame duck' industries were to be left to the mercies of market forces. By these means inflation was at first brought down, until in February 1972 the sheer industrial strength of the miners prevailed over the government. The coalfields dispute brought a new character on to the stage, one who was to epitomise 1970s man. At the gates of the Saltley coke depot in Birmingham the police retreated in the face of a superior force of flying pickets from Yorkshire, estimated to be some ten thousand men. The young Yorkshire militant, Arthur Scargill, clambered on to the roof of a public lavatory and proclaimed: 'This is the greatest victory of the working class in my lifetime.' The miners' pay claim was settled at 27 per cent. 'A little blood-letting may do no harm,' Lord Carrington was advised. 'What do you mean?' he demanded indignantly. 'This is true blue Tory blood and it's been spilled all over the carpet.'

Other workers followed on the militant coat-tails of the miners. The workers of the Upper Clyde Shipbuilders were occupying their bankrupt yard. The local Chief Constable advised the government that he could no longer be responsible for public order. Meanwhile unemployment was rising towards the million mark. In January 1972 it had reached 928,000. A million was the round number at which it was widely believed unemployment would threaten social and political stability. The events on the Clyde gave support to this view. Heath was too much the political child of the 1930s to regard that prospect with equanimity. He performed a U-turn far more spectacular than Macmillan's in 1962. In February the Upper Clyde Shipbuilders were rescued with new subsidies. The Budget that spring was strongly reflationary; monetary policy was relaxed. In August a powerfully interventionist Industry Bill was enacted. Meanwhile, Heath sued for a new compact with the trade unions. When his series of talks at Chequers failed he went ahead, and on 6 November 1972, a fateful date, legislated statutory controls on pay and prices. The times were not favourable to incomes policies. World commodity prices were exploding. The Yom Kippur war[14] in October 1973 resulted in a quadrupling of the world price of oil. By the beginning of 1974 inflation was running at 13 per cent. The incomes policy could not possibly take the strain. Inflation was by now in the blood. This time the miners advanced in the wake of the Gulf Sheiks. In December 1973 industry had to be put on to a three day week. In February Heath went to the country asking, 'Who rules Britain?' He lost. The miners ruled Britain.

Heath had tried first to escape from the Post-war Settlement, then to prop it up. The crisis had deepened since Wilson's days, even before OPEC took a hand. 'We have to find a more sensible way of settling our differences,' he had said at the end of the first miners' strike in 1972. But his bid for an incomes policy was made more difficult by his Industrial Relations Act of 1971. At first the unions refused to talk at all, especially when in June 1972 five dockers' pickets were committed to Pentonville Prison in contempt of the Act. The law had to be bent in a hurry to get them out before they became martyrs. The law was now an ass. However, the Industrial Relations Act remained on the Statute Book and Heath was not prepared to lose face by repealing it. This gave the TUC its excuse to break off the Chequers talks.

The point had been reached at which it was probably politically impossible for the unions to enter into any kind of effective agreement on pay with a Conservative government. The legal status of the trade unions had become too contentious an issue. Following the débâcle of 'In Place of Strife' the unions had moved towards a still closer relationship with the Labour Party. The object was to prevent anything like the Battle of Downing Street from occurring again; the effect was to increase the power of the unions within the Labour Movement. Rather than come to terms with Heath the TUC leaders preferred to await the return of a Labour government.

When the Tories had returned to power in 1951 the TUC had declared its readiness to work with the elected government of the day whatever its political complexion and Churchill had seized the outstretched hand with a kid glove. Now, in 1973, the unions were entirely hand in glove with the Labour Party, part of the government when it was in power and an extension of the Opposition when it was not. In this way the politics of the 1970s became polarised around the union question.

Moreover, the fall of the Heath government dealt a blow to the authority of government itself. When Wilson had been prevented from legislating against the unions, that had been a crisis of the Labour Movement. When the unions moved into confrontation with an elected government it was altogether a more serious matter. And when Heath had had to resort to the ultimate deterrent by a dissolution of Parliament and his bluff was called, he had disarmed not only himself but his successors. The country had taken a massive step towards the condition known in the 1970s as 'ungovernability'. Parliament was no longer sovereign. The courts could be flouted. Violence had become a feature of the industrial scene. Power could be exercised only if shared with non-elected bodies such as the TUC. Or so it seemed in the aftermath of the Heath débâcle. 'No Government in Britain can hope to succeed today without the good will of the unions,' wrote Norman St John Stevas in 1976.[15]

Trade unionism was one of the chief growth industries of the 1970s. This was largely due to the burgeoning of the public service bureaucracies. Between 1961 and 1975 central government employment had increased by 27 per cent and local government employment by 70 per cent. For example, the National Union of Public Employees (NUPE), which was to play a leading role in the Winter of Discontent of 1978–9, grew from a membership of 265,000 in 1968 to 712,000 in 1978. This trade union expansion was also an unforeseen consequence of the incomes policies of the 1960s and 1970s. In order to ensure that their noses too were in the corporatist trough, the middle classes unionised themselves. Even the top civil servants, who included the people running the incomes policies, affiliated themselves to the TUC in brotherhood with the Transport and General Workers' Union. Clive Jenkins organised Midland Bank managers. In 1973 there took place the first ever major strike in the National Health Service. Doctors now learnt to engage in what they pleased to call 'industrial action'. Recorded in my notebooks is a BBC-TV news bulletin which began: 'Tonight militant consultants . . .' Thus were the professions proletarianised. We were all militants now.

Who governs? Heath had asked. Many now thought the answer was the leaders of the TUC, whom they saw on their television screens, coming in and out of Downing Street. With Wilson's return to office in the wreckage of Heath's confrontation with the miners the Social Contract came into force. This Rousseauistic euphemism was the brainchild of Jack Jones, militant shop steward turned left-wing statesman. After the Labour Party split of 1931 Ernest Bevin had acted to enlarge the influence of the unions within the Party to prevent such a débâcle from happening again; after the débâcle of 'In Place of Strife', Jones, Bevin's successor at Transport House, had done likewise. He had established a Liaison Committee consisting of representatives of the General Council and the 'Shadow' Cabinet and National Executive Committee of the Party. It was there that the Social Contract was hatched.

The notion was that if a Labour government pursued economic and social policies acceptable to the unions a positive response would be forthcoming. 'A government which is prepared to tackle the problem of prices in the shops, rents and housing costs and put up pensions will certainly get the co-operation of the trade union movement and there will be moderation,' Jones had promised as Labour moved back into power. In the first year of the Social Contract inflation soared to 27 per cent. The miners had been bought off for 22 per cent. By the June of 1975 earnings had increased by an average of 26·6 per cent, weekly wage rates by a staggering 33 per cent. In exchange for their restored legal immunities and for the food subsidies, price and rent controls contained in Denis Healey's first Budget, and the 'howls of anguish' he had promised to extract from the rich, the unions had delivered nothing. The Social Contract, said the *Daily Mirror*, was 'a shameful flop'. Joel Barnett, the Chief Secretary to the Treasury, wrote later: 'To my mind the only give and take in the contract was that the government gave and the unions took.'[16]

Who governed? A Gallup Poll found that 52 per cent thought Jack Jones the most powerful man in the country, only 34 per cent the Prime Minister. The truth of the moment was that no one had power. With inflation soaring frighteningly out of control, the Cabinet committees concerned with economic matters 'merely watched passively the slide towards hyper-inflation during the spring and early summer of 1975,' according to another inside witness.[17] People began to imagine they could hear not the tumbrils but the wheelbarrows of Weimar rolling in the streets. In fact it had been mass unemployment, and not the earlier hyper-inflation, which paved the path for Adolf Hitler and brought down the Weimar Republic. Nevertheless, amid now fast-rising unemployment, Weimar with its hooligan violence, aimless sexual freedom, its superstitions and cults, and intellectual proletarianisation, offered tempting analogies to pessimists.

By the summer of 1975 something had to be done. The government now had a majority at Westminster, though a slender one. The referendum on Britain's continuing membership of the Common Market was safely out of the way. A run on the pound in July helped to concentrate the minds of the unions. Jack Jones was converted to the need to restrain wages below the level at which prices were rising. The pay restraint was to be voluntary; everyone was to get a flat £6 a week up to £8,500 a year, and above that nothing. For two years the policy worked not badly. By the summer of 1977 average earnings were increasing at an average of 14 per cent while price inflation was down to 13 per cent.

By that time, however, the real living standards of the average family had fallen in two successive years, by about £7 a week in total. In December 1973 the real weekly take-home pay of a family (a married couple with two children) averaged £70.20, in 1977 £63.10. Deteriorations on this scale were quite unprecedented. Annual increases of two or three per cent a year in real incomes had come to be regarded as a standard feature of post-war capitalism. The French philosopher and commentator, Raymond Aron, had dubbed this the 'revolution of rising expectations'. In 1973 55 per cent of people looked forward to higher living standards in the following year; by 1977 this figure was only 23 per cent. The counter-revolution was in progress.

Not only were average wages failing to keep up with inflation but the first two phases of the policy, combined with a new militancy among the unions of the unskilled, had put a fierce squeeze on differentials. The gap was narrowing between skilled and unskilled, manual and non-manual, male and female, older and younger workers. Income tax was up from 30 to 35 pence in the pound. No wonder the pay policy was beginning to break down. Meanwhile, something else had happened. When Labour returned to power in 1974, full employment was not as full as it had been, but with unemployment figures standing at just over half a million (less than 2·5 per cent of the work force) it could not be claimed seriously – although some did – that the goal of full employment had been abandoned. Some fifteen months later unemployment topped the million mark for the first time since 1940. Now the cornerstone itself of the Post-war Settlement was crumbling.

Not only in Britain was this happening. The recession was world-wide, and the deepest by far since the 1930s. At first governments had struggled to keep growth going but one by one they gave in. Deflation was back in business. Keynes was proclaimed dead: monetarism became the new orthodoxy. The Labour government held out until the last. As Joel Barnett recorded: 'The Chancellor . . . made the fundamental decision to react to the oil crisis in a different way from the Germans and the Japanese, and indeed from many other developed countries. Instead of cutting expenditure to take account of the massive oil price increase of 1973 . . . [he] decided to maintain our expenditure and borrow to meet the deficit.'[18] By 1976 public expenditure and borrowing were both out of control. In July there was a run on the pound, stemmed for a while by expenditure cuts and another tranche of borrowing from the International Monetary Fund. In the autumn a crisis broke out again. Healey was on his way to Heathrow Airport listening in his car to the news of the fall of the pound. Instead of heading for Manila, where the IMF was meeting, he diverted to Blackpool, where the Labour Party conference was meeting. There, to boos and catcalls, he stood amidst the debris of his policy and announced his application to the Fund for what would this time have to be a conditional loan. All other credit was exhausted. A conditional loan meant that the conduct of the British economy would be placed under surveillance. That was something which happened to Third World countries.

For Labour, 1976 was the year of the U-turn. In his Budget that spring Denis Healey, as we shall see later, had taken the decisive step towards monetarism. At the Labour Party conference that autumn Callaghan spoke words which effectively buried Keynes. 'You cannot spend your way out of a recession,' he asserted. But now, in November, while the bailiffs from the IMF waited in a London hotel, the Cabinet faced the bankruptcy of Croslandite socialism. Everything that he had predicted would be the consequence of nil growth and rampant inflation now came about. The Welfare State could no longer be sustained on its existing scale, social spending had to be curtailed.

The alternative approach insisted upon by the Treasury under pressure from the IMF made no sense to Crosland; to deflate when 1·25 million were unemployed stuck in his Keynesian throat; deflation would mean falling tax revenues, unemployment would increase the cost of benefits; the fiscal crisis of the Welfare State would deepen. But the government was no longer its own master. 'Even if the Government survives, does it make such a difference if Labour measures can't be implemented?' he wondered.[19] For Croslandite socialism had little or nothing to say about the creation of resources; it was concerned with their distribution. Now it stood empty-handed, offering sympathy and the dole. It was worse than that, for public spending was not an end in itself but one of the means to a broader social equality in which the cards of opportunity would be re-dealt.

The goal of revisionist socialism was equality. Nothing had happened to invalidate its goals, only the means were no longer available; and as Crosland, in his love of liberty, had always insisted, revisionism was a doctrine as much about means as about ends.

The Cabinet agreed to cut public borrowing from a planned £10·5 billions to £8·7 billions. The proportion of national wealth consumed by public spending (which in 1975 had reached 50 per cent) was reduced to 44 per cent by 1977. The world did not end. In fact the immediate crisis passed remarkably swiftly. The balance of payments was restored to surplus. Unemployment was rising but so were real living standards once more. By 1978 inflation was at last down in single figures again. But then, as Burckhardt said of the French Revolution, 'did the curtain rise on that great farce of hope.'

In the first weeks of 1979 a wave of industrial militancy spread across the land. In the months which preceded it economic logic prevailed over political prudence; greed and envy burst from beneath the skin, as is their way; and folly, vanity and cowardice played their familiar roles. These were the immediate causes of the events of the Winter of Discontent as it soon became known. Nothing that happened was quite inevitable, yet the roots of what happened can be seen stretching deep into the post-war period. They were a manifestation of what we shall call the politics of decline (see Chapter 2). The Winter of Discontent put the finishing touches to the destruction of the Post-war Settlement. It made a fitting obituary to the Old Order.

In the summer of 1978 the pay policy had been due to enter its fourth stage. One problem with pay policies is that they are more useful as temporary instruments of crisis management than they are as tools of regular government. It is relatively easy to impose a period of crude restraint in moments of grave emergency. The British are good at that sort of thing, going back to war-time rationing and the Blitz. But as the policy has to be relaxed and refined, made necessarily more flexible, resentments and envies mount. One consequence of pay policy is to draw attention to what others are being paid. Pay is news. As the official negotiators go slow, the initiative passes to the unofficial negotiators. The moguls of the TUC, observed coming and going on television, are seen to be in collusion with government and employers; even the authority of the shop floor leadership can become undermined, giving rise to the *unofficial* unofficial strike. Two years is about the limit of effective wage restraint; then comes the problem of 're-entry', how to return to normal collective bargaining without inflationary burn-out. Almost by definition re-entry has to be attempted when circumstances are improving, partly as the result of temporary wage restraint. As real living standards rise again, so do expectations. Invariably it is when things are looking up that heads appear above the barricades. All these factors were at work in 1978 and, in addition, there was a smell of North Sea oil in the air. Having already largely broken down in the public sector, the pay policy was now threatening to break down in the private sector. The spending cuts forced upon the Cabinet in 1976 had excited the militancy of the burgeoning public service unions. Callaghan's fears were amply justified when he warned: 'I say to those who are calling for a return this year to free collective bargaining that in my view that would be a return, this year, to free collective chaos.'

pay policy = income policy

The writing was on the wall in the largest letters when, at the last conference of his union before his retirement, Jack Jones was repudiated by his members, who insisted on a return to 'unfettered collective bargaining'. Nevertheless, from the government's point of view there was no avoiding a fourth stage of the pay policy. Not only was it necessary for keeping up the fight against inflation but also the authority of the government depended upon it. Labour no longer had a majority in the House of Commons and was depending on Liberal support. Its credibility was heavily invested in its claim to a special relationship with the unions. Incomes policy was its alternative to confrontation of the kind which had developed under Edward Heath and which would surely be the result of the policies proposed by Margaret Thatcher. If the unions could not agree to a further phase of voluntary restraint they must be seen to acquiesce in the government's more responsible view of the matter. By implication the government was now saying that the country could not be governed effectively without some permanent substitute for free collective bargaining, some alternative to free collective chaos. Its policy was rejected by the annual Trades Union Congress and repudiated by the Labour Party conference. The government could act in what it took to be the national interest and appeal to the electorate as a whole only by defying the Labour Movement: it could appease the party and the unions only by alienating the country. The contradictions were closing in.

It is the unfortunate logic of incomes policies that they become more restrictive in money terms as they become more relaxed in real terms. Logic in this case required the 'norm' to be pitched below the Treasury's forecast of the rate at which earnings were actually likely to rise, which was estimated at 10–11 per cent. Nevertheless, when the Cabinet endorsed – which it did with some foreboding reluctance – the Treasury's figure of 5 per cent it did so in the expectation that this would serve more as a campaign point in an autumn election than as a realistic target for the coming pay round.[20]

However, on Thursday, 7 September, Callaghan flabbergasted his Cabinet by announcing that he had that morning informed the Queen that there would be no election that year. We may guess that the Queen was scarcely less astonished, for an October election had been regarded as a racing certainty. Transport House had started to press the buttons. Plans for election night television coverage were already under discussion with the broadcasting organisations. When Callaghan sang, 'There was I, waiting at the church', to the annual Trades Union Congress in Brighton earlier that week few took the hint, least of all the luminaries of Trade Unions for a Labour Victory, who on the way down had discussed battle plans at the Callaghan farm in Sussex. But behind the scenes there had been some frantic lobbying by a 'cold feet' group at the centre of which was Michael Foot, who thereby performed one of his many disservices to the Labour Movement. While no one can say whether Callaghan would have won in the autumn of 1978 – my own opinion was that he would not have – at least he would have been in with a chance. The discretion vested in a Prime Minister to obtain a dissolution of Parliament at a moment of his own choosing gives him an immense advantage over his opponents but it places an awesome responsibility upon him to get the timing right. Callaghan's problem as he pored over the entrails of the opinion polls was that he could not be certain of winning, and if he went for an election and lost he alone would be blamed; there was the risk that come the spring he would be certain of losing but, on the other hand, you never could tell . . . So he funked it. He put off the evil day and, when it came, it was indeed he who was blamed.

To set off into a final winter without secure means of parliamentary support and without proper defences against inflation was foolhardy in the extreme. As William Rodgers puts it, 'having embarked upon a courageous but fraught pay policy, the wise course was to submit to the electorate rather than to invite the unions to tear it apart.'[21] That is what they proceeded at once to do. With Jack Jones gone the Transport and General Workers' Union was out to smash the incomes policy. The 5 per cent target which the government had declared served not as a restraint but as a red flag to the inflationary bull. In December one Cabinet Minister was lamenting, 'Five per cent originally meant seven or eight, now it means nine or ten.' To the TGWU it meant 22 per cent. That was what it was claiming for the road haulage drivers who, having duly turned down a 13 per cent offer, came out on strike in January 1979. That was the beginning, in full earnest, of the Winter of Discontent.

Industrial disorder spread as by contagion. It was far from being a simple display of class grievance or trade union solidarity. In the 1970s the banner of tax revolt had been carried from California and Massachusetts into the social democratic fastnesses of Scandinavia. It was an aspect of 'overload' and 'ungovernability', one of the responses to the rising curve of government expenditure in conditions of economic recession. In Britain some 2½ million more people were paying tax in 1979 than in 1974 and the same number had passed from the lowest into the higher tax bands. 'Go anywhere in the country,' Thatcher told Callaghan in the no-confidence debate which finally brought him down, 'and the demand will be for two things – less tax and more law and order.' Healey's 'howls of anguish' were coming not from the rich but from the mortgage-paying, car-driving, foreign-holiday-taking affluent working classes.

Not only did the Winter of Discontent have the character of a tax revolt but also that of a peasant revolt. On the coat-tails of the proverbially acquisitive Ford workers, the tanker drivers and the general haulage drivers, came the low-paid in their hordes, the swollen armies of local government and health service employees. A recent estimate had put the number of male workers, manual and non-manual, earning £50 or less a week at some 600,000. Their pay compared with an average industrial earning of £78.40. There were now well over 2 million local authority employees in England and Wales of whom the bottom 10 per cent earned £40 a week. Dustmen were better off than this, averaging £56. In the National Health Service the bottom decile earned £48 a week. The government's own definition of a poverty line was £55 a week for a married man with two children. There were a million working men in Britain earning less. We were paying ourselves more than we could afford, said the bankers and the economic journalists. Our decline had reached the point at which we could not afford to pay ourselves enough to hold a decent society together.

The winter was cold. Snow lay on the ground. Callaghan was in Guadeloupe for an economic 'summit' meeting. He was photographed sitting under a palm tree. At the airport on his return he was asked about the crisis and is reputed to have asked (although there is no record of it) 'Crisis? What crisis?' This attempt at Macmillan-style nonchalance went down badly. Members of his Cabinet were under no illusions about the predicament now facing the government. Its authority was on the line. The question, 'Who governs?' had been

Winter of Discontent = widespread strikes/labor unrest

asked again. It had brought Heath down. It would bring Callaghan down unless he acted. If the unions would not allow him the authority to govern the country he must appeal to the country for the authority to govern the unions. That was the position. Everyone knew it. 'Either Jim must stand up and read the Riot Act or he must go to the bloody country,' said one of his oldest and most loyal friends. He did neither. He appealed in vain to the TUC but the TUC had little or no authority over affiliated unions. At Congress House, the TUC general-secretary, Len Murray, was near to despair: this was not trade unionism, this was 'syndicalism'. It was taking over from trade unionism as he knew it. Just as the TUC had no control over the unions the unions had lost control of their members. In the trade union boom of the 1970s NUPE had recruited members faster than it could train organisers. Local militants were a law unto themselves, many of them self-appointed. A local officer of the TGWU in South Wales said, 'Talk about bloody-mindedness, this is bloody-mindlessness!' The unions, quite simply, were out of control.

A Callaghan aide at Number 10 complained, 'We're trying to hold the line with no weapons at our disposal.' There were weapons but the government was not prepared to use them. The crisis it faced in the January and February of 1979 was nothing like as serious as the one with which Heath had had to deal in 1974: then the power supplies of the nation were in jeopardy and workers had had to be put on a three-day week; but in January 1979 there were relatively few lay-offs (about 250,000 by the end of the month) and essential supplies were moving. There was some panic buying in the shops but little cause for it. There was no need to risk intensifying the conflict by declaring a State of Emergency as Heath had done in 1974. Even Rodgers, who as Transport Minister was the most 'hawkish' member of the Cabinet, agreed with that. But he wanted to use troops to take out what he called 'soft targets', for example to move a consignment of pharmaceutical drugs bottled up in the docks at Hull. Instead, the Home Secretary, Merlyn Rees, requested the permission of the TGWU leaders for the supplies to be moved. Even they were taken aback by this display of Ministerial subservience. The government stood petrified in the face of the trade union power it had done so much to promote – power now turned to anarchy. The Cabinet solemnly considered whether the troops could dig graves. But the use of troops in any contingency was anathema to Rees. Damage limitation was the government's only policy – in other words, appeasement. After 1975 anything which smacked of confrontation was not to be thought of. 'By God I'll confront them,' said Thatcher on the

Jimmy Young show. Her demeanour was in sharp contrast to the
Prime Minister's. Would he call the unions to order? 'No,' said a
Cabinet colleague, slightly misquoting Byron:

A little still he strove and much repented,
And whispering, 'I will ne'er consent', consented.

In the circumstances he faced it was not in his character to do
otherwise.

No man alive better personified the old Labour Movement now
dying than James Callaghan. He had grown up with it and of it. The
son of a seaman and a domestic servant he owed everything to it,
including his education. While each of Labour's three post-war
leaders had been Oxford men he had had no university education at
all, a fact he seldom forgot. Few who dealt with him as Chancellor of
the Exchequer, Home Secretary, Foreign Secretary and, finally, as
Prime Minister held his intellectual powers in the low esteem in which
he held them himself. That made him a chippy sort of character. Born
in 1912, his political apprenticeship was served against the background of mass unemployment and degrading poverty; he was the last
of the 1930s generation to reach the top. It is one of the paradoxes of
post-war politics that the men presiding over an era of expansive
optimism were men haunted from their earlier lives by a sense of
pessimism. He was of a foreboding bent of mind and it was appropriate, perhaps, that he should have come to the top as the 'long boom'
ended, in time to preside over the passing of the *ancien régime*.

He had entered Parliament in 1945 wearing his Naval Lieutenant's uniform. The navyman in him accompanied him through his long
career and he exercised his high offices with a jaunty authoritarian-
ism. He was the first professional trade union official to become
Prime Minister and almost certainly the last. He was the last of
Bevin's breed. However, he had held no high office in the union
movement and such were its snobberies that as a former organiser for
the Inland Revenue Staff Federation, a collector of tax collectors, he
was regarded by the vanguard of the working class in much the same
way as the Service Corps or the NAAFI would be regarded by a crack
regiment of the line. In the 1950s he made his career on the right of
the Labour Party, which in those days was where the union leaders
stood and where the power lay. He supported Hugh Gaitskell
politically but was never a member intellectually or socially of the
Gaitskell set. On Gaitskell's death in 1963 he played third man in the
election in which Harold Wilson beat George Brown. His interven-

tion helped to put Wilson in. At that time Callaghan had no base either in the party, the Movement or the country. It was later that he built the remainder of his career around an alliance with the trade union movement. 'Rebuilt' is a better word for what he had to do, for his career as Chancellor of the Exchequer ended in the ruin of devaluation. In 1967 there would have been few takers for Callaghan as Prime Minister. 'Policeman Jim' became Home Secretary – he had been a parliamentary adviser to the Police Federation. He gave more time and thought to his farm in Sussex. The controversies around the White Paper 'In Place of Strife' gave him his chance to establish, for the first time in his career, a real political base. By then, perhaps, the tanks of his ambition had been refuelled with sour grapes – Harold Wilson and Barbara Castle thought so. Be that as it may, both opportunism and tribal instinct placed him on the unions' side. Moreover, his political judgment told him that Wilson and Labour would not win another election by biting the hand which fed the ballot boxes. He knew his Labour Movement. He was a traditionalist – the 'Keeper of the Cloth Cap'.

When he became Prime Minister seven years later he was sixty-four. His position was weak in every respect. He had scarcely a majority in Parliament. He had been elected to the leadership of his party only narrowly, by 141 votes to Michael Foot's 133 and Denis Healey's 38. He had no mandate from the people, having not fought or won an election. The National Executive Committee and the party conference were no longer under the control of the parliamentary leadership. With the incorporation of Michael Foot within the Cabinet, Callaghan now faced in Tony Benn a much more formidable enemy on the left. He inherited a worsening economic crisis. Within a year he was governing by permission not only of the IMF but of the Liberal Party with whom he had been obliged to form a parliamentary pact. For all that, James Callaghan now found his métier. He was a good Prime Minister.

Vastly experienced by now, of solid conservative temperament, ungiven to ideological predilection, possessed of sound populist instinct, his talents were appropriate to a world rapidly falling apart, as it seemed to him it was. Wilson, by the end of his career, had become a master at avoiding unpleasant problems, most of which were familiarly insoluble. Callaghan preferred to take them on bluntly. He restored Cabinet government in some degree, even in the conduct of economic policy; he used his Cabinet as it should be used, a tool of government by consent. The great IMF trauma occurred within months of Wilson's hasty departure, like a day of reckoning come. Callaghan skilfully played both wings of his Cabinet, Keynesian and socialist, against the middle, himself; he managed at the same time to avoid calamity and face the inevitable. He steered his government through a change of policy more drastic than the U-turns of the Macmillan and Heath governments and did so without a resignation.

Mellowed by power, ambition now all spent, more confident in himself, or perhaps by now resigned to the limits of what might be achieved, he took to addressing the nation as if leaning – somewhat sternly – over a farmyard gate. He was the Stanley Baldwin of his day. Much of what he said was at variance with the policies of his party but in tune with the aspirations of the people. His populist instincts told him which way the wind was blowing. When he told the 1976 party conference that it was no longer feasible for a government to spend its way out of recession it was not that he had been converted to monetarism, which he would have regarded as too new-fangled for an old fuddy-duddy such as himself; it was Polonius speaking, not Milton Friedman. He had always had a keen ear for the concerns and prejudices of ordinary people. As Home Secretary he had understood well that concern for law and order was not the monopoly of Tory ladies in their hats. When he called for a 'Great Debate' about the quality and the content of teaching in schools he was voicing a widespread and growing dissatisfaction among working families. He told the ideologues on the NEC, 'If you want to retain power you have got to listen to what people – our people – say and what they want. If you talk to people in the factories and in the clubs, they all want to pay less tax. They are more interested in that than the Government giving money away in other directions.' Callaghan was one of the first to grasp the populist roots of Thatcherism.

He spoke his mind, 'Honest Jim', and restored to politics some of the dignity lost in the last Wilson years. The public liked his old-fashioned style. To his pleasure, and probably to his surprise, he found himself well liked, even fondly regarded – a bit of a national character. He was the popular Prime Minister of an unsuccessful government.

Like Baldwin, and Cincinnatus before him, 'Farmer Jim' enjoyed speaking of his return to the plough. No one took him very seriously, for he also enjoyed being Prime Minister. That was until the events of January and February of 1979. Now he meant what he was saying. The heart went out of him as the world he knew was stood upon its head. He was utterly perplexed by the things that were happening, paralysed and powerless. Everything he had stood for, and every-

Crisis of J. Callaghan, 1979

thing he was, was now in peril. 'Policeman Jim' was appalled by the lawlessness which now took place in the name of the Labour Movement. He was shocked, and deeply hurt – for his skin was always thin – at what he took to be the ingratitude of the trade union leaders. He, above all men, had championed them and now they were busy losing him the election. Yet psychologically he was incapable of acting, petrified by all of his past. How could he, a Labour Prime Minister, take on the unions? The Labour Party *was* the unions. As the Labour Movement tore itself apart that winter it was James Callaghan who was torn limb from limb.

In the Winter of Discontent television did for class war what it had done for war in Vietnam. The nation was brought nowhere near to its knees; people were not even seriously inconvenienced. It was nothing like as bad as it had been in 1974 when the lights went out. Outrageous acts there were, but many fewer than legend would have it. Not many emergencies were turned from the hospitals, schoolchildren came to no great harm, and only in parts of Lancashire were the dead unburied. It was the spectacle that was presented to the public which made the Winter of Discontent such an unmitigated disaster for Labour. For many years the unions had been unpopular in the land. High proportions of respondents to opinion polls agreed with the pollsters that the unions were 'too powerful'. With the signing of the Social Contract they had been admitted to an even more privileged and powerful role, or so it seemed. Their leaders strode through the corridors of power as if they owned them. Now, the spectacle, as seen on television, was not so much of power – as embodied in the coal miners – but of anarchy and pettiness. The country seemed to be in the hands of self-appointed Gauleiters, pickets and strike committees, who officiously decreed who and what should pass. Their permission was required for medical supplies to move or for ambulances to take the sick to hospital. 'If it means lives lost, that is how it must be,' said one of them. They decided whether or not heating fuels would enter hospitals or whether schools would open their doors to shivering children. The country seemed to be caught in the grip of a militant trade union psychology, with everything politicised and proletarianised. The National Union of Teachers felt obliged to instruct its members not to cross NUPE picket lines. Mr Geoff Davies, head of Parson's Down junior and infants' school at Thatcham, Berks, asked the parents of children who normally had school dinners to arrange for them to go home for dinner. He told them in a letter, 'We cannot allow you to provide packed meals instead, as this

could be regarded as a form of strike breaking. Children who
normally bring a packed lunch will not be affected.'

Hundreds of thousands of commuters, nursing their accumulated
rage at ASLEF and the NUR, now saw acted out before their eyes on
television everything that trade unionism had come to mean for them.
The same must have been true of many motor workers sick of being
press-ganged out on strike by militant stewards, of doctors (themselves far from blameless), nurses and patients who knew the sort of
things that had been going on in hospitals, of council tenants with
dripping walls awaiting the attention of Direct Labour departments,
of ratepayers fed up with overflowing dustbins. Seen on television it
may have all looked more dramatic and awful than it was, but to claim
that the Winter of Discontent was created by the media is to ignore
and demean the daily experience of millions of Britons at that time.
What they heard and saw rang true. It is the people who best know
what is going on among the people.

The Winter of Discontent was the moment when the Old Order
crumbled. From the latter part of the 1960s and throughout the 1970s,
the last and best hope of preserving the Post-war Settlement had
seemed to lie with the trade unions. Barbara Castle and Harold
Wilson had inaugurated the attempt to bring the unions within the
law and make the practice of collective bargaining compatible with
the achievement of prosperity. For a decade this project obsessed and
eventually destroyed successive governments. As the 1970s advanced
the co-operation of the trade union movement became increasingly
indispensable if the Keynesian circle was to be squared in order to
make possible full employment, economic growth and universal
welfare, all at stable prices. Too much was asked of the unions in this;
in return they asked too much of government. Neither side could
deliver. For each side the negative aspects of their too ambitious
bargain came to outweigh the positive: the unions practised wage
restraint according to their lights but full employment was abandoned
none the less and social spending cut; the government conferred all
manner of privileges upon the unions, enhancing their negative
power, but wage inflation continued none the less and there was no
bonus in productivity. If there was something aspiring to be called a
'consensus', in the sense of a general disposition to uphold the
Post-war Settlement by co-operation across the class divide between
government, employers and trade unions, it was the events of the
winter of 1979, not Margaret Thatcher, which put an end to it.

Could it have succeeded? In principle, yes it could, for something
of the kind had succeeded in Sweden, the most socialist of the West

European democracies, and in Germany, one of the least socialist. But Britain was not a Sweden, or a Germany: the great Social Democratic project of the 1960s and the 1970s was attempted against, as we shall see in a moment, a backdrop of accelerating decline; moreover, it was superimposed upon a society in many ways mal- formed for modern purposes, whose traditions and folk memories were at war with the enterprise in hand. The pretension of the unions to become a partner in government was, to be fair to them, never wholehearted. Some of their leaders saw it as the only way of reconciling full employment and free collective bargaining but others did not, and correctly predicted that this enterprise would end in tears or something worse. The unions did not so much aspire to corporate status; they found it thrust upon them. It was an unhealthy and corrupting role. The Winter of Discontent was a comment not only on a failed government but on a union leadership which had comprom- ised its independence. Moreover, if what the Labour Movement represented was an alternative and morally superior culture to the one which offered its embrace, then that too became a casualty. For after what had taken place in the hospitals and schools it would not be possible for some while to regard the collectivist thrust of the Labour Movement as synonymous with the forward march of humanity. The *ancien régime* and the old Labour Movement brought each other down.

2

The Politics of Decline

The Winter of Discontent was at the same time a manifestation of the politics of decline. For economic failure had gradually taken its toll on the social cohesion and stability which had made Britain for so long one of the political wonders of the world. The word 'decline' crept into the political vocabulary some time towards the end of the 1970s, although the condition it described had long been present. Slower growth than in other countries results in relative decline, and that had been the British condition not only throughout the long post-war boom but also throughout the twentieth century. More insidious are the consequences of persistently slow growth: the weakening of the industrial base and the deterioration of the human resources available to it. By this means slow growth engenders slower growth, and relative decline can lead in the end to absolute decline. This occurs when output falls or becomes insufficient to maintain the living standards of the people. Except for cyclical recessions it had never happened in the modern world. Could Britain be the first country to go from developed to under-developed?

The Establishment was slow to recognise the condition, and slower still to admit it. The political fiasco of Suez in 1956 had been a big jolt, not to the British people, who were quick to forgive and forget and to re-elect the Tories, under Harold Macmillan, in 1959, but to the governing class. The Empire had always been predominantly a ruling class affair, a point which eluded the many foreign observers who attributed Britain's post-war difficulties to the shock of losing it. The Suez incident, however, did administer a severe shock to the confidence of the governing class, bringing home some of the reality of Britain's post-imperial position. Yet Britain's leaders, misled by the Commonwealth and the much celebrated 'special relationship' with the United States, continued – well into the 1960s – to suppose that

Britain remained a Great Power. In the year following Suez the signing of the Treaty of Rome by France, Germany, Italy and the Benelux countries was viewed complacently in Britain and almost with indifference.

When the war ended in 1945 nobody predicted decline. To be sure, the country had been greatly enfeebled by the war – half of her overseas earnings had been wiped out, her export trade halved, and formidable debts accumulated – but the defeated and occupied powers of the continent had suffered far worse devastations. In the euphoria of victory there were few doubts that Britain would recover and hold her position politically as a member of the Big Three and industrially as the world's third greatest power. Policy was based on those assumptions. According to Kenneth Morgan, the historian of the Attlee government, later historians of decline have antedated their diagnosis. 'The post-war problems of the British economy should always be related to the belief, as widespread in Washington and Moscow as in London, that Britain between 1945 and 1951 was still a great power, and the leader of a struggling, exhausted continent in trying to generate a new and more stable international political and economic order.'[1]

Indeed, given the long years of relative decline which had preceded the war, the recovery after 1945 was remarkable. In the 1950s the decline in exports was halted and, for a time, reversed, and the balance of payments for the most part balanced. By Britain's own past sluggish standards the growth of the economy in the 1950s was good but nowhere near as good as that of others. Taking advantage of their access to American technology and of the favourable Keynesian economic environment of the post-war years the war-damaged economies of Europe recovered in remarkable fashion. While Britain grew at an average of 2·5 per cent per annum through the 1950s, growth in the rest of the industrialised world averaged 4 per cent. Germany was growing at more than twice the British rate. In the 1960s Britain, again by her own standards, did better still. Her economy grew at an average rate of 3·75 per cent but, again, the rest of the industrialised world averaged 5·5 per cent. Over the whole period of the 'long boom' (between 1950 and 1973) Japan averaged 9·7 per cent annual growth, Germany 6·0 per cent, France 5·1 per cent and Britain only 3·0 per cent. 'There is no record of any other power falling behind at such startling speed.'[2]

In terms of wealth per head of the population Britain grew between 1950 and 1973 at half the rate of Germany and France. In 1950 she had ranked among the very wealthiest nations of Europe, a little behind

Switzerland and Sweden, who had escaped the war, but comfortably ahead of Germany, France and all the others. By 1960 Germany was at the point of overtaking, by 1970 France had also moved ahead. In 1978, on the eve of the Winter of Discontent, the following countries were all more than 50 per cent better off than Britain in terms of per capita wealth: Germany, the Netherlands, Norway, Denmark, Belgium, and Sweden. By then France was exactly half as well off again and Japan very nearly so.

In 1950 Britain's 25·4 per cent share of world export trade in manufactured goods was artificially high as a result of the war. But already by 1953 it had fallen to 20 per cent as other economies recovered. Between 1951–5 her share of world markets averaged above 20 per cent while in the four years 1973–7 it had fallen to an average of 9 per cent. Over the same period Germany increased her share from 13 to 21 per cent, Japan from 4 to 14 per cent, while France held hers at above 9 per cent.

By all these measures of actual performance Britain experienced a steep relative decline during the twenty-three years of the 'long boom'. When it ended in 1973 the pace of relative decline accelerated. In the 1960s a growth rate of 3·75 per cent had compared with an OECD average of 4 per cent. In the 1970s Britain's 2 per cent compared with an average of 3·5 per cent. The growth in manufacturing industry was down to 0·1 per cent per annum, from an average annual 3·3 per cent during the previous decade. That compared with Germany's 3·6 per cent (6·6 per cent, 1960–70) and France's 2·1 per cent (5·4).

The measures of underlying economic performance tell a still more dismal tale. During the years of the 'long boom' productivity had grown at an annual average of 5·6 per cent in Germany, France and Italy while in Britain the growth rate had been only 3·1 per cent. After 1973 the growth of productivity in the three major west European economies slowed to 3·4 per cent but in Britain to 2·7 per cent. In manufacturing the deterioration in relative productivity growth was still worse. After 1973 Germany continued to improve by 2·5 per cent a year, France by 3·8 per cent but Britain by only 0·2 per cent. By 1980 output per head in manufacturing was only two-thirds that of Italy, half that of France and less than half that of Germany.

Economists quarrel about whether lack of investment is a symptom or a cause of Britain's decline. It is not disputed that we reinvest less of our wealth than others do. In the 1960s Britain devoted 17·8 per cent of her GDP to investment compared with an average of 20·8 per cent among industrialised nations belonging to the OECD. In the

1970s the proportion had grown to 18·7 per cent but the OECD average by more, to 22·2 per cent. Japan invests more than 30 per cent of her national product. A better measure of Britain's decline, perhaps, is the lag in *new* manufacturing investment. Between 1953 and 1960 we invested in new plant at half the rate of Germany. In the 1970s the British rate of capital investment per worker was half that of Germany and Japan and considerably lower than everybody else's.[3]

Britain lost not only her share of world markets but, increasingly after 1973, her share of her own domestic market. Others did not want our goods but neither did our own people. In 1963 we exported manufactured goods of twice the value of those we imported. By 1973 the surplus had almost gone. This was not due only, or in the 1970s even chiefly, to uncompetitiveness as measured by price but rather to uncompetitiveness in design, delivery, after-sales service or marketing. The British became increasingly habituated to the purchase of foreign goods in preference to their own. As this deterioration progressed, the providential oil from the North Sea began to flow in quantities sufficient to mask the deficit. Nevertheless, by 1983 Britain, once the proverbial workshop of the world, had become for the first time since the Industrial Revolution a net importer of manufactured goods.

A modern society cannot easily embrace the idea of decline. The idea of progress is too deeply embedded in the twentieth-century consciousness. In the post-war period Western Europe underwent a remarkable renaissance, literally a rebirth from the ashes of its civilisation. If progress could survive the experiences of the twentieth century then progress was indestructible. This belief was reinforced by the secular faith of the age. God was dead but hope of a heavenly kingdom had been replaced by hopes of an earthly one. Belief in the supreme power of science encouraged belief in the efficacy of social science too. Socialism became the religion of the age but a broader church grew up around faith in economic management and social engineering. It was complete with a clergy of experts of which the economist was the highest priest. John Maynard Keynes provided an Anglican version of the new religion and in the mixed economies and Welfare States of the West a generation grew up which took the advance of prosperity for granted. For these reasons the notion of decline was alien to the contemporary mind.

The Ancients of Greece and Rome had not made this assumption. They always took it for granted that States must rise and fall. For them it was written in nature that oceans flowed and ebbed, the sun rose and set, and wheels turned in their full circle. Man's own mortality provided a compelling model for the life and death of States and medical metaphors abound of which the 'English disease' is the latest in a long line. States are 'injured by time', said Aristotle, which is a view not very different from our contemporary theories of 'mature' and 'sclerotic' economies. Machiavelli, who lived through an age of decline, believed that 'since nature has not allowed worldly things to remain still, when they arrive at their final perfection, they have no further to climb and so they have to descend.' The belief that decline was more natural than stability had its psychological base in man's fallibility: he could be relied upon to sow the seeds of destruction within the city he had built. For the men of the Renaissance, as for many of the Romans, decline was thus a moral and, therefore, a political question. Luxury was commonly the corrupting agent. 'With greatness, riches increase, and with riches, vices increase, luxury, arrogance, lust . . . kingdoms which have been brought to the top by frugality have been ruined by opulence,' said the Venetian historian Giovanni Botero. 'It rarely happens that external forces ruin a state which has not first been corrupted by psychological or social ones.'[4]

Decline in those days almost invariably ended in the loss of liberty as the result of military defeat. Machiavelli, who lived to see the Italian Republics overrun by the outside powers of France, Germany and Spain, identified another aspect of political fallibility, what today we would call the boredom factor: 'Ancient writers were of the opinion,' he noted, 'that men are wont to get annoyed with adversity and fed up with prosperity, both of which passions give rise to the same effect.' His study of politics led him to the conclusion that it was virtually 'impossible to constitute a republic that shall last for ever.' Experience showed that cities 'had never increased in dominion or riches except while they had been at liberty.' But how was liberty to be preserved? Adaptability was Machiavelli's answer. The capacity to change was the key to a republic's survival. Modern economists give an answer very similar to Machiavelli's and make adaptability the key to economic survival. 'All empires seem eventually to develop an intractable resistance to the change needed for the required growth of production.'[5]

Following the example of seventeenth-century Spain the moral account of decline gave way to explanations of a more economic or social kind. In the earlier part of the seventeenth century the decline of imperial Spain was generally perceived in terms of the decline of Rome, but by the eighteenth century it was ancient Rome which was being seen in terms of modern Spain. Spanish critics of the time, the *arbitristas*, focused on inflation, over-taxation, the absence of a work ethic and many other factors which today are part of the diagnosis of the 'English disease'. Spanish gold was seen by some as a curse in blessing's disguise, in the same way and for, essentially, the same reasons that some have seen North Sea oil as an agent of de-industrialisation. But once more it was failure to adapt, above all, which was the downfall of imperial Spain. 'It was one of the tragedies of Castile's history that it found itself, by the end of the reign of Philip II, in a position where it seemed that readjustment to the new economic realities could be achieved only at the price of sacrificing its most cherished ideals.'[6]

Gibbon, writing in the shadow of imperial Spain's decline and fall, a haunting event for a European of his time, treated many aspects of decline but in the end preferred the moral to the economic explanation. His version of Rome's demise was similar to the Romans' own: decadence, luxury, effeminacy, despotism and military weakness were no match for barbarian frugality, discipline, manliness, freedom and military strength. In their turn those of the Victorians who saw the challenge which faced them at the very moment of their pre-eminence saw it in remarkably Gibbonian terms. Haldane for example: 'The name of the little territory which encloses Weimar and Jena stirs the imagination of thousands of our youth of both sexes, even as the name of Jerusalem moved the hearts of men in the centuries behind us.'[7] For barbarians read Prussians. The virtues which Gibbon so admired, and what Adam Smith, influenced by him, had seen as 'the irresistible superiority which the militia of a barbarous has over a civilised nation' were now applied not only to the military arts, although they were not lacking, but to the development and organisation of production in the service of the State. Meanwhile, it was Britain which was succumbing to the Roman disease.

An intimation of Britain's decline as a manufacturing power was given to the Victorians with the Paris International Exhibition of 1867. There the advances of German engineering (we would now say technology) were on display. One observer, Dr Lyon Playfair, reported: 'I am sorry to say that, with very few exceptions, a singular accordance of opinion prevailed that our country had shown little inventiveness and made little progress in the peaceful arts of industry since 1862.' Playfair, who was a campaigner for industrial education on the continental model, noted that all the major European countries possessed 'good systems of industrial education for the masters and managers of factories and workshops, and that England possesses none.'[8] The following year, 1868, a Royal Commission – they were legion – was established, and it reported in terms which echo in the words of James Callaghan and Sir Keith Joseph in the 1970s and 1980s: 'our industrial classes have not even that basis of sound general education on which alone technical education can rest.'[9]

Here then are two recurrent and interwoven themes of British decline and, most likely, two of its chief causes – technological laggardliness and inappropriate education – manifesting themselves at the very apogee of Britain's industrial power. Why did Britain begin to fall behind at about this time? 'This sudden transformation of the leading and most dynamic industrial economy into the most sluggish and conservative in the short space of thirty or forty years (1860–90/1900) is', in the words of Eric Hobsbawm, 'the crucial question of British economic history.'[10] There are many theories and all bear upon the crucial question of our own times which is why, during the 'long boom' of the post-war years, did Britain fall so disastrously behind?

Hobsbawm puts his question in a way which implies that virtues which were present in the first Industrial Revolution, say between 1740–1850, were absent during the second, from say 1870. But this is now disputed. We are told that the first Industrial Revolution was no miracle of enterprise or innovation but rather a slow plodding affair. Britain's rate of economic growth rate was slow then, later and now. Investment rates were low and too narrowly based on cotton, coal, iron and steel; incomes grew only slowly and the workers who left the land for industry were mere factory fodder and remained the most ignorant industrial peasantry in Europe. Britain emerged from the Industrial Revolution less than fully transformed; the earliness of industrialisation had meant that it had taken place within an obsolete institutional structure and was superimposed upon a still aristocratic society.[11]

In any case, the capacities required for success in the second Industrial Revolution were not those which had been required in the first. The day of the craftsman engineers was over. Their heyday had been in the early phase of the Industrial Revolution, in the eighteenth century when James Watt's steam engine and the early textile machinery and machine tools were designed and made. By mid-Victorian times the mechanical engineer, the romantic hero of the early industrial revolution, had become the victim of social snobbery. In 1847 the engineers split into professionals, who were the civil engineers, and mechanicals. The chief reason was the rise to prominence of George Stephenson, who could scarcely read and was not a 'gentleman'. More than a century of industrial decline is encapsulated in this professional exclusion of the engineer which typifies the 'gentlemen' and 'players' syndrome, of which Harold Wilson was to make much in his modernising campaign of 1964. Stephenson warned at the time: 'Unless the talent of England is concentrated, it is not unlikely that some of the continental talented men might take part of the business of this country.'[12] In 1977 a Department of Industry study reported: 'in manufacturing industry generally the status of mechanical engineering is low in itself, and production engineers are regarded as the Cinderella of the profession.'

In the second Industrial Revolution, out of which came the electrical and chemical industries and the motor car, it was the application of science to industry which was at a premium. In that Britain was already a laggard. Continuity may be the clue to the history of British decline. Certainly there is a continuity of lament. Many of the letters written to *The Times* in the late Victorian or Edwardian era could have been reprinted in the 1960s and 1970s, or indeed today. Educational failure, particularly in the matter of producing an adequately trained labour force, and the failure to apply technology to production were then, as again now, seen as the chief national weaknesses. For example, it was not until 1902 that Britain at last arrived at a national system of secondary education and even then local authorities were only empowered, not required, to provide post-elementary education in addition to that provided by the churches. The statutory school leaving age remained at 12, although local authorities could, if they wished, raise it to 14. Until 1876 not even elementary education had been compulsory. The Foster Act of 1870 created school boards to fill the gaps, if they thought fit, in the voluntary system. Until then elementary education had been re-garded as a matter of charity rather than of national duty or purpose.

Prussia, in contrast, took education to be a duty of the State from birth to adulthood. Elementary school, secondary school and university were integrated into a national system. By late Victorian times the *Gymnasia* (grammar schools) had been complemented by the *Realschulen* (technical schools) which were given an equal status. Classics and science were provided on an equivalent basis and held in equal esteem. In Britain no start was made on technical education until 1889. Another Paris Exhibition had brought another shock of discovery and another Royal Commission had been instituted. At that time the Polytechnic at Zürich had 600 students, half of whom were foreign but none British. The Commission was told by the Professor of Civil Engineering at University College, London, 'I believe the reason is that among the English the class of boys does not exist who could take these examinations.'[13] By the turn of the century technical education was still only rudimentary. According to Halévy by Edwardian times it was widely agreed that the failure of the State to provide adequate technical education was the chief cause of the 'decline, or at least stagnation of British industrialism'.[14] Yet a government White Paper of 1956 approached the subject with all the thrill of discovery. 'From the USA, Russia and Western Europe comes the challenge to look to our system of technical education to see whether it bears comparison with what is being done abroad.' It concluded, 'we are in danger of being left behind.' Playfair had warned of that as early as 1853. At the time about which Halévy was writing, Germany was producing some 3,000 graduate engineers per year, while in Britain in 1913 only 350 graduated in all branches of science, technology and mathematics. Another sixty years on it was the same story. At the end of the 1970s there were 15,000 professional engineers graduating in Britain each year compared with, for example, 30,000 in France and 70,000 in Japan.

This paucity of technologists must have played a part in Britain's technological falling-behind in the late Victorian and Edwardian years. However, there was more to it than that. A sympathetic German observer, Wilhelm Dibelius, writing in 1922, blames not so much the educational system as 'the national aversion of the English people to systematic thinking.' Or, he might have added, to any form of systematic instruction. Samuel Smiles was pandering to the popular prejudice of his times when he wrote in *Self Help* (which, published in 1859, sold 55,000 copies) that, 'Anybody who devotes himself to making money, body and soul, can scarcely fail to make himself rich. Very little brains will do.' In 1974, at an examiners' meeting at the University of Birmingham, one of the examiners said of a poor student, 'Give him a third and let him be a businessman!'

Very little brains would do also for the gentlemen. When Harold Wilson hung the 'grouse moor image' round the neck of his Conservative opponent, Sir Alec Douglas-Home, in 1963, he was reviving the complaint first heard in 1909, in Arthur Shadwell's *Industrial Efficiency*, that the entrepreneur, the salt of the Industrial Revolution, had succumbed to the aristocratic embrace and the lure of English country life. Wilson, as we have already mentioned, invoked the image of the annual Gentlemen *v.* Players cricket match at Lords as a way of contrasting the professionalism of the technologist against the amateurishness of much of British management. Did he realise, I wonder, that it was in exactly those terms that Halévy had pronounced his epitaph on Victorian Britain?

It was no longer possible to pass over the fact that a young Englishman on leaving school was intellectually two years behind a German of the same age with the consoling reflection that he made up in character what he lacked in information and that, if more ignorant, he was better equipped for practical life. How was it that in London itself the business houses of the City employed a host of Germans whose presence was unwelcome but whose industry compelled admiration? If English bankers and merchants preferred them to their fellow countrymen, it was because they found them less devoted to sport, more industrious, more methodical, and better educated. Victorian England was beginning to lose confidence in herself. A nation of amateurs was being forced to recognise that they could not compete with a nation of professionals.[15]

The 'cult of the gentleman', the 'cult of the practical man': the English vices do not change.

Wilson in his modernising zeal of the early 1960s, frequently gave examples of 'brain drain' and of British failure to apply to industry the technology even of its own devising. Like the Tibetans who could find no better use for clockwork than the prayer wheel, or the Chinese for whom the invention of gunpowder led to nothing more than a firework industry, so the British had failed to exploit – in Wilson's favourite example – even the hovercraft. The very same complaints were being made at the turn of the century. For example, in 1896 a vogue book was published with the title *Made in Germany*. The *Daily Express* launched an 'England Wake Up!' campaign, the *Daily Mail* ran a series on the 'American Invaders'. *The Times* printed articles on the 'Crisis of British Industry'. There were complaints about the design and adaptability of British goods, of catalogues available only in English, of prices quoted only in sterling, and about the English weights and measures system which was a forbidding mystery to all metric-minded foreigners. The first inquiry into the shortcomings of the Foreign Office as an agency for commercial support was in 1886. Similar inquiries were held in the 1960s and 1970s. In a French magazine in 1903 this story was told:

There was a period, not more than thirty or thirty-five years ago, when England led the way in applied chemistry. A new era was opened up by the researches into the products of coal tar carried out by the celebrated chemist, Hofmann, when he was teaching in London. His pupil, Mr Perkins (now Fellow of the Royal Society)

discovered the first aniline dye. Why has the benefit of this new
branch of applied science been reaped by Germany? Simply
because Professor Hofmann, meeting with no encouragement,
returned to Germany and took with him his band of assistants. The
coal tar industry . . . left with Hofmann.[16]

When war broke out in 1914 Britain was wholly dependent on
Germany for aniline dyes. By then, says Correlli Barnett, we were
'well on the way to becoming a technological colony of the United
States and Germany.'

Between 1870 and 1913 British industry doubled its output. World
output grew fourfold. Some historians have sought to blame the
entrepreneur himself for the failure of Britain to keep up with the
Second Industrial Revolution. The 'cult of the practical man' had
succumbed to the 'cult of the gentleman'; the grandsons of the men
who from their backyards had made Britain the workshop of the
world were now public schoolboys, proficient in team spirit and,
perhaps, in Latin but lacking in the spirit of enterprise which had
made England what it was; nowadays they spent their time in
gentlemanly pursuits, leaving the mill to their foremen; in this way
the battle for industrial survival was lost on the croquet lawns of
Edwardian England. The theory of 'entrepreneurial failure' re-
appears, as we have already seen, as a lament of our own times, in
which the shortcomings of management are explained in class or
cultural terms. Hobsbawm points out that most of the Edwardians
were not gentlemen but, in any case, they did what is expected of
entrepreneurs: they maximised advantage and profit. They are not to
blame if the easiest way of doing this was to find new outlets for old
staples in the captive markets of the Empire, leaving the tougher
competition to the Germans and Americans. Even if we exonerate
the late Victorian and Edwardian entrepreneur for taking the easier
path but still argue that Britain lacked what today we call an 'enterprise culture', we are merely saying that this lack of drive and
foresight was not new – then or in our own times.

What did happen in the period between 1870 and 1914 was that the
whole system of the State re-formed itself around the dominance
which Britain had achieved. This was done at the very moment at
which that dominance was coming to an end. A new chapter of
modernity was opening in which Britain would fall behind, eventually
losing her Empire and her markets. It was in this period that we
'retreated from industry into trade',[17] and began to live off our past
and what had been accumulated.

Great Britain had emerged from the Industrial Revolution, as we have seen, a less than modern State. The middle classes had been strong enough to obtain on a piecemeal basis the reforms they wished to see: there had been no centralising revolution of the kind which had taken place in most of the States now emerging as industrial competitors. The year 1870 brought a great surge of Disraelian reform. The civil service, opened now to competitive entrance by examination, was reformed into a bureaucracy appropriate for the government of an Empire and its mother country. The trade union legislation of 1869 and 1871 was the beginning of the process, culminating in 1906 and 1912, by which class war was institutionalised within the framework of the Liberal State with disastrous results for industrial relations and industrial growth. Similarly, the educational system, centred by then on the public schools, was designed to produce the cadres of the governing class appropriate to the richest country in the history of the world and the hub of an empire on which the sun never – and would never – set.

The State apparatus created after the Second Reform Act of 1867 was not intended to perform the functions required of government in the nascent industrial nations of the continent. What need was there to imitate others? Britain's liberal institutions were widely admired and envied, seen as the secret of her success as the world's wealthiest and most powerful nation. Liberal institutions, and the liberal mind, were inimical to the growth of State power. Centralising forces, and the bureaucratic tradition, were weak. There was thus a failure of the State, at the very moment of modernisation. Britain remained, in Norman Stone's phrase, the 'last of the *ancien régimes*'.[18]

Correlli Barnett contrasts the late-Victorian State with countries such as Prussia which 'still believed, like Elizabeth and Cromwell, that a nation was a single strategic and commercial enterprise and that the national interest as a whole came before private profit.' He blames *laissez-faire* for a legacy of 'decaying industrial power, a brutalised and ignorant urban race, a ruined agriculture.'[19] In this he echoes the 'Prussians' of the times, the social imperialists. He is Gibbon-like in his contempt for the Evangelicals as the 'wets' of their day and, later, still more contemptuous of the Bloomsbury set who, it must be said, were the antithesis of a Prussian-style élite.

Pragmatism was the English vice. Lecky exemplified it. He saw politics as a process of 'perpetual compromise'.[20] The belief persisted down the years. So much was peculiar about the British system, its historical development so untypical, that there were always reasons for grafting the present on to the past. Even the disastrous 1870

Elementary Education Act Lecky hailed as a splendid example of the art. In fact by leaving unresolved the question of who is responsible for the schools and what they teach – the State, local authorities or the churches – it bedevilled English education for a century.

Some time around 1970 Britain's downward progress gathered pace. Britain's growth rate fell from 70 per cent of the OECD average in the years 1967–73 to only 45 per cent of a reduced average in 1973–8. The factors contributing to the vicious circle of slow growth were by now chronic. Slow growth resulted in low investment, low investment contributed to slow growth; inflation was rising but so also was unemployment, the result – Iain Macleod coined the word for it – 'stagflation'. Attempts to expand were constrained by recurrent balance of payments difficulties; rising public expenditure meant rising taxation and heavier borrowing; union militancy stoked up inflation, inflation stoked up union militancy. At about that time, however, a step-change seems to have taken place: Britain began to lose market share with alarming rapidity. In 1964 her share in world trade in manufactures had been still 14·2 per cent, by 1969 it was 11·2 per cent, by 1974 it had slumped to 8·5 per cent – a decrease of nearly 50 per cent since 1960. Stop-go had been seen as a cyclical phenomenon: now the evidence pointed towards a secular (i.e. long continuing) decline. Britain made her living by exporting manufactured goods while importing her food and raw materials. World trade in the former had grown more rapidly than trade in the latter and, although the import of manufactures had been doubling every five years or so, the scale of Britain's surplus remained a cushion against the trend. That is until around 1970 when the absolute gap between imports and exports began to close rapidly. Between 1961 and 1971 manufactured imports increased their share of the British domestic market from 8 per cent to 13 per cent. By 1976 their share had soared to 21 per cent. At the opening of the decade the value of exports exceeded imports by £6,000 million, in 1977 by only £1,000 million. 'The external constraint began to grab us by the throat.'[21]

Writing in 1976 two Oxford economists, Bacon and Eltis, asserted that Britain's economic performance had become 'incredibly worse' over the past decade:

In 1965 . . . the examination question, 'Can economies have simultaneously, zero growth, rapid inflation, substantial unemployment and a balance of payments deficit?' was set in Oxford. Undergraduates answered that this combination of failures was only possible in an underdeveloped country. It has now been achieved in Britain.[22]

Manufacture was in relative decline in all the industrialised economies as their service sectors expanded and they moved towards what the American sociologist Daniel Bell had dubbed the 'post-industrial society'. The world-wide trade recession brought about by the quadrupling of the oil price after 1973 also slowed the pace of manufacture in all countries. Only in Britain, however, did manufacture go into *absolute* decline.

'De-industrialisation', as this phenomenon came to be called, and a precipitous fall in Britain's share of world trade, now came to present an alarming prospect. Wynne Godley and his Cambridge colleagues repeatedly warned that this deteriorating trade imbalance was no longer susceptible to periodic devaluations; it would become increasingly difficult to maintain full employment without balance of payments crises and the prospect would be of 'chronic recession'. Bacon and Eltis, by a different route, arrived at a similar conclusion. As the result of de-industrialisation, they said:

> . . . the plant is just not there to meet the country's requirements for goods. Hence articles which are normally produced in Britain have to be imported and the goods are just not available to exploit export opportunities . . . In consequence attempts by governments to move towards full employment produce vast balance of payments deficits, which make continued expansion impossible.[23]

What the 'New Cambridge' economists and Bacon and Eltis had diagnosed was the condition we now call by its name: *decline*. Still into the 1970s, the Establishment flinched from the word. It had too ominous a Gibbonian ring about it, too strong moral undertones. 'De-industrialisation', which sounded bad enough, could be presented as a natural structural shift, something which was happening to everybody; 'relative decline' was only a fancy way of talking about slow growth, a perennial complaint; and the Cambridge diagnosis was an excitable way of describing the balance of payments constraint which was an equally familiar symptom of the British disease. The word 'decline', on the other hand, suggested a cumulative process, a general and systematic falling behind, qualitative as well as quantitative. Britain's malperformance could be quantified easily enough in terms of growth rates, share of world trade, and so on, but less easily when it came to the factors which might determine future competitiveness. Persistent slow growth has cumulative consequences: for investment, for productivity, for the trade balance, and for social cohesion and political stability. At the point at which slow growth, or relative decline, results in an incapacity to sustain production and living standards, decline becomes absolute. By definition, absolute decline has to be a temporary phenomenon, otherwise output would dwindle to nothing in a black hole economy. What had happened to Spain in the seventeenth century was that relative decline, in the form of persistent failure to adapt to a changing world, brought about a phase of absolute decline, lasting from about the 1620s to the 1680s, a calamitous experience which ensured a long future of further relative decline.[24]

If the word 'decline' was uncongenial to the governing class, the thought of it had not escaped its mind. Macmillan's turn towards Europe in 1961 was born not out of belated enthusiasm for the European Economic Community which had been launched without Britain in 1957, but rather out of a growing lack of confidence in Britain's own future. In 1959, in his famous lecture on the 'Two Cultures', C. P. Snow anticipated the mood which was to pervade the ruling élite over the decade which followed:

> I can't help thinking of the Venetian Republic in their last half-century. Like us, they had once been fabulously lucky. They had become rich, as we did, by accident. They had acquired immense political skill, just as we have. A good many of them were tough-minded, realistic, patriotic men. They knew, just as clearly as we know, that the current of history had begun to flow against them. Many of them gave their minds to working out ways to keep going. It would have meant breaking the pattern into which they had crystallised. They were fond of the pattern, just as we are fond of ours. They never found the will to break it.[25]

In 1961 Iain Macleod, then Leader of the House of Commons, told the author of *The Anatomy of Britain*, Anthony Sampson, that if Britain did not join the European Economic Community: 'No question – we'll just be like Portugal.'

The economic failures of the 1960s forced a belated recognition of Britain's strategic over-extension. The withdrawal from east of Suez, decided upon in 1968, was – for the ruling élite if not for the mass of the public – an event scarcely less traumatic than the Suez incident of 1956. Loss of Empire tends to be regarded as something which happened at a stroke with the ending of the war and the independence of India, leaving Britain thereafter struggling, in Dean Acheson's always quoted phrase, to 'find a role'. In fact, the dissolution of the Empire was a slow, drawn-out business which to this day, in the form of the Falkland Islands, has been a drain on resources, a distraction from the real predicament facing the country and the source of much nostalgia and delusion. Strategic over-extension contributed to Britain's economic difficulties, as it had with Rome and Imperial Spain, and Britain's economic difficulties made it increasingly impossible for her to keep up her position in the world; but more important, perhaps, than the mutual causality at work here was the concurrent, and reinforcing, demoralisation of the governing class. For the people of Britain the 1960s were years of material advance, cultural excitement and individual liberation, but for their rulers it was a decade in which it slowly became more evident that Britain was experiencing a decline beyond their ability to arrest.

Although by the early 1970s those concerned with the management of the economy were only too aware of the intractable and chronic aspects of the British disease, it was still not politic to speak the language of decline. For example, in 1973 – the year in which Britain did at last join the Common Market – Edward Heath publicly reprimanded Lord Rothschild, the head of his own 'Think Tank', for predicting that on existing trends Britain's Gross Domestic Product would by 1985 be half of Germany's and France's and about on a par with Italy's. Rothschild had warned:

> Unless we take a very strong pull at ourselves and give up the idea that we are one of the wealthiest, most influential, and important countries in the world – in other words that Queen Victoria is still reigning – we are likely to find ourselves in increasingly serious trouble.

A year later the Wilson Cabinet had met at Chequers to review the economic situation. Denis Healey, then Chancellor, had said jokingly, 'If we do join the Third World it will be as a member of OPEC.' Crosland had said that they did not know how such a relative decline had taken place: 'All we can do is to press every button we've got. We do not know which, if any of them, will have the desired result.'[26]

Foreigners, perhaps, were better able to see the seriousness of the British condition or, at least, to speak more frankly and openly about it. In 1974 the Paris-based Hudson Institute made explicit the analogy with seventeenth-century Spain, quoting in a report on Britain the words of the British Ambassador to Madrid in 1640:

> Concerning the state of this kingdom, I could never have imagined to have seen it as it is now, for their people begin to fail, and those that remain, by a continuance of bad successes, and by their heavy burdens, are quite out of heart.[27]

On his return in 1979 from a tour of duty in Paris as British Ambassador to France, Sir Nicholas Henderson reported in his valedictory despatch: 'In France we have come nowadays to be identified with malaise as closely as in the old days we were associated with success.'[28] When, in a conversation with the Federal German Chancellor, Helmut Schmidt, I referred to Britain generically as among the developed nations, he pulled me up and said, 'Britain is no longer a developed nation.'

By the mid-1970s just about every mix of remedy had been tried, apparently to no avail. Many of the specific diagnoses offered did not stand up to comparative test: other countries were taxed more heavily than Britain, had more strikes, spent more on their Welfare States, and so on, and yet were capable of faster and more sustained economic growth. It seemed increasingly probable that the explanation lay somewhere in history, in class animosities or cultural attitudes towards industrial production, or in the shape of British institutions. Scholarly studies of the period 1870–1914 took on contemporary relevance and encouraged this view that there was something ineluctable about Britain's long slow decline. The sheer length of it invited cultural explanation; many of the weaknesses – investment deficiency, for example – seemed to persist through differing economic circumstances, while in other countries similar economic factors seemed to produce different results. 'An effective economic strategy for Britain will probably have to begin in the cultural sphere,' wrote Ralf Dahrendorf, the German director of the London School of Economics.

Correlli Barnett's *The Collapse of British Power*, which I have several times referred to, was published in 1975 and sought to demonstrate that, 'The English disease is not the novelty of the past 10 or even 20 years . . . but a phenomenon dating back more than a century.' The Hudson Institute saw Britain in the 1970s as 'very largely the creation of the mid-Victorian period'. The Marxist historians Perry Anderson and Tom Nairn noted how the aristocratic *ancien régime* had absorbed the new bourgeoisie to produce an élite

[margin handwriting: Penny A. explanation 'decline'?]

in which capitalist values vied with the aristocratic in a State half modern, half feudal. This failure to produce a full-blooded capitalist class was perhaps a cause of the weaknesses of the industrial spirit so frequently lamented. The American scholar, Martin Wiener, gathering together this long literature of lament into what became an influential vogue book, attributed both Britain's political success and economic failure to 'the containment of the cultural revolution of industrialism' from towards the end of the nineteenth century. The late Victorians had laid the foundation for social stability but at the price of a lack of industrial innovation.[29]

The American economist Mancur Olson constructed a theory of 'the rise and decline of nations' around the paradox that war and political instability may be favourable to innovation and peace and social tranquillity conducive to stagnation. The reason for this is that stability strengthens in time the hands of interest groups, or 'distributional coalitions', and produces in societies 'an institutional sclerosis' which slows their adaptation to changing technology or circumstance. This, he suggests, 'helps to explain why Great Britain, the major nation with the longest immunity from dictatorship, invasion and revolution, had had in this century a lower rate of growth than other large, developed democracies.'[30]

In the first edition of his best-selling and influential *Anatomy of Britain* Anthony Sampson quoted a passage from J. H. Elliott's study of the decline and fall of imperial Spain. The words were clearly intended to have contemporary relevance:

> Heirs to a society which had over-invested in empire and surrounded by the increasingly shabby remnants of a dwindling inheritance, they could not bring themselves at the moment of crisis to surrender their memories and alter the antique patterns of their lives. At a time when the face of Europe was altering more rapidly than ever before, the country that had once been its leading power proved to be lacking the essential ingredient for survival – the willingness to change.[31]

Machiavelli's explanation of decline as failure to adapt became the common diagnosis of the British disease.

Cultural explanations were adduced also for Britain's class-divided industrial relations. Ronald Dore, the student of comparative technology, writing in 1973, concluded: 'It will be a long time before Britain loses the marks of the pioneer, the scars and stiffness that come from the searing experience of having made the first, most long-drawn-out industrial revolution.'[32] This, he argued, had led to the classes drawing apart and retreating into their separate cultures. Richard Caves of the Brookings Institution, Washington, reported that: 'Britain's economic malaise stems largely from its productivity problem whose origins lie deep in the social system.' Because of this, he added, 'one needs an optimistic disposition to suppose that a democratic political system can eliminate that problem.'[33] Chancellor Schmidt's advice to me at about this time was: 'You must get rid of that damned class system of yours.'

Our own people were slow to grasp the notion of decline. That was and had always been a part of the problem. How is one to speak of decline when output is growing and living standards improving? The seeds of decline are easily mistaken for the fruits of prosperity. Between 1870 and 1914 the industrial falling-behind was concealed behind the wealth and splendour of the imperial heyday. Between the wars the structural weakness in the economy was masked by the world-wide recession. During the long post-war boom which continued until 1973 Britain's relative decline was an undercurrent to a rising tide of prosperity. After 1973 the ending of full employment and the onslaught of inflation across the whole of the industrialised world obscured the extent to which Britain's cumulative decline had made her more vulnerable to, and less able to adapt to, the world-wide recession. Finally, North Sea oil, like a providential windfall, gave Britain a new lease of life beyond her means, and a new excuse not to adapt to a changing world, just as had done the accumulated assets of the Victorian climacteric.

However, as the underlying crisis in the economy grew deeper, and as the country was brought to the verge of ungovernability, the nature of the British disease became more clearly understood, more explicitly recognised – at least within informed opinion and among the governing élites. The 1979 General Election was fought openly on the issue of decline. The new Chancellor of the Exchequer, Sir Geoffrey Howe, said in his first Budget address:

In the last few years, the hard facts of our relative decline have become increasingly plain, and the threat of absolute decline has gradually become very real.

The Bank of England agreed. It warned in 1979:

The consequences of failure to arrest the country's industrial decline are likely to become more pressing and more obvious as time goes on. Now condemned to very slow growth, we might even have to accept, if present trends continue, decline in real living standards.

In 1970 decline was still the unmentionable. Now it was official.

3

Consensus or Conviction Politics?

Margaret Thatcher and Tony Benn were the twins of their time. Between them in the 1970s they set out to smash what they alleged to be a collusive conspiracy between the political parties, the so-called consensus politics of the two previous decades. For Thatcher consensus meant the appeasement of socialism and the ineluctable advance of collectivism. For Benn it meant the collaboration of Labour governments with capitalism and the betrayal of the working class. In order the better to assault the consensus both of them exaggerated it. In retrospect, Benn minimised the achievements of both the Wilson and the Callaghan governments and Thatcher the differences which existed between the parties, especially in the first years of the Heath administration, in whose Cabinet she served. They both thrived upon the air of conspiracy which was implicit in their critique of consensual politics. 'Thatcherism' and 'Bennism' were founded in a theory of betrayal, the stab-in-the-back which is a common feature of the mythology of revolutions or revanchiste movements.

For Benn the betrayals were by Labour Prime Ministers who, once in office, soon became the tools of the City of London, the international bankers, the IMF, NATO and the Brussels bureaucrats of the EEC. Their treachery consisted in disregarding or defying the democratic decisions of the party conference. Hence the cry, 'all power to the conference', which was at the heart of the extra-parliamentary politics of the 1970s and 1980s of which Tony Benn became the champion.

For Thatcher the stab-in-the-back was Heath's U-turn on 6 November 1972, the day on which the Cabinet, of which she was a member, introduced statutory powers to control pay, prices and profits. That, together with the profligate reflation which had become the economic policy of the government, was, for her, to collaborate once again with the Social Democratic or Keynesian consensus which had ruled in Britain since the war with increasingly disastrous results.

Betrayal theories require that there be something to betray, an ark of the covenant, a tradition of some kind: grace to fall from, a Golden Age to recall. Where these do not exist they must be invented. In the case of 'Thatcherism', Edward Heath's specific act of treason was incorporated into a more general rewriting of history in which successive Conservative governments in the post-war period had departed from the true principles of Conservativism and collaborated in the advance of collectivism. Whoever was in office, Social Democracy had been in power. A certain confusion entered here, for Thatcher herself also spoke admiringly of Winston Churchill's post-war administration and, especially, of R. A. Butler's 1952 'set-the-people-free' Budget.[1] It can be argued that it was Heath who had thrown the first stone at the Post-war Settlement in 1970 with his Selsdon Park programme,[2] allowing inefficient firms to close, driving up unemployment, and legislating against the unions. In that case, the U-turn of 1972 was not a betrayal of any true Tory tradition, merely the abandonment by Heath of his own programme. Nevertheless, post-war Conservativism was alleged to have fallen from grace, to have departed from the true ark, and it was the Victorian age – although that of *laissez-faire* liberalism rather than Tory paternalism, the age of Gladstone rather than of Disraeli – which came to play the role of Golden Age in the nostalgia of Thatcherism.

For Benn the Labour government of 1945 served a similar purpose. He too was liable to be confused, putting the Attlee government forward sometimes as a reassuring model of moderate socialist reform and at others as an encouraging example of how true socialism could win popular support. He told an interviewer in 1981:

> the amazing thing was the extent to which we were able to mobilise young and old, left and right, men and women, Scots, English and Welsh, the trade union members and the Labour Party . . . Unfortunately that spirit escaped and evaporated during the period of successive Labour governments after 1951.[3]

Thatcher and Benn, each of them, came to preach a politics of new departure, a break from the recent past and a rejection of the notions which had governed it. They formed unholy alliance to dance on the grave of John Maynard Keynes, Thatcher because Keynesianism was an engine of socialism, Benn because it was the crumbling prop of capitalism. She, the shopkeeper's daughter, hated socialism with the same passion that he, the peer's son, had learnt to hate capitalism and his own class.

Both of them had experienced conversions. She, it seems at some point on the road between the February and October elections of 1974, turned from her past ways as an unprotesting member of Edward Heath's Cabinet and saw the true light by then emanating from Keith Joseph. Sir Keith was later to declare dramatically, 'It was only in April 1974 that I was converted to Conservativism. I had thought that I was a Conservative but now I see that I was not one at all.' Benn's conversion had occurred shortly after laying down the seals of office in 1970. He had been radicalised in office, he was later to say, but his moment of revelation came during the 1971 sit-in by the workers at the Upper Clyde Shipbuilders, a yard which he had endeavoured to save while at the Department of Technology. The occupation of the yard was conducted in a style reminiscent of the events in France in 1968; the cry was for workers' control. It was there, on the 'red' Clyde, that the Honourable Anthony Wedgwood Benn consummated his love affair with the working class. Looking back, he expressed his gratitude to:

> The shipyard workers who organised the work-in at Upper Clyde Shipbuilders, the brave men and women who fought so hard to set up Meriden and Kirkby Manufacturing and Engineering as co-operatives, and the brilliant and humane shop stewards at Lucas Aerospace combined with hundreds of others to give me an education in the real meaning of practical socialism which no books or teachers could have matched.[4]

In all countries at about this time a new radicalism was emerging on both right and left in response to the breakdown of the old Social Democratic order. Influenced as Benn and Thatcher were by the events and spirit of those times, they were revealed to have certain beliefs in common. One was their attitude towards the State. For Thatcher the power of the State had usurped the responsibility of the individual to the point at which not only economic enterprise but moral choice had atrophied. For Benn bureaucracy had become one of the enemies of socialism and he saw in participatory democracy the means of rebuilding society from the bottom up. Their common animus against government at the centre gave both of their politics a strong tinge of 'populism'.

The word populism is much misused to mean demagogic – although both of them could be that – or merely popular. The word properly should mean a direct appeal to the people, often above the heads of existing political institutions, Parliament or party. In its American forms, populism can be of the Right or of the Left and has often involved novel coalitions – blacks and poor whites against plantation owners, farmers and workers against the banks and railroad companies. Benn and Thatcher could both be said to be 'populists' in their fashion. Benn, for example, appealed directly to the shop stewards' organisations over the heads of the trade union Establishment and took up the cause of workers' control. He made common cause with the excluded elements and groups of society – blacks, students, women, sexual minorities – in the hope of constructing a new and broad progressive alliance. He inveighed in true populist manner against what he saw as an effete, corrupt and defeatist ruling class:

> The Vichy spirit in the top echelons of the establishment is quite astonishing. If you listen to those who inhabit the golden triangle of the City of London, Fleet Street and Whitehall, there is a lot of defeatism. Compare that with the mood at Lucas Aerospace, at Meriden, at Kirkby, at the shop stewards' committees up and down the country. They may be angry, worried, disappointed but they are not defeated. Compare them with the gloomy men who go to City luncheons and dinners in their boiled shirts for ever calling upon everybody else to face the harsh realities of technical change.[5]

Thatcher, a true outsider unlike the patrician Benn, shared his contempt for the Establishment, especially for civil servants and, more especially still, for Brussels bureaucrats and the Foreign Office. Her populism took the form of a direct appeal to the working class. She appealed to its acquisitive and patriotic instincts. 'Today,' she said in 1976, 'it is the Conservatives and not the Socialists who represent the true interests and hopes and aspirations of the working people.' In this she was echoing the radical Toryism of Lord Randolph Churchill and Joseph Chamberlain except that theirs was a paternalist appeal and there was nothing paternal, or maternal, about the Thatcher-style. Rather she presented herself to the working class as the champion of the taxpayer against the Treasury, the worker against his trade union, the council tenant against the landlord and the citizen against the State. Shortly before she became leader the High Tory grandees feared she would be too petty bourgeois to command a majority in the land. In a speech at Amersham, January 30, 1975, Ian Gilmour warned against 'retreat behind the privet

hedge into a world of narrow class interests and selfish concerns.'
They could not have been more wrong about her.

One other thing she and Benn had in common was zeal. Together
they raised the temperature of British politics, arousing new passions
and inspiring new idealism. They were the twin agents of the polarisation which came to characterise the party politics of the 1970s and
1980s. She called her approach 'conviction politics' which was a way
of declaring that she was not bound by the consensual wisdom but
would be guided by her own passionately held beliefs. Benn admired
her for this and determined to put forward his own socialist beliefs
with similar conviction. It seemed not to occur to him that her
convictions were striking popular chords which his were not. Nevertheless, Benn – eyes gleaming – filled halls with huge audiences as he
travelled the land preaching his gospel of left-wing socialism.

Fundamentalism would seem to flourish in the rubble of collapsed
belief. Thatcherite and Bennite enthusiasm coincided with the revival
elsewhere of Christian and Islamic fundamentalism. Everywhere
people were groping for new certainties in an uncertain world. The
consensus which Benn and Thatcher so despised had been founded in
rationality: the age of Social Democracy had been the age also of the
social scientist as the age of Keynes had been the age of the economist. The Keynesian notion of 'managing the economy' suggested that
government was a technocratic business, comparable to the science of
management. But now, in the 1970s, as things went badly and as
economies declined to be managed and the governed to be governed,
the priesthood of the expert fell into disrepute and the magic men
were deserted by their skills. There now took place a retreat from
rationality. Monetarism was a mystical creed at the heart of which lay
the search for some Holy Grail of authority which would serve as
surrogate for God or gold. Marxism, reviving at the same time,
answered a similar need for a project which, unlike Keynesianism or
Social Democracy, was capable of transforming the human condition. It was amid this intellectual and spiritual ferment, born of a
dawning social pessimism, that Margaret Thatcher and Tony Benn
arose as peddlers of new and simple faiths. Between them they
changed the political vocabulary of the times. She placed herself at
the head of an intellectual offensive against 'a generation and more of
collectivist theory' which she blamed largely on Keynesianism, in
Nigel Lawson's words, 'that great engine of creeping socialism.' For
Benn, Keynesianism was the creed of declining capitalism, devoid of
remedy for ailing manufacturing industry. They were the first political leaders to face squarely the issue of decline.

Their alternative in each case to Keynesian macro-economic management was to approach the problem from the supply side: they
looked to micro-economic inputs to increase the efficiency of products, whether through the intervention of planners or the freer play of
market forces. By Thatcher's diagnosis the remedy was to let the
market work its cure within a framework of monetarist discipline with
supply-side measures chiefly directed at the rigidities of the labour
market. For Benn, at the core of the decline was manufacture – it was
he who coined the word 'de-industrialisation' – and the cause of it
was a deficiency of investment. The patent failure of its economic
strategy – if strategy is not to glorify it – had set in motion a re-
appraisal after the defeat of the Labour government in 1970. Benn at
that time was shopping for new thoughts and inspirations, susceptible
to the Pauline light. At an early stage of his conversion, as we have
mentioned, he had been attracted by the idea of participation –
one of the three P's studied in the Class of '68, the others being
permissiveness and protest. Indeed, in a pamphlet published in
1970 and sub-titled 'A Socialist Reconnaissance', which was the
result of consultations in the library with various gurus of the age,
he had already reached the hard conclusion about participation,
namely:

> Workers are not going to be fobbed off with a few shares –
> whether voting or non-voting. They cannot be satisfied by having a
> statutory worker on the board or by a carbon copy of the German
> system of co-determination. The campaign is very gradually crys-
> tallising into a demand for *real workers' control*. However revolu-
> tionary the phrase may sound, however many Trotskyite bogeys it
> may conjure up, that is what is being demanded and that is what we
> had better start thinking about.[6] (My italics.)

The device of the 'planning agreement' became the quintessential
instrument of Bennite socialism. The one hundred largest companies
would be obliged to enter into planning agreements with the government, for which purpose a Ministry of Planning was envisaged. They
would be obliged at the same time, and as a condition of the State
investment they might receive, to involve their workers, through
their unions, in the planning process. By this means the government
would obtain the firm-by-firm information necessary to draw up a
plan, information hard to obtain at the centre; at the same time it
would have the benefit of the knowledge, wisdom and ingenuity of
the workers; and by so involving the workers it would break down the

factory class system and obviate any need for wage restraint or 'incomes policies'.

The Bennite package was innovative in a number of ways. It addressed the problem of over-centralised Statism; it appealed to fashionable desires for participation, accountability and an end to secrecy; it could be presented to the Right as a substitute for nationalisation and to the Left as a major step towards it; it got round some of the unions' hostility to any form of industrial democracy which smacked of shared-managerial responsibility; and it appeared to be addressing the problem of de-industrialisation. In the decade between 1973 and 1983, the concept of the planning agreement exercised a powerful fascination upon the left-wing mind. It became the point of reference for economic debate within the Labour Movement. It was the radical alternative to Thatcherism and, together with Thatcherism, one of the radical alternatives to the bankrupt Croslandite version of Social Democracy and to the Callaghan-style corporatism practised after 1975.

Whether it offered a real answer to the decline of British manufacture is another question. Economists would dispute that under-investment was a central problem. Resources might be inefficiently applied but that was another matter. The Bank of England pointed out in the mid-1970s that the real rate of return on investment, excluding stock relief, was zero. Why should anyone invest if there was no profit to be had? The Marxists, to the left of the Bennites, agreed. Moreover, Bennite socialism was based on a sentimental vision of the working class. Benn had been much excited by his dealings with the Lucas shop stewards. They were a talented, ingenious lot who might well have managed better than their managers; but most workers had no desire to be managers, and their unions most certainly did not want them getting their collective bargaining lines crossed. It might be one matter to plan the expansion of, say, the electronics industry but how likely were coalminers or steel workers to plan the contraction of their own hopelessly uneconomic industries? Benn spoke of the 'self-discipline of full democratic control'. Participation plus planning was his socialist remedy for decline, rather in the way that Lenin had supposed, or so he said, that the 'Soviets plus electrification' was all there was to socialism.

Somewhat later a third element was added to what became known as the Alternative Economic Strategy of the Bennites – protectionism. The Cambridge School of economists, by whom Benn was much guided, had argued that no amount of Keynesian reflation on its own could save British industry because the propensity to import had grown so great that a balance of payments crisis was the swift and certain outcome. De-industrialisation tightened this constriction and was a vicious spiral. Import control – 'planned trade' was the pre-fered euphemism – was the only way out. Benn gave protectionism a patriotic twist. He was not interested in import controls in them-selves, he insisted, only in saving British industry and British jobs. Like Thatcher he was a nationalist, or had become one. In 1970 he was explaining to his electors in Bristol why Britain must join the European Economic Community (in 1963 he had been against it) but in Opposition again he soon sensed which way the wind was blowing. It was he who manipulated the 'Shadow' Cabinet into the promise of a referendum on Britain's continuing membership of the Community and in so doing wrong-footed the Revisionist Right of his party for the next decade. Increasingly he spoke the language of left-wing nationalism. The British ruling class had 'defected to Brussels', he said. The Common Market, NATO and the IMF were reducing Britain to the status of a colony. They were the agents of de-industrialisation and would make Britain into a 'Salazar-like society'; we would become the 'Kirkby of Western Europe'. (He had forgotten that, back in the 1960s, Barbara Castle, opening a housing estate in that benighted overspill from Liverpool, had said: 'This is your chance to build a New Jerusalem.')[7] 'If you say to nation states there is nothing you can do,' Benn said, 'you will end up with withdrawal of consent from elected governments.' By joining the Common Market, he solemnly warned the Cabinet, we had 'lit the long fuse to revolution'. Did he himself believe it? Who knows? But, like Enoch Powell, he plainly believed himself to be speaking great truths which were concealed from the people. 'You once called me an Old Testament prophet' (he said to Wilson) 'and that is just what I am. There are just certain ideas that I think ought to be spelt out and I spell them out.'[8]

By 1975 Benn was in the wilderness, where prophets belong. He remained a member of the Cabinet but had been sacked from the Department of Industry, where his industrial strategy had been progressively watered down by Wilson and the Cabinet, and exiled to the Department of Energy on Millbank. There, using his powerful position within the party apparatus as chairman of the home policy sub-committee of the National Executive, he concerned himself chiefly with preparing a socialist programme for a future Labour government. The events of 1975, traumatic for Benn and important for the future, compounded the myth of betrayal. As the Left saw it, the Bennite programme adopted at the party conference of 1973 had been the blueprint for socialism. Benn had told delegates, 'We are saying at this conference that the crisis that we inherit when we come to power will be the occasion for fundamental change and not the excuse for postponing it.' At that time history had seemed for once to be going the Left's own way. The quadrupling of the price of oil in 1973 produced a crisis of capitalism, at least of a sort; working class action by the miners had brought the Heath government down, although some would say Heath had brought himself down; miraculously Wilson, or so it seemed to him, was suddenly back in Number 10. But this time, the Left believed, Labour was equipped with a socialist programme, a programme which Wilson then proceeded to emasculate. Labour in 1974, Benn later insisted, had been armed with 'policies that had been fully worked out to open up a really new vision of industrial life that would have transformed the situation in a decade.'

The year 1975 saw Margaret Thatcher's accession and Tony Benn's banishment. Shortly before his dismissal he said at a luncheon:

> If I got knocked down by a bus as I left the Café Royal after this lunch, I don't believe anything would be changed one way or the other . . . There is a wind of change blowing gale force through British industry . . . I am no more than the weather cock showing which way it is blowing.

He certainly believed at that time that history was on his side. He had worked out that great radical change occurred in approximately forty-year cycles and that after 1945, which he chose to regard as an authentically socialist moment, 1984 would be the year, his year. He had an air of destiny about him in the 1970s but we had seen the same glint in the eye of Enoch Powell and that had taken him from high office to the farthest fringe of British politics. All the same, if I had had to have chosen one of them in that year, Thatcher or Benn, rival exponents of the politics of decline and the twins of their age, I think I would have given the future to Tony Benn.

While the New Left was busy taking over the Labour Party the New Right had been busy capturing the Conservative Party. The leftward shift in the Labour Party had been in part a response to the rightward shift by the Heath government. 'Stand on your own two feet' was the slogan of Heath Mark I. Then came the U-turn which produced a pay and prices freeze and the débâcle of the miners' strike in February 1974. Between the two General Elections in that year Sir Keith

Joseph had begun to develop a radical critique of Edward Heath's style of Conservativism. The moment the October election was lost Heath's leadership was at issue. It is the custom of his party to show no mercy to losers and Heath was now a three-time loser. Moreover, in February 1974 he had lost on an issue of class confrontation, a most serious setback for a party which saw itself as the natural governing party. Since the enfranchisement of the working class the Conservative Party had been remarkably successful in keeping Labour out of office, and socialism out of power even when Labour was in office. Now Heath had played into the enemy's hands. The débâcle, or so it could easily be alleged, never need have happened had it not been for the notorious 1972 U-turn which had brought in the statutory incomes policy, which led to the fatal show down with the miners two years later. It could equally be argued that the attempts to put into action the Selsdon Park programme during the first two years of the Heath administration had brought about a class confrontation which the 1972 U-turn was intended to avoid. In any case, Heath was unloved by his party.

A tetchy, uncomfortable figure, he was the first leader of the Conservatives in modern times who was outside the traditional mould. A grammar school boy, the son of a jobbing builder, and an organ scholar at Balliol, his background was similar to Margaret Thatcher's. Snobbishly nicknamed 'the grocer' because of his supposedly shopkeeper's bent of mind he was, in truth, a man of vision who had seen clearly at an early stage of his career that the future of post-imperial Britain lay with the nascent European unification movement. Brought up on the south Kent coast he had as a young man looked across the narrow English Channel to the Continent, and bridging that gap became his life's mission as a politician. He had been foiled by General de Gaulle in 1963 when he had been Macmillan's negotiator in Brussels, and the overriding goal of the administration he formed in 1970 was Britain's belated accession to the European Community.

By then Europe had become also Heath's remedy for Britain's decline. He saw the Common Market as a cold douche which would brisken British industry into competitiveness. Like Wilson before him, Heath was a moderniser. But whereas Wilson was a politician of infinite pliability, for whom party management was the first prerequisite of governing at all, Heath was full of impatience. For him ten days was a very long time in politics. Wilson had made a famous speech about the 'white heat of technology' but it was Heath who in his spirit and character was the technocrat. He adopted a brisk managerial response to government, expecting things to happen when buttons were pushed. Caught in a London traffic jam, he telephoned the chairman of the Greater London Council, who was visiting Tokyo at the time, and shouted at him about it. The style was 'abrasive', a word he first used himself, a characteristically Heathite word. But he rubbed too many people up the wrong way. For a man who had served his apprenticeship in the Whip's Office he was remarkably deficient in conducting normal human relations, although he inspired the loyalty and affection of his personal entourage. Much of his manner may have been due to gaucheness, shyness perhaps, for he was a kindly man and could be funny when relaxed although even when he laughed, the shoulders heaving, the appearance was of a man imitating laughter.

Heath was the last of the 1930s generation to lead his party. He had been moved and shocked as a young man by the unemployment and poverty which had so disfigured Britain in the years between the wars. When in 1971 unemployment spurted towards the – at that time unthinkable – million mark, he lost his nerve. He had no stomach for the class confrontations which his industrial policies were provoking. Being a man of no fixed ideology, he turned in his tracks. The policy of refusing all succour to 'lame duck' industries gave way to massive interventionism; stringent monetary and fiscal policies gave way to a new burst for growth; the policy of resisting inflationary pay claims one by one gave way to an ambitious and elaborate incomes policy which, when agreement with the TUC proved impossible, he imposed by statutory edict. A believer in the power of reason, Heath expected reason to prevail. He found it difficult to grasp that people, and at times society as a whole, could be thoroughly unreasonable. It was all very irritating. When he went to the country in 1974 asking, 'Who rules Britain?' he asked a silly question and received a silly answer. His political adviser at the time, Douglas Hurd, has testified that his real reason for going to the country was that the energy crisis threatened Britain with catastrophe and that his government required a new mandate to preside over a severe but inevitable decline in real living standards, something which had not occurred since the war. 'People would have to understand, because only with that understanding could their government do what was needed.'[9] So once more, seeing things clearly himself, he appealed to reason. He told the truth. He lost. Heath was the first victim of the politics of decline.

When he lost again the following October he would have to go. Sir Keith Joseph was the obvious challenger from the Right but he had embarrassed the Conservatives with a speech in Birmingham on 19 October in which he had suggested clumsily that the breeding habits of the poor threatened what he called 'our human stock'. Not only had he embarrassed his party but himself. A pathologically sensitive and nervous man, given to agonising intellectual and moral self-doubt, he was deeply upset by the reaction from press and public to what he had said. He peered into the kitchen and decided that it was too hot in there for him.

Sir Keith Joseph had played the Baptist's role in Mrs Thatcher's coming. The analogy is apt because in conversations at that time he (like Benn) had compared himself with a prophet come down from the mountains. Indeed, there was an Old Testament ring to his cries of woe from the wilderness as he urged repentance from the wicked ways of socialism and beat his breast in immolation for his own part in the betrayal of the ark of the Conservative covenant. Characteristically he was able to identify the exact moment of his conversion and date it, as we have seen, to April 1974. When there was a similar Damascan moment for Margaret Thatcher we do not know. According to one of her biographers it may have been at the election press conference on 1 October 1974 when she publicly disassociated herself from Heath's notion of a government of national unity which had been hinted at, though vaguely, in the Conservative manifesto. *Her* policies, on housing, she asserted with what was to become characteristic spirit, were not negotiable. She was a Conservative, not a coalitionist.[10]

After Heath's defeat in February 1974 she had joined with Sir Keith Joseph in setting up the Centre for Policy Studies, with its remit to 'secure fuller understanding of the methods available to improve the standard of living, the quality of life and the freedom of choice of the British people, with particular attention to social market policies.' This move had been regarded with extreme suspicion by Heath and the CPS was to serve as a Thatcherite 'Think Tank'.

That summer Sir Keith had become more openly critical of the direction which the Conservative Party had taken under Heath's leadership. His criticisms of the policies pursued by the government of which he had been a member, and on which Heath now proposed to fight another election, broadened into a critique of post-war Conservatism. At Upminster, in Essex, on 22 June, he said:

Our industry, economic life and society have been so debilitated by thirty years of socialistic fashions that their very weakness tempts further inroads. The path to Benn is paved with thirty years of intervention, thirty years of good intentions, thirty years of disappointments.

The reality is that for thirty years, Conservative governments did not consider it practicable to reverse the vast bulk of accumulating detritus of socialism.[11]

However, it was during the election campaign in October 1974 in a speech at Preston that Joseph delivered what was to become at once a seminal text. In it he challenged the very foundation of the Post-war Settlement – full employment. This was the speech in which the monetarist credo was first set out: inflation had been brought about by governments printing money in illusory pursuit of full employment.

> To us, as to all post-war governments, sound money may have seemed out of date: we were all dominated by the fear of unemployment. It was this which made us turn our back against our own better judgment and try to spend out of unemployment.

The speech was a political event. *The Times* published the text verbatim. Full employment, according to the post-war standard, had been effectively abandoned by the Wilson government after 1967 but nobody had dared to say so. Here was Joseph seemingly abandoning the very goal, tearing up the sacred Beveridge text. Denis Healey, who was currently Chancellor of the Exchequer, denounced the speech as: 'A disastrous prescription for a social breakdown on a scale unknown in this country.' Joseph had made the election issue clear, he said; the British people could 'vote either for a slump and class conflict on an unprecedented scale or for national unity in the fight for full employment and justice.'

In subsequent speeches, Joseph tried to correct the impression that he was a crude or vulgar monetarist who believed, or had suggested, that control of the money supply would alone cure Britain's ills. At Preston he had described monetary control as a 'pre-essential'. He was to elaborate on this later in his Stockton Lecture of 1976 which was titled, 'Monetarism is Not Enough'. 'Monetary contraction in a mixed economy,' he argued, 'strangles the private sector unless the state sector contracts with it and reduces its take from the national income.' Public expenditure must be cut therefore and also the taxes, a climate of entrepreneurship had to be created and restrictive practices broken down. 'We are over-governed, over-spent, over-taxed, over-borrowed and over-manned.' These were to become the familiar themes of Josephism, and of Thatcherism, for he was Mrs Thatcher's mentor. He repeated his prophet's message over and over, with hymns to the beauty of the free market and sermons against the evils of socialism.

Governments, he preached, were to blame for Britain's long decline, for it was they who printed the money. He attributed much of the mischief to war. War was the midwife of socialism. War not only resulted in greater intervention by the State but also excited expectations of a land fit for heroes when it was over. At the same time it burdened the country with expenditure and debt. In 1945 the euphoria of victory had reinforced the illusion that governments could do anything. He himself, he confesses – for he enjoys confessions – had been caught up in that climate. He had 'wanted to believe' that full employment, rapid growth rates, and price stability were simultaneously within grasp. He confesses also to class guilt. 'We found it hard to avoid the feeling that somehow the lean and tight-lipped mufflered men in the 1930's dole queue were at least partly our fault.' A failure to examine the implications of full employment, and of the Welfare State, had led to a failure to recognise the symptoms of the failure of these economic policies. For even though it was not immediately evident, artificially stimulated demand and high taxation were eating into the sinews of the economy. One of the first symptoms was slow growth. But the Keynesian cure had been applied, only to worsen the disease until, eventually, stop-go gave way to stagflation and, worse still, slumpflation.

Contained within this confession of personal error was an indictment of all Conservative governments since the war. In the course of it Joseph set about the systematic rewriting of history. Lord Blake, the High Tory historian, also a critic of the Heath government, dated the Fall to 1958 when in what Macmillan had called a 'little local difficulty' Peter Thorneycroft, Enoch Powell and Nigel Birch had resigned from the Treasury in protest against a lack of monetary stringency. Thereafter, the Tory Party had moved too fast and too far into the centre ground and had come 'too near to socialist policies'.[12] Joseph, however, went further. As Ian Gilmour puts it:

The sans-culottes of the monetarist revolution also wished to strengthen the party's new leadership by denouncing the alleged follies of the Ancien Régime. Ideally, perhaps, this could best have been achieved by a bell, book, and candle condemnation of the Heath government alone. The snag was that some of the leading monetarists had served without demur in that government. The

trail of heresy had, therefore, to be extended back to the thirteen
years of 1951 to 1964.[13]

Having endeavoured to rewrite the history of the post-war period
Joseph next embarked on a revision of its political geography. The
'middle-ground' which the parties rushed to occupy at election times
was no more than a chimera of the politicians' imaginations: it existed
only as an ephemeral compromise between them but bore no relation
to the true aspirations of the people. This so-called middle ground
was 'simply the lowest common denominator obtained from a calcu-
lus of assumed electoral expediency, defined not by reference to
popular feeling but by splitting the position between Labour's position and the Conservatives.' Not at all was it 'rooted in the way of life,
thought and work of the British people, nor related to any vision of
society, or attitude of mind, or philosophy of political action.' What
Joseph called, in contrast, the 'common ground', consisted of what
the people really thought and actually desired. 'The people', or so
Joseph claimed to know, 'were far closer to Conservative instincts on
many issues' than they were to the supposed consensus. He went on
to lambast his own party's 'obsession with the middle ground' which,
far from providing a secure base, was a 'slippery slope to socialism
and state control'. He arrived at this conclusion by a curious route.
The consensus was formed, he argued, by splitting the difference
between the Conservatives and the Labour Party; because the
Labour Party itself is a compromise which shifts constantly to the left,
the dynamic of the consensus – or its dialectic, he might have said –
is to drag the Conservative Party always to the left. Note how the
Labour Left used exactly the same argument in reverse to blame
electoral expediency for the betrayal of the working class by successive Labour governments. Joseph's argument is here hard to follow.
Wilson captured the centre ground in 1964 by trimming to the right.
By occupying the centre ground on their own terms the Conservatives
had held office for the previous thirteen years. When Heath defeated
Wilson in 1970 it was on the most right-wing programme presented by
the Conservative Party since the war. His 1972 U-turn had nothing to
do with the centrifugal pull of Labour but, rather, with his judgment
of the social and political consequences of the policy he was pursuing.
Labour's lurch to the left after 1970 was no reason for the Tories to
abandon the centre ground. As Gilmour said in his speech at Amersham on January 30, 1975: 'There is no reason in logic, history,
philosophy, or expediency why the Tory Party should join the
Labour Party in moving towards the extreme.' But for Joseph, and

for Thatcher, it was necessary to establish a Great Betrayal and the great betrayal was the *consensus*.

Because the policies emanating from the consensus were, he argued, doomed to fail, consensual politics could only breed still greater dissatisfactions. 'Far from achieving social harmony and strengthening the centre, it has created resentments and conflict, has moved the centre of gravity of the whole Labour Movement to the left, strengthening the left-wing, the irreconcilables, the revolutionaries.' By this argument the post-war Conservative Party, through its collusion with consensual politics, stood accused of actively promoting the cause of left-wing socialism.

Decline – although he did not here use the word – became the motor of party polarisation. For, 'paradoxically socialism advanced thanks to its own failures, not by successes.' He argued that the expectations for full employment and welfare excited by the war were not only extravagant but actually 'irrational'. Post-war promises were incapable of fulfilment by the adopted means because the mixed economy with all its interventionist ways was incapable of accelerating economic growth. The worse things became, the worse things were made. Joseph in this way diagnosed a crisis of Social Democracy which shares with the left-wing socialists' version the conclusion that the means are inadequate to the ends or, as the Marxists would say, are in contradiction. For a long while, however, there was a conspiracy to avoid examining the 'true causes' of slow growth (or relative decline) which were excessive State expenditure, nationalisation, job subsidisation and 'excessive State reactions to exaggerated expectations':

> The socialists were inhibited because it was their creation. We were inhibited because we had accepted these policies as the middle ground, so that to criticise them would be regarded as 'immoderate', 'right-wing', 'breaking the consensus', 'trying to turn the clock back', in short unthinkable taboo.

The indictment was complete. The collective guilt of consensus politicians was established. Post-war history was rewritten. The Post-war Settlement was exposed as a fraud. Heath's great betrayal was a culmination of a long saga of misguided interventionism.

4

A Moral Issue

Not only the intellectual but the moral foundations of the *ancien régime* were crumbling, or so the Thatcherites believed. In the way of all revolutionaries or counter-revolutionaries possessed of a simple truth, they embarked upon a crusade to restore lost virtue. See 'just how far we have fallen', she said, shortly after her victorious entrance to Number 10; there was a 'crisis in the nation'; society was 'sick – morally, socially and economically'. She instanced the events of the recent Winter of Discontent as a 'reversion towards barbarism'. She went on to attribute this moral malaise to a generation and more of collectivist thinking. 'The moral fallacy of socialism is to suppose that conscience can be collectivised.'

Decline was also a moral question. We have seen how the Ancients regarded this as a self-evident truth. Gibbon replanted the idea firmly in the modern mind. Every schoolchild knew about the bread and circuses. Note the implication that dependency and moral degradation are the two sides of the coin of corruption. In our times, 'welfarism' and moral decay go hand in hand. Thus Mrs Thatcher, addressing the Greater London Young Conservatives in 1976:

> A moral being is one who exercises his own judgment in choice on matters great and small . . . In so far as his right and duty to choose is taken away by the State, the party or the union, his moral faculties – his capacity for choice – atrophy and he becomes a moral cripple. A man is now enabled to choose between earning his living and depending on the bounty of the State . . .

It was in this speech that Victorian values made their first appearance in the repertoire of Thatcherism. Her moral agenda could have been written on a sampler. The individual owed responsibility to self, family, firm, community, country, God. She would put it in that order of ascent, for self-regard was the fount of all virtue; what else could have been meant by the injunction, 'love thy neighbour as *thyself*'?

Victorian values 'were the values when our country became great'. Implication: departure from Victorian values had something to do with decline. Decline she was pledged to arrest and reverse. 'Somewhere ahead,' she said in her final election broadcast of 1979, 'lies greatness for our country again.' Economic regeneration and moral regeneration were now to go hand in hand. Collectivism is the corroding culprit for both economic failure and moral decay. 'The truth is that individually man is creative; collectively, he tends to be spendthrift' she said in Cardiff in 1979. Earlier, from the pulpit of St Lawrence Jewry in the City of London[1] she had declared, 'The role of the State in Christian society is to encourage virtue, not to usurp it.' Inflation was both a symptom and a cause of the malaise. If the value of money was allowed to decline so would other values. Printing money was the equivalent of State-provided bread and circuses. Inflation was morally sapping, undermining all the Victorian virtues, and was ultimately the destroyer of liberty. Labour governments had:

> . . . impoverished and all but bankrupted Britain. Socialism has failed our nation. Away with it before it does the final damage . . . The very survival of our laws, our institutions, our national character – that is what is at stake today.[2]

But Victorian values implied something more than a nostalgia for lost civic virtue, for the entrepreneurial spirit, frugality and the authority of the family, all of them rooted in individual responsibility: it was the code also for repudiating the 'permissiveness' of the 1960s, that iniquitous decade. Others were explicit, Dr Rhodes Boyson, for example:

> Some people look with amusement or even horror at the self-help of the Victorian age, but its virtues of duty, order and efficiency have been replaced in the muddled thinking of our age by a belief in individual irresponsibility . . . The predictable outcome is seen in disorder, crime and lack of civic duty and in the palsied inefficiency so often visible throughout the public service . . .[3]

By blaming the 1960s for the 1970s the distempers of the time could be laid at the feet of socialism. The indictment was long: crime, especially juvenile crime; violence, personal and political; industrial militancy and public disorder; flouting of the rule of law; loss of parental control, of authority generally; the decline of learning and discipline in the schools; divorce, abortion, illegitimacy, pornographic display, four-letter words on television; the *decline of manners*. This fall from grace had occurred during the Wilson government, and in particular during the time at the Home Office of Roy Jenkins, who had presided over the abolition of capital punishment, legalisation on homosexuality and abortion, the liberalisation of divorce, and the abolition of theatre censorship. 'The End of Victorianism' is how the social historian, Arthur Marwick, describes this period. Exactly. Before long, however, the Swinging Sixties had joined the Naughty Nineties and the Roaring Twenties in the hall of notoriety. In his 'history of respectable fears', *Hooligan*, Geoffrey Pearson contrasts these generational alarms with what he discovers to be 'a seamless tapestry of fears and complaint about the deteriorated present'. He argues not that lawlessness and disorder are myths of our time, far from it, but that real and present fears are incorporated into a myth of moral decline.

> The twin mythologies of 'law-and-order' and 'permissive' rot . . . arise out of the way in which the facts of disorder are paraded within a historical idiom of decline and discontinuity. Whereas if we reinstate the facts of the past it becomes clear that the preoccupation with lawlessness belongs more properly to a remarkably stable tradition.[4]

By the same process, the myth of moral decline was incorporated into the Thatcherite account of Britain's all-too-real economic decline.

The myth was multi-layered. It was compounded of the explosion of youth, the flowering of pop culture, the 'permissive society' so-called, and the concurrent waves of industrial militancy and political protest. The youth explosion was, as Marwick has pointed out, at heart an economic phenomenom. Why this should be thought to belong among the annals of decadence is not clear, for the flowering of the pop culture of the early 1960s was at the same time a flowering of enterprise culture, and the boutiques and the Beatles were among the more successful export industries of the age. Perhaps it was because money buys freedom and independence as well as jeans and records. In 1951 there had been 14·5 million people under the age of 19; by 1968 there were more than 17 million. By then the sons and daughters of the newly 'affluent' workers of the 1950s had money to spend; the youth revolts of the early 1960s were not anti-materialist, far from it, but they undermined established authority to the extent that the middle aged and middle class were no longer the sole arbiters of popular taste: culture was now made from the bottom up. The sexual revolution was harder for the older generation to take. Philip Larkin spoke for middle age in the famous lines:

> Sexual intercourse began
> In nineteen-sixty-three
> (Which was rather late for me) –
> Between the end of the *Chatterley* ban
> And the Beatles' first LP.

But as Kenneth Leech has observed, attitudes change more rapidly than behaviour. The sense of new freedom generated by the 1960s was greater, perhaps, than its gratification, certainly if such surveys as there were are to be trusted. For example, at the University of Durham in 1970, according to a *New Society* survey, 93 per cent of girls coming up to the University were virgins and 49 per cent continued to be so in their third year. However, it was the idea of sexual freedom combined with the statistics of divorce, illegitimate birth, abortion, and single-parenthood which made up the indictment against the 'permissive society'. The Abortion Act came into force in 1968. A year later there were 53,000 abortions and in 1980 137,000. Thereafter it levelled out. How many illegal abortions took place before 1969 is unknown. Illegitimate births increased from 48,000 in 1961 to 81,000 in 1981. In 1961 however, 38 per cent were registered in joint names, and 58 per cent in 1981, suggesting an increase in stable extra-marital relationships. Divorces rose from 27,000 in 1961 to 80,000 in 1971. In that year the Divorce Reform Act of 1969 came into effect and by 1980 divorces had increased to 160,000. Single-parenthood, a function of both divorce and illegitimate births, increased from 367,000 in 1961 to 515,000 in 1971 and to 890,000 in 1981. By 1981 there were almost 1½ million children brought up in this fashion. The reforms in all these cases were designed to accommodate human behaviour rather than to shape it; the upward trends, admittedly, in divorces, abortions, etc., were steep but in each case levelled off after a while; the absolute numbers do not suggest that marriage as an institution is threatened. It must be said, however, that the new freedoms of the 1960s became the new servitudes of the 1970s and 1980s for large numbers of women whose 'liberation' consisted in bringing up children alone, having been divorced or deserted.

The 'counter culture' of the latter part of the decade was altogether more subversive than the commercialised pop culture of the early 1960s. The youth revolts of the 1950s and early 1960s had not been revolts against materialism; this counter-culture, although – or, more likely, because – it was a revolt of the affluent and the privileged, bit viciously at the hands which had reared it. Generational war broke out. According to Robert Hewison, in his excellent cultural history of the age, the use of drugs was the 'symbolic and actual *casus belli* between the authorities and the underground' and was one cause of the political explosions of 1968.[5] 'Sex and drugs and rock-and-roll' as the Rolling Stones proclaimed at the time, were 'in'. Authority became alarmed. The Wootton Report which had distinguished between 'hard' and 'soft' drugs and recommended the decriminalisation of cannabis was rejected. Homes of pop stars were raided. The counter-culture, in the words of Stuart Hall, came to be seen as:

> a moral conspiracy against the State: no longer simply getting and spending, clothes and records, fun and games – but drugs, crime, the withdrawal from work, rampant sex, promiscuity, perversion, pornography, anarchy, libertinism and violence. It became a source of moral-political pollution, spreading its infection in its every form; the conspiracy to rebel. In a profound sense, the dominant culture – face to face with this spectacle – felt itself out of control.[6]

This passage may over-dramatise the sense of confrontation at the time but, written in 1978, it catches the flavour of the *post hoc* view of the 1960s as a source of all that was decadent in the declining Britain which was to turn to Margaret Thatcher for salvation.

The counter-culture was founded on the idea of alienation. According to one fashionable guru of the day, Theodore Roszak, the source of the alienation was technology, which had provided society with a total power to manipulate its members and smother them with affluence. The affluent privileged young drew comfort from the discovery that they were the victims of repression as total as any of which the Nazi or Stalinist regimes had been capable. 'Repressive tolerance' it was called. Herbert Marcuse was the chief corrupter of that generation of youth. A philosopher of the Frankfurt School who had taken refuge in the USA, he turned the world upside down as a revolutionary should: it was affluence, not immiseration, which had beaten the working class into submission; welfare, rather than exploitation, had dried the sap of revolution; what passed for liberalism was in truth repression by another name; the permissive society was tantamount to a Fascist society. The next stage in this thought-process was to justify violence – 'demystify' was the cant word – by identifying the liberal State as the source of all violence. 'State violence' legitimised 'counter-violence'. The inhabitants of the affluent society owed their 'comfortable servitude', according to Marcuse, to the export of 'terror and enslavement' throughout the world. Encouraged by this thought, the students imported the techniques and style of Third World wars of liberation into the politics of the affluent society. Their white guilt about the Third World, and about their own affluence, was channelled into hatred of the West. In Vietnam they had a unifying cause and a bountiful supply of images of violence. 'Racism' within their own societies was a form of violence inviting counter-violence, and Black Power was a part of the struggle of all colonial peoples. Che Guevara was their romantic hero and he had made hatred an element of the struggle, 'relentless hatred of the enemy that impels us over and beyond the natural limits of man, and transforms us into effective, violent, selected and cold killing machines.'[7] The students, together with the blacks, were metaphorically – some believed literally – the guerrillas of the affluent society. Hence they dressed in jungle fatigues and marched upon the American Embassy in Grosvenor Square, and advanced on the offices of their Vice-Chancellors, chanting 'Ho, Ho, Ho Chi Minh.'

The intellectuals, among whom the students were pleased to number themselves, had been promoted to the vanguard of the revolution by Marcuse. For, with the working class no longer revolutionary, they were the one group within the affluent society who, 'by virtue of their privileged position, can pierce the ideological and material veil of mass communication and indoctrination.' It could not quite be counted a revolutionary class – the nostrum that the intelligentsia was the 'new working class' was 'at best premature' but, nevertheless, he told the Congress on the Dialectics of Liberation held at the Roundhouse in London in July 1967, the intellectuals had a 'decisive preparatory role' to play, as the catalysts of revolution.[8]

It was an immensely flattering role. It was also profoundly undemocratic. For no longer was it the role of the vanguard to anticipate the wishes, or the *consciousness*, of the working class but rather to overrule it in the name of history and 'liberation'. The events of 1968 in Britain were peaceful by the standards of those which took place in Paris, Berlin and Berkeley. There were big

anti-Vietnam demonstrations in Grosvenor Square, one of them violent, and campus disturbances notably at the LSE and the newer plate-
glass universities of Essex and Sussex, which the architects seemed
to have designed for purposes of confrontation. The revolutionary
project was well summed-up in the metaphor of masturbation with
which Trevor Griffiths began his play *The Party*. There was never the
slightest prospect of socialist revolution in Britain between 1968 and
1979. Nevertheless, the excitements and turmoils of the years from
1967 to 1974 – embraced by the notion of '1968 and all that' – left
lasting legacies. The student revolts after 1967 and, perhaps too, the
concurrent wave of shop-floor militancy in industry were in part
expressions of disillusion with Labour government under Harold
Wilson. A generation too young to have remembered the disappointments of 1945–51 were experiencing what passed for socialism in
Britain for the first time, and their disillusion had all the passion of
new discovery. After 1968 the Marxists gained intellectual ascendancy over the Reformists until the oil shock of 1973 put paid to Anthony
Crosland's vision of socialism without socialism. Revisionism, as
Crosland had said, was 'a doctrine about means as well as ends'. To
the true believers, if socialism was not to come about by parliamentary means it would have to come about by extra-parliamentary
means, for come about it would.

Thoughts of revolution, however delusory, were part of a new
ambivalence towards democracy, the rule of law, and political violence. During the 1970s it became increasingly difficult to accommodate conflict within a growing general prosperity. Liberal society was
torn apart as people were either pulled to the right or pushed into
condoning activities which had no place in liberal society. This was
another consequence of the snapping of the Social Democratic
consensus; for if the reformist approach towards socialism was now
bankrupt, the reformer was obliged to choose sides somewhat in the
way that the constitutionalists in the last days of Tsarist Russia were
obliged to choose between autocracy and revolution. Of course, the
predicament was nowhere near as hopeless or extreme, but the same
fascination with the Left could be observed among the liberal intelligentsia. For example, the cause of the Viet Cong was widely
espoused. The Palestinian Liberation Organisation was regarded
with sympathy and acts of terrorist violence, although not usually
condoned, were regarded with a certain ambivalence. Closer to
home, when five London dockers were committed to Pentonville
Prison in 1972 for defying a court order under the Heath government's Industrial Relations Act, Labour's attitude was ambivalent in

the extreme. Reg Prentice, a Labour MP who later became a Tory, was the only voice raised on behalf of the rule of law and he was castigated in consequence. Tony Benn congratulated those 'who would rather go to jail than betray what they believe to be their duty to their fellow workers' and Barbara Castle said that it was no solution 'to say that we must all obey the law. Lawmaking should be an expression of the democratic principle.' 'How long will it be before the cry goes up, "let's kill all the judges?"', Michael Foot asked a miners' rally. When Arthur Scargill and ten thousand flying pickets prevailed over the police at the gates of the Saltley coke depot in 1972 the event could be seen either as an heroic victory for trade unionism or as a triumph of political violence against the rule of law. No Labour leader sided with the police. When the councillors of Clay Cross, a mining village in Derbyshire, defied the 1972 Housing Finance Act, and were disqualified from holding office and were surcharged[9] in consequence, the Labour conference of the following year resolved to indemnify them retrospectively. Crosland, then the 'Shadow' Minister responsible, said, 'As a democratic socialist proudly committed to the rule of law, I could not condone, let alone encourage, defiance of the law.' Yet when Labour was returned in 1974 it enacted a measure to end the disqualification and indemnify all councillors against future surcharges arising from refusal to implement the 1972 Act.

It seemed to some that law and order was breaking down in all directions and that society was about to be engulfed in a general wave of violence. In addition to political violence, there was hijacking and terrorism. Protesters were protesting and marchers marching. Violent picketing was an increasingly frequent accompaniment of industrial disputes. Violence was sweeping the football terraces. Mugging was rife in the streets. While Labour was in power in the 1960s the Tories had been ready to link the rise in crime and disorder with the rise in unemployment, a view which after 1979 became the worst of heresies. But, in fact, crime had been on the rise, and not only in Britain, since the mid-1950s, perhaps because affluence had intensified the relative deprivation of those who could not afford the goods and pleasures which were everywhere displayed, advertised and enjoyed. Crime would seem to be among the distempers of prosperity. Conservatives were inclined to blame it on the deterioration in the cohesion and authority of the family and the associated lapsing of discipline in the schools. 'Many of our troubles stem from a lowering of family standards which were once the pride of this nation,' said William Whitelaw as 'Shadow' Home Secretary. Such explanations

were more easily accommodated within a general theory of decadence and decline. Yet complaints about the decline of the family had
been heard for a hundred years or more, especially 'from that
well-heeled section of the community which segregates its own
children away from the family in private schools and preparatory
schools as soon as it is decently possible to do so.'[10]

It may be that relative prosperity, working mothers (who were an
important source of that prosperity), changes in manners, education
(for the most part improved) and the general climate of opinion
concerning freedom and authority had together resulted in the family
becoming a less effective agency of control on behalf of society.
Bringing up children had been made a more difficult business because
they were more financially independent and were subjected to the
influences of the mass media, greater sexual freedom and the tempta-
tions of drugs. The sociologist and educationalist A. H. Halsey,
himself of working class upbringing, was struck when re-reading
Richard Hoggart's classic *The Uses of Literacy*, which describes the
working class world before the affluent 1950s:

> by the integration of ordinary families in those days with the moral
> traditions of the old class and Christian society which he so
> accurately and lovingly described. That moral structure had ebbed
> away fast under the assault of the classless inequalities and the
> secular materialism of the post-war world and, in the process, the
> familial controls over upbringings have steadily attenuated.[11]

The increase in crime which was the cause of such anxiety was real
enough, even when allowances are made for increases and changes in
the reporting of crimes. Violent crime had turned sharply upwards
from the mid-1950s and rose steeply through the 1960s. Reported
crimes against the person increased from 38,000 in 1969 to 95,000 in
1979. The rise was especially alarming among young persons. Law
and order was an issue in the 1966 General Election. It figured
prominently in the Selsdon Park programme of 1968. Nor was it the
only thong to the backlash. The coming of the permissive society and
the reaction against it were concurrent events. The clampdown on
drugs dates from 1968, the reaction against egalitarianism in education from the first Black Paper[12] in 1969. Mary Whitehouse's campaign against violence and sex on television dates from 1964. 'Let us
take inspiration from that remarkable woman,' Keith Joseph was
later to say. Another remarkable woman did. The backlash against
the 1960s, or, we should say, the myth of the 1960s, took on a new

force with the advent of Margaret Thatcher to the leadership of the Conservative Party.

Concern about law and order, however real in itself, is a symptom also of more general angst and there was much to be anxious about as the 1970s wore on. Inflation itself was a source of anxiety. Crime on the streets, and its vivid reporting in the newspapers, seemed to be part of an epidemic of violence. Colour television brought the atrocities of war, hijacks and acts of terrorism – such as the massacre at the Munich Olympic Games – into every home. Outside were a host of pickets and protesters – for example with confrontations at London rail termini between angry commuters and railmen because Southern Region trains seldom ran on time.

The Labour leaders, or some of them, saw which way the public mood was moving. Thatcher had made law and order (Dame Laura, the young 'wets' at the Conservative Central Office called it) a populist issue. Callaghan in his call for a 'Great Debate' on educational standards had already identified discipline in the classrooms as a matter of proper parental concern. At the conference of 1978 Labour hardened up its line on policing and crime. Labour had joined in the backlash, but to no avail. The Conservative Party Manifesto said:

> The most disturbing threat to our freedom and security is the general disrespect for the rule of law. In government, as in opposition, Labour have undermined it. Yet respect for the rule of law is the basis of a free and civilised life. We will restore it, re-establishing the supremacy of Parliament and giving the right priority to the fight against crime.

'Rome itself fell, destroyed from inside,' warned Sir Keith Joseph. Was that true of the *ancien régime* in Britain in 1979? Not, I think, in the sense of a moral decay emanating from the 'permissiveness' of the 1960s but true, perhaps, to the extent that the changes in attitudes and behaviour which had occurred made it more difficult to manage an accelerating economic decline. The 1960s are easily caricatured as some kind of 'happening' or fantasy, a last fling, a final spasm of delusion, before reality set in. But the 1960s, as I saw them, were a time in which a reforming Home Secretary did more for the sum total of human happiness than the combined endeavours of the Department of Economic Affairs and the Treasury. More than that, they were a period in which people did more for themselves than the government did, in which society changed – and changed quite profoundly – from the bottom up. And, in the end, the ceiling seemed a little higher. That Britain became more difficult to govern as a result does not mean that it changed for the worse – not at all. Some of the new freedoms brought new miseries and new anxieties, but freedom is freedom and freedom is good. The 1960s were boom years for freedom. As Britain's decline accelerated, life got better – more open, more varied, more fun, noisier, better designed, funnier, sexier, more exciting, adventurous, dangerous – better in almost every way. If we were not becoming a more classless society at least we thought we were, or at least the fashionable attitude towards the working class changed quite profoundly.[13]

Orwell had said that the English working classes were 'branded on the tongue'. The 1960s made working class accents into marketable brands. Growth, albeit sluggish by continental standards, was a motor of egalitarianism, although not quite in the way that Crosland had envisaged: consumerism was the equaliser, not the provisions of the Welfare State which was much exploited by the middle classes. Men are what they eat, that ultra-materialist Feuerbach had said, but the 1960s helped to make men and women into what they wore, what they drove, what they listened to, how they cut their hair and where they spent their holidays. What was so wrong with that? The equalities engendered by materialism are of greater importance than the inequalities which may be involved in its achievement. A man behind the wheel of his car or sunning on a Spanish beach feels both more equal and more free, and so he is.

Hope was the other mass market of the 1960s. Material hope, spiritual hope, revolutionary hope, all were in demand at the same time: people hoped for more goods, more love, more happiness, for transcendence and transformation. Perhaps prosperity itself raises non-materialist expectations. It would seem that societies cannot live by consumer goods alone and that some prospect for improvement or salvation must be entertained. For many centuries people expected nothing in improvement of their lot on earth but looked to heaven for a better life. Then with God so inconveniently dead, expectations were transferred from heaven to earth and, in the early years of the century, hope became an altogether more dynamic quantity. Science and socialism were its chief vehicles through the twentieth century.

Hope, of course, is inflationary and in all sorts of ways. The wages explosion which burst across all Europe after 1967 was, one suspects, an expression of raised expectations rather than a response to the endeavours of governments to dampen them. But wages were only a part of expectations and when the music stopped in 1973 the game went on, as people demanded more and more from a system capable of providing less and less. This was the essence of ungovernability. For expectations to be lowered again the power of the State would be needed, the State acting within its proper role, that is as policeman not as nanny. Repression, the Left called this. 'Fascism!' some said, to keep their revolutionary courage up. The National Council of Civil Liberties issued a poster which proclaimed: '"The streets are in turmoil. The universities are filled with students rebelling and rioting . . . We need law and order." They got it! (The words were Hitler's in 1932.)'

But more than a stick was required. A new religion was necessary, for one hope can only be knocked on the head by another. The money religion offered a means of social redemption provided people could be persuaded that the laws of economics were written in heaven and not the Treasury. But monetarism, as old Hayek complained from Vienna, was in truth no different from what had gone before in that it still excited expectations of economic management by the State. And so it was, for in 1979 the Thatcher government promised more by promising less. Expectations must be lowered, the satisfaction of wants postponed, hope contained. Yet a hundred years of decline was to be arrested and reversed! How? By a cultural counter-revolution, a transformation of attitudes. Decline, it seems, *was* at heart a moral issue.

2
THE MOULD BROKEN?

5

Unconventional Wisdom

As Margaret Thatcher stepped through the doorway of Number 10 Downing Street no doubt she considered herself to be making history. And so she was. She was the first woman to become master at that august address and, what was more, a local grammar school girl made good. Moreover, she was a woman with a mission: to arrest and reverse her country's ineluctable decline and to save it from a fate worse than death – socialism.

She paused on the way to evoke St Francis of Assisi. 'Where there is discord may we bring harmony,' she said. 'Where there is error, may we bring truth. Where there is doubt, may we bring faith. Where there is despair, may we bring hope.' The quotation has been held to be singularly inappropriate in the light of the style of government which was to follow but, apart from the bit about discord and harmony, these words (though not St Francis's but a Victorian attribution) serve as an accurate enough manifesto of her intentions. St Francis, after all, was a conviction politician of a kind.

Her 'conviction politics' were what came to be known as 'Thatcherism'. 'Thatcherism' is more usefully regarded as a style than as an ideology: an ideology is a consistent system of ideas whereas what she called her conviction politics were largely instinctive and very much the product of her own experience. These instincts were narrow in range, dogmatically voiced; that she came to be credited with an 'ism', a most un-Tory achievement, is a tribute to the force of her beliefs rather than to their coherence.

She did not need to read books by Milton Friedman or Friedrich von Hayek to learn the importance of sound money or that the power of the State was the enemy of freedom. She had learnt these self-evident truths at her father's knee. For her they were not the abstractions of an ideologue but the products of experience; what set her apart from the empirical and pragmatic Tory tradition was not the source of her convictions but their unchangeability in the face of all subsequent experience. Ralph Harris, the supreme ideologist of market forces, describes how he first recognised her as a co-religionist at a lunch at the Institute of Economic Affairs:

> I can remember her falling on one rather stupid Conservative MP who was asking why we thought that people should value choice. She got up and spoke like a Finchley housewife about the choice of going shopping, and being able to go to one shop and then to another shop, and being able to make a choice, rather than being registered with the butcher as some of us remembered during the war and having no choice.[1]

It is that phrase *registered with the butcher* which rings so true. The leaders who had come before her – Callaghan, Heath, Wilson – being men, had been formed less by direct experience of handling ration books than by the economic and political experiences of the 1930s, brought up as they were under mass unemployment and in the shadow of war. With her arrival at the top a profound generational change took place. Born in 1925, fourteen when war broke out, at Oxford 1943–7, her formative memories were not of the dole queue but of the queue outside the butcher's, not of the means test but of the ration book. Her crucial political experiences were gained under socialism at home and communism abroad; she was a daughter of the age of austerity, a child of the Cold War.

Her anti-socialism was deeply rooted not only in time but in place. I myself was brought up a shopkeeper's son in a small East Anglian town. I know Margaret Thatcher. For someone of her background the election of 1945 was a shattering event, as if anti-Christ had come to power. The Attlee government was regarded with fear, loathing and almost total incomprehension. How could something so alien have come to pass in England? Edward Norman, chaplain of Peterhouse and Reith lecturer in 1979, has described how 'like most English lower middle class people' he was brought up 'with a savage view of working class life'.[2] It was a view based on an almost total lack of knowledge, due to the fact that in small towns in the southerly part of England the working class scarcely existed as a sociological entity. In my own town there was one council estate on which were segregated an alien race of people who frequented certain disreputable pubs and the dog track down by the gas works and whose children threw stones and attended the secondary modern school. For the rest there were the working people of the town – labourers, artisans, gardeners, delivery men and so on – sons and daughters of their fathers and grandfathers, who lived in their own streets and houses and treated their betters with proper respect and had nothing to do with trade unions and (or so it was fondly believed) with the Labour Party.

To the petty-bourgeois mind what was still more appalling than that the working classes should elect a socialist government was that they should be aided and abetted in this evil and unpatriotic enterprise by upper middle class people. In small market towns such as Grantham the upper class consisted of the 'county', titled folk and gentlemen farmers, Tory to the core. Then there were professional people, a cut above 'trade' ('business' was the preferred word), whose sons attended public schools, though usually minor ones, and a few of whom 'went on to the university', though rarely to Cambridge or to Oxford. Indeed, Oxford and Cambridge were words spoken in awe not merely of the scholastic achievement required to gain admission but for what they represented in terms of social class – the 'varsity', an idyllic world of blues and toffs and gowns and punts where servants still existed to make the beds and clean the shoes of the 'young gentlemen'. That the products of such pinnacled privilege, Balliol men no less, old Etonians even, should turn traitors to their class and, as members of a socialist cabinet – Mr Attlee was a Haileybury boy himself – preside over the demise of shopkeeping, middle class England was as incomprehensible as it was enraging.

The Roberts of Grantham were Methodists and I can speak to that too. 'Methodist means method', she told an interviewer. My own headmaster was always saying the same: 'There is method in our Methodism', a claim which he elevated to a par with God moving in mysterious ways His wonders to perform. East Anglian Methodism was of a very different temper from the Methodism to which the Labour Party, according to Morgan Phillips, its then General Secretary, owed more than to Marx. Occasionally at my school we would be visited by a fiery preacher from Lancashire, but in East Anglia Wesleyan enthusiasm had given way to a smug non-conformity. Methodism was the religion of prosperous shopkeepers and farmers, a pious celebration of the work ethic and discharge of the religious duty which accompanied the ownership of property. East Anglian Methodism was the petty bourgeoisie at song in a part of the country where the Church of England tended to be the 'county' at prayer.

Later, upwardly mobile, she abandoned the Methodism of her childhood and its memories of gloomy Sundays – her father was a lay preacher and strict Sabbatarian. She became C. of E. Religion merged into politics. Conservativism and Christianity were synonymous, and that was all there was to it. Socialism was the anti-Christ. But she seldom prays the name of God in aid. 'Rejoice' she commanded, at that tense moment of the Falklands war, not 'Thank the Lord'. Her intellectual friends at Peterhouse took her to task for this lack of religious interest; for them monetarism was too earthly a creed and, like Keynesianism, liable to excite secular expectations when the task of government should be to restore authority and a spirit of acceptance.[3] Religion offers no special clue to the make-up of the latter-day Margaret Thatcher, although the evangelical certainty of her parents' church may have contributed something lasting to the style which we are calling 'Thatcherism'.

More to the point is the contribution of her upbringing to the religion of herself. To take her at her own word as a 'conviction politician', to see her as an ideologue engaged upon some lifelong crusade, would be to miss entirely the force of her ambition. It is of the small town variety and there is none more ardent. According to one of her biographers, it was not until she had escaped from Grantham that she revolted against it. Perhaps it is true, perhaps she was too conventional a girl to revolt against the excruciating tedium of petty bourgeois life in a small provincial town, although we are told she was carried away by the excitement of a week with family friends in London which included a performance of the *Desert Song*.[4] Perhaps she too would never quite live down the excitement of arrival at one of the great London termini, in those days grimy cathedrals of steam and clatter, the taxi ride with luggage strapped in, past the dome of St Paul's or down the Mall towards the Palace where, perhaps, the guard was being changed. That feeling is never quite extinguished: it is the exhilaration of escape.

Whether or not escape was consciously on her agenda she was plainly most strongly motivated by the circumstances of her childhood. There are stories of deprivation of the kind which grow up around all fairy tales of self-improvement: modern prime ministers need, like American presidential candidates, their equivalent of the log cabin. In her case it was the outside lavatory. It sounds an unlikely tale; there was, I remember, some similar story about Harold Wilson having no shoes as a boy. Her father, Albert Roberts, could perfectly well have afforded a proper lavatory; nor is he likely to have seen any special virtue in an outside one, the prime status symbol of the working classes and not something which a self-respecting shopkeeper would want to own up to. His shop, by her own account, was 'quite a big shop. It had a grocery section and provisions section, with all the mahogany fitments that I now see in antique shops, and beautiful canisters of different sorts of tea, coffee and spices. There was a post office section, confectionery section and cigarettes . . .'[5] Her father came to employ five assistants and, later, he opened a second shop. It is hard to believe that there would have been a real problem about the fees of £13 a year in 1935 when she was admitted to Kesteven and Grantham Girls' School or even about her taking up her place at Somerville, with the aid of a college bursary, in 1943. Her father was a substantial man in the town, a councillor and Alderman. Shopkeepers for the most part did well out of the war, and even better under the Attlee government, when there was more money around than goods to spend it on. Rationing and shortages affected them less than others as they were in a position to help each other out in an informal barter economy. Margaret Thatcher's childhood may have been repressed but it cannot have been deprived.

She was driven on and upwards not by the spur of poverty but by ambition and a spirit of acquisitiveness. Chemistry was her first choice (her elder sister had settled for physiotherapy) but she was soon to regret it. She raised her sights to the Bar, the highest ambition for a small-town girl or boy, but read chemistry none the less on discovering that, combined with the law, it would enable her to make money at the patents bar. Professional politics became a possibility for her when a Labour government raised the salary of an MP from £600 to £1,000. She became a barrister in 1953. By then she had married a rich man, ten years her senior. Indeed, she passed her Bar Finals within four months of the birth of twins. In 1955, with the children not yet two, she began looking again for a parliamentary seat. She was adopted for Finchley in 1956, elected to Parliament in 1959. Her children were then just six.

Already she had come a long way from Grantham. Within ten years since coming down from Oxford she had begun a lucrative practice at the tax bar, married a rich man and obtained a safe parliamentary seat. The idea that the family is the true centre of her moral universe, that she was a paragon of motherhood and wifely virtue, does not fit easily with the speed and determination with which the Grantham girl made good. Even more preposterous is the view that representing Finchley somehow made her into a suburban housewife. On marrying she moved into Flood Street, Chelsea, and from that day she was untouched by financial worry of any kind, spared from the economics of housekeeping, and materially for ever removed from the shop-keeping world in which she had grown up. Her little shopping expeditions, the apron at the sink, Denis's special breakfast bacon, were aspects of the politician's image. Moreover, she had brought with her from her girlhood a whole armoury of homely virtues with which to justify and explain her good fortune, and the less good fortune of others, and to protect her from any pangs of petty-bourgeois guilt which might from time to time impinge upon the paramountcy of her ambition. For ambition, in small-town girls and boys, is like genius in a writer or a painter – a demonic force, harnessing all vices to one transcending virtue, in this case self-improvement and self-advancement, the creative art of success.

Workaholicism is the most common symptom of this condition in later life. At school she was notorious for the thoroughness of her homework. As a Minister she soon became famous for her attention to her boxes. Ministerial boxes are the politicians' drug, their escape from life into work, the expiation of familiar guilt. She would sit at hers into the night until every piece of paper was dealt with – sidelined, initialled, scribbled on – still the scholarship girl attending to her homework. It was in this way that the word 'wet' entered into the terminology of politics; it was her frequent comment on papers from colleagues and officials which she found lacking in true doctrine or true grit. Her addiction to homework may have saved her life, for she was still at her boxes when the bomb went off in the Grand Hotel, Brighton in 1984.

Her early political ambitions are often attributed to the self-educating, self-improving zeal of her father. There are touching descriptions of her family life in this regard – the insatiable borrowing from the library, current affairs eagerly discussed around the dinner table, her father's dissertations, ears tuned to the radio – a habit that stayed with her. But she did not derive from this the intellectual curiosity, or any of the originality of mind, which the self-improving drive of the Workers' Education Association excited in so many Labour leaders of an earlier generation. Rather, or so it seems – it equipped her with a neat set of prejudices, like a twin-set and court shoes, with which to pursue her ambition into politics.

At Oxford, the rags-to-riches version of her youth not withstanding, she was free with the sherry bottle in the service of her career. She became president of the Oxford University Conservative Association. The anti-socialist zeal she had brought with her from Grantham was appropriate to those times. When she turned to Von Hayek's *Road to Serfdom* it was not for revelation but rather to have her prejudices confirmed. She was much moved by Churchill's open-air speech at the great rally at Blenheim on 5 August 1947, in which he fulminated against the iniquities of socialism. That same year was one of Crippsian austerity, a heatwave summer after a worst-ever winter freeze up, a winter of fuel shortage and power cuts. The dollar loan was exhausted, Marshall Aid yet to come. The rations were cut again – meat from 1s. 2d. to a shilling's worth a week. The sugar ration was 8 oz a week, bacon, cheese and tea 2 oz.[6] Even the basic petrol ration was abolished, and the foreign currency allowance was cut from £75 to £35. The coal industry had been nationalised but the Yorkshire miners were on strike – over a demarcation dispute. At midnight on 15 August India became independent. Britain could no longer hold the line against communism in Greece; Palestine was in turmoil. *Picture Post* published a crisis issue. It portrayed Britain in decline. America had taken advantage of the First World War to industrialise. Markets had been lost. Now, after another war, Britain was a debtor nation while America prospered again. Why, *Picture Post* asked, were 40 per cent of directors drawn from the peerage and squirearchy? It was later that year that the British middle classes resumed the habit of wearing evening dress. In that year, too, Margaret Roberts came down from Oxford and embarked on her political career.

She had held junior office during the last days of Macmillan and was statutory woman in the Heath Cabinet. She became famous chiefly as 'Thatcher the milk snatcher' (Crosland's soubriquet) when, as Secretary of State for Education, she abolished free school milk. This was not an early 'Thatcherite' stroke but was done, ironically, at Iain Macleod's suggestion.[7] However, certain Thatcherite traits were at that time noted or, at least, with hindsight recorded: her immense capacity for work, a profound mistrust of civil servants, and a penchant for getting her way. But her biography is more of a piece if one proceeds from the young Margaret Thatcher, Grantham and Oxford, to the woman who in 1975 seized the leadership of her party in 1975. Keith Joseph as we have seen, flinched from the challenge. The Conservative Party by then wanted anybody but Heath, even if it were a woman. William Whitelaw, who had risen as his loyal lieutenant, was far too loyal – too public school, too cricket – to stand against him. There was a paucity of other challengers. Thatcher put up and humiliated Heath on the first ballot. The eccentric rules of the newly introduced procedure for electing Conservative leaders permitted new runners to declare for the second ballot, but by the time Whitelaw was into the starting gate Thatcher had stolen the race. It was a brilliant piece of opportunism, a successful *coup d'état*. Four years later she entered Number 10.

[margin handwritten note: She rose in the party in a vacuum of leadership]

Addressing the House of Commons for the first time as Prime Minister on 15 May 1979 she proclaimed the election of that year to have been a 'watershed'. Was it? It was true that, for the first time since 1974, Britain had a government with a secure majority (43 over all) and the country had voted decisively for change. The campaign had made quite explicit the Conservative intention to make a deliberate break with the policies of the post-war era, and especially those which had been followed since 1964. But was it really a 'watershed' or 'critical' election, comparable to 1886, 1906 or 1945, an election which permanently altered the political landscape? The study of the election carried out by Nuffield College, Oxford, thought not. To be sure, the Conservative gain of 7 per cent in its share of the vote was the highest since the war but its 44 per cent was still the lowest percentage support for any post-war government save in 1974. The Tories had recovered from the débâcle of that year, but no more than that; there was no evidence of a growth in underlying support. Indeed, they seemed to be losing ground among the middle classes and any claim to have become the natural majority party once more would rest on the lasting allegiance of the skilled workers and trade unionists who had abandoned the Labour Party. Moreover, it was only with the Winter of Discontent that the Conservatives had moved into a decisive lead in the opinion polls on the key issues of prices and trade unions. In other words, the Labour Party had lost the 1979 General Election, as governments often do. As the Nuffield College study said:

> The Conservatives were well placed to catch the plum that fell into their laps. But it was the Labour movement that shook it off the tree. It is worth stressing that since 1959 no British government had won re-election at the end of a full term in office. In the country's declining position, the old rule about governments losing elections may apply more forcefully than ever. As one of Mr Callaghan's advisers complained, 'In today's world, it's jolly difficult for a government not to lose.'[8]

Callaghan shared the Nuffield College view. 'People voted against last winter, rather than *for* the Conservatives,' he said afterwards. And it seemed not improbable at the time that whoever presided over such high unemployment – 1·2 million – and over double-digit inflation would be punished by their electorates. Governments were going down all over Western Europe. The election came at the end of a decade of dissatisfaction. Real living standards had failed to rise during much of the Callaghan government's time; redistributive taxation had bitten hard on the working classes and the consequences for Labour in 1979 were exactly as Anthony Crosland had predicted (see Chapter 1). This analysis could be reinforced by the course and character of the campaign. In spite of all that had happened Callaghan remained the most popular of the contending leaders. 'We are winning in spite of an unpopular leader and an uncharismatic team,' said one Tory candidate from his constituency. 'Events have made Tory voters.' The Conservative policies were the most popular on the doorsteps – especially on taxation and law and order – but on other key issues, notably unemployment, Labour continued as the preferred party; there was no sign of any willingness to break with the Welfare State.

However, these electoral straws can be read in more than one way. The fact that it was Callaghan who fought his campaign using Conservative arguments – 'We are the party of roots, of tradition' – perhaps indicates that the country was in the mood for a radical break. If Margaret Thatcher was an unpopular leader, and Labour's unpopularity the temporary consequence of that winter's disasters, then, perhaps, all the more reason to suspect that the result of the 1979 election was the result of a subterranean earthquake.

Today we have the benefit of hindsight. We can see more clearly that the 1979 General Election *was* some kind of watershed. The re-election of the Thatcher government in a parliamentary landslide in 1983 made that clearer, although there were again special factors to cling to – the 'Falkland Factor' and the 'Foot Factor'. If the present helps us to explain the past, the past helps us to understand the present and, for that purpose, 1979 remains a seminal year in which the decline of the Labour Party opened the way to the realignment of British party politics.

There were some – Margaret Thatcher apart – who saw this at the time. Among the first to do so clearly was the Marxist Left, which lives in the expectation of ideological backlash. Writing in *Marxism Today* in January 1979, before the election in May of that year, Stuart Hall placed Mrs Thatcher in the context of a pervasive shift to the right which he dated from the late 1960s. 'It no longer looks like a temporary swing of the pendulum in political fortunes,' he wrote. He explained this in terms of reaction against the 'revolutionary ferment of 1968 and all that,' the populist appeal of Enoch Powell, the appearance of 'Selsdon Man'[9] but, above all, to the crisis of social democracy, or 'labourism', as it deepened through the 1970s. As befits a left-wing social commentator, Hall sees this in Gramscian terms as the establishment of class 'hegemony' in new form but, be that as it may, he spots Thatcher as the 'mould-breaker'. Thatcherism, of course, 'aims for the construction of a national consensus of its own. What it destroys is that form of consensus in which social democracy was the principal tendency.'[10]

Hall's sense of a re-alignment in progress in an ideological, or hegemonical, sense was confirmed in more precise terms by some of the studies of the 1979 election results. Although the Nuffield study was sceptical of the 'watershed' verdict, it nevertheless remarked on some far-reaching trends. One, which we shall come to, was the further tendency towards regional and demographic polarisation, the increasingly sharp distinction between north and south, city and countryside. More important still was 'the continued inversion in the relationship between class and party', a phenomenon observable elsewhere in Europe. While the middle class had been shifting to Labour, the Conservatives were increasing their strength among the working class.[11]

Marx had predicted that the inevitable result of universal suffrage would be the 'political supremacy of the working class' although Engels, commenting on the elections of 1868, complained petulantly, 'once again the proletariat has discredited itself terribly'. It went on doing so: out of 26 General Elections since 1885, the Conservatives have won 14; only on three occasions has the party of the Left won decisive victories, in 1906, 1945 and 1966. The Conservatives have been more often in power than their opponents and, when in power, have remained there longer.[12]

As some two-thirds of the electorate can be socio-economically classified as working class, it is to the working classes that the Conservatives owe this remarkable record of survival and success as a party of power. It is often said, with much truth, that the Labour Party is the party of the working class but it would be truer to say that there are two parties of the working class, Labour and Conservative.

Customarily about a third of the working class has voted Conservative, vastly outnumbering the middle class voters who have supported Labour. This, as Philip Norton and Arthur Aughey remark in the best recent book on Conservativism, 'is something that causes little surprise to a Conservative'.[13] Many theories have been advanced to explain this 'fact' of British politics. Deference was one explanation. The working classes, Disraeli's 'angels in marble', knew who their rulers and betters were and, with a touch of a forelock or cloth cap, would vote cheerfully and dutifully against their class interest. This theory was open to the criticism that such voters might be deferential because they were Conservatives, not Conservative because they were deferential. In any case, if ever this had been an explanation for working class Conservativism, the spirit of deference seemed singularly lacking in the Britain of the 1960s and 1970s; indeed, one commentator was to attribute Britain's increasing ungovernability in large part to what he called 'the collapse of deference'.[14]

Another explanation consists of a highly sophisticated version of W. S. Gilbert's famous verse:

> I often think it's comical
> How nature does contrive
> That every boy and every gal,
> That's born into the world alive,
> Is either a little Liberal,
> Or else a little Conservative!

According to this, the 'generational cohort theory' developed by David Butler and Donald Stokes in their seminal *Political Change in Britain*, children pick up their politics from their parents in much the same way as they learn their table manners. Moreover, they go on being socialised by their environment – neighbourhood, workplace, friends and so on – well into their adult lives. This theory helps to explain not only why voters vote according to their natural class circumstance but also why they do not; allegiances formed before the rise of the Labour Party continued to be handed down through the generation scale, postponing the fulfilment of Labour's natural class base. By the 1960s, with the pre-1918 generation slowly dying off and the post-1945 generation entering the electorate, Labour's socio-demographic prospects seemed good. When Labour then lost the 1970 General Election (the first edition of *Political Change* was published in 1969) many were eager to point out that the Butler–Stokes theory had been disproved. But it is just as likely that a generational effect was slowing the pace of Labour's secular decline and, if Butler and Stokes were right, Labour's class base may wither more slowly than the working class itself.

A tendency working in the opposite direction to childhood socialisation is that of *embourgeoisement*. According to this idea, working class families become more likely to vote Conservative as they become more middle class in their life styles, especially in the ownership of goods such as cars and labour-saving household appliances. This theory was particularly popular after Harold Macmillan had won the 1959 election, telling people they 'had never had it so good'. Washing machines, televisions, and holidays in Spain were thought to be eroding old class loyalties, and Labour – according to an influential attitude study of the time – suffered in this age of affluence from its 'cloth cap image' and reputation as the party of the underdog. Subsequent research cast serious doubt upon whether *embourgeoisement* in the kitchen translated into *embourgeoisement* in the polling booth; a study of affluent Luton car workers found no evidence of it. In any case, consumerism among the working classes had increased much more rapidly than Conservativism; and in spite of the continuing boom, the Tories lost the 1964 and 1966 elections.

The Conservative victory in 1979 was won against the background of a decade of recession in which materialistic expectations were disappointed and, in four years out of ten, average real living standards did not rise at all. Nevertheless, something very similar to what was thought to have happened in the late 1950s showed signs of happening in 1979. Labour suffered what Ivor Crewe called 'a massive haemorrhage of working class votes'. Its policies were out of tune with the aspirations of a significant section of its natural class base who wanted to own their own house and pay less of their income in tax; and the swings against Labour were particularly pronounced in high-wage working class areas such as the new towns, the Yorkshire and Lancashire coalfields, and the car-worker suburbs.[15]

Class voting, it seemed, was in decline. Butler and Stokes had spotted this at the same time as they were elaborating their generational cohort theory. It was in 1967 that another Oxford political scientist, Peter Pulzer, uttered his much-to-be-repeated dictum that 'Class is the basis of British politics; all else is mere embellishment and detail.' Yet already at that time it was ceasing to be true. Butler and Stokes, writing in 1969, noted the importance of housing tenure in influencing how people voted: owner-occupiers were more likely to vote Conservative than council house or private tenants. In part this was due to the socialising effects of neighbourhood; a Wates estate, it seemed, was an agent of *embourgeoisement* even if a modern kitchen was not. And as Butler and Stokes foretold, 'An electorate which saw politics less in class terms could respond to other issues and analyses.' And so, in 1979, it seemed the electorate did. Certainly class was out of fashion among the psephologists: issues were in. The most influential theory was by now Ivor Crewe's theory of 'partisan de-alignment'. In the early 1970s Crewe and his collegues at the University of Essex had taken over the British Election Study from Butler and Stokes, who had inaugurated it in 1963. Crewe pointed out that not only was the aggregate share of the vote commanded by the two parties steadily reducing but, more significant, voters' identification with parties was growing weaker; and, as loyalties weakened, this made them more likely to decide their votes according to the issues. The theory applied to both major parties but, in practice, its implications for the Labour Party were greater because the Labour Party was the class party *par excellence*. Until around 1974 working class voters had continued to think of themselves as Labour even if not voting Labour; but, from about that time, there was a weakening of party identification. The same tendency could be observed among Conservative voters but it was less pronounced and was more easily explained by temporary disillusion with the Heath government. In Labour's case a much more profound and ominous alienation was at work, it seemed, whether Labour was in or out of office. 'For a substantial number of Labour identifiers,' says Crewe, 'February 1974 appears to have been a "last straw" election, confirming doubts and fears that had originated in the preceding decade.'[16]

At every election since 1951, with the one exception of 1966, the Labour vote had declined – in total by about one-third between 1951 and 1979. The election of 1979 was the third successive occasion on which the Labour vote had fallen below 40 per cent of the votes cast, compared with 49 per cent in 1951, 46 per cent in 1955, 44 per cent in 1964, and 48 per cent in 1966. This, Crewe notes, had occurred in spite of the demographic factors favourable to Labour identified by Butler and Stokes and in spite also of a decade in which social and economic conditions ought to have favoured the Labour Party. Macmillan's 'Affluent Society' had given way to the worst recession since the 1930s and, after the events of 1968, the age of deference was no more.

Labour's seemingly-secular decline could be explained in part by the gradual contraction of the working-class base on which it traditionally relied. Manufacture was in decline and the service sector was growing, blue-collar was giving way to white-collar employment. The world in which the Labour Party had grown and flourished, the world brought about by the Industrial Revolution, was slowly disappearing. Between 1964 and 1979 the proportion of manual workers within the electorate had shrunk from 63 per cent to 56 per cent. But, according to Crewe, the news for Labour was worse than that: it was the erosion of support for Labour *within* the working class that was crucial. At the 1979 election manual workers, supposedly natural Labour supporters, were slightly more in favour of Conservative policies than of Labour's own policies. Crewe's researches showed a chasm opening up between Labour and the electorate, not least among its own traditional supporters. In 1979 manual workers were more in favour of reducing the highest rate of income tax (a Tory policy) than of introducing a wealth tax (a Labour policy). Crewe found among Labour ranks 'a spectacular decline in support for the collectivist trinity of public ownership, trade union power and social welfare'. In 1964, for example, 57 per cent of Labour supporters approved of more nationalisation while 59 per cent repudiated the idea that trade unions were too powerful. By 1979 these two opinions were held by about only one-third of its voters. Labour fought the 1979 election in opposition to the sale of council houses to their tenants but 85 per cent of the electorate, and 86 per cent of the working class, were in favour of this Conservative proposal. Only 39 per cent of the electorate, and 48 per cent of the working class, favoured Labour's plan to complete the elimination of the grammar school.[17]

Before the election of 1979 Crewe had written: 'It is difficult to conceive of a party avoiding a long-term electoral decline if the majority of its surviving supporters reject the majority of its basic policies.' The results gave support to his thesis that Labour was indeed in secular decline and to the belief among political scientists that class-voting, or the working class itself, was in decline. Among skilled manual workers there was an 11 per cent swing to the Conservatives, 6·5 per cent among semi-skilled, and 7 per cent among trade union members. In consequence Labour commanded less than half (45 per cent) of the votes cast by the working class (no more than 37 per cent, counting those who could have voted but did not) and barely 50 per cent of the trade unionists who turned out.[18]

'Watershed' or not, the 1979 General Election transformed the political geography of Britain. One reason for supposing that the Conservatives had done less well than Labour had done badly was their poor showing in the north. When Disraeli first said that the Tory Party was a national party he meant that it was the English party. He was referring to the fact that the Liberals nearly always owed their majorities at Westminster to the Scots, Welsh and Irish. Labour had inherited this Liberal ascendancy in Scotland and Wales and some parts of the north of England. Yet the Conservatives had never been an exclusively southern party. For example, there was a strong paternalist Tory tradition in Lord Derby's Lancashire, of which Lord Randolph Churchill was a part, and the progressive Chamberlain tradition in Birmingham. In 1979, however, the Conservatives were reduced to a mere seven seats in the cities of the north. In 1959 they had held 18. Altogether they finished with 20 fewer seats in the north (and 14 fewer in Scotland) than in 1955. But in the south and the

Midlands they had 34 more than in 1955 (and five more in Wales). The 1979 election saw the country divided along a line running roughly between the Humber and the Mersey, the northern part of it swinging by much less to the Conservatives than the southern part of it, and nowhere more than in Wales, which in 1979 joined the south for political purposes. However, to see this as simply a north–south divide would be to miss the polarisation which was taking place at the same time between town and country, and city and suburb. Like the growing divide between north and south, this also had been going on since 1959. In 1955 the Conservatives could win two out of five big city seats; in 1979 fewer than one in four. What was happening was that Labour was becoming the party of decline, the Conservative Party the party of growth. Slowly the political culture of the south was moving northwards (and this although the recession was moving southwards), colonising the Midlands, ghettoising Labour's strength in the inner cities and the urban centres of manufacturing decline.[19]

In 1983, if we may jump ahead for one moment, these tendencies accelerated and left the country even more sharply polarised along the lines we have indicated. Conservatives made further substantial gains in the Midlands in spite of that area having suffered badly from an accelerated decline in manufacture while in the south, outside London, Labour was virtually wiped out, holding only three seats – Bristol South, Ipswich and Thurrock. Yet, at the same time, the Conservatives for the first time since 1885 failed to win a single seat in Glasgow and in Liverpool. The political map of Britain corresponded still more closely to the map of unemployment and the contours of affluence and poverty. Labour, more than ever, had become the party of the poor and unemployed. Or, to look at it another way, Labour was in decline but its decline was not national. Rather, it was concentrated in certain parts of the country. In the south in 1983 it became the third party, with the newly formed SDP–Liberal Alliance[20] the chief challenger to the Conservatives; but in Scotland the Labour Party still enjoyed a huge lead, and in the north was only marginally behind. It was no coincidence that in Scotland the old manual working class accounted for nearly twice the proportion of the electorate than in the south, that 54 per cent were council tenants compared with only 20 per cent in the south. One result of this geographic polarisation and concentration was to cushion Labour's decline: its loss of seats was not commensurate with its loss of votes across the country as a whole.[21]

This regional voting pattern was one factor which helped to

obscure the significance of the 1979 General Election. A much more fundamental cause was that an influential section of Mrs Thatcher's own party continued to regard her as an aberration. She was a mistake of history, rather as the Stuarts are sometimes seen as an unnecessary break with the continuity of English history as embodied in the Tudors. She had become leader of the Conservative Party only because of its passionate desire to be rid of Heath. She was a usurper, who stood outside the true Tory tradition; some said that she was not a Tory at all but a neo-nineteenth-century Liberal. Had the party greybeards made the choice of Heath's successor it would not have been her; as the leading historian of the Conservative Party, Lord Blake, has pointed out, Disraeli, Bonar Law, Heath – previous outsiders – had all been embraced by the party establishment before rising to its leadership: 'She alone had captured it by direct assault.'[22] And outsider she remained. 'I am the Cabinet rebel,' she is reputed to have said. It was true, at least for a while, as we shall see; more important, it was how she saw herself.

Neither had she been the voters' choice; they were heavily for Whitelaw. Until the Winter of Discontent many in her party believed that she would lose the coming election and were preparing to blame her; she herself believed that she would have just the one chance, if only because her party would not give a woman a second chance. The most frequent complaint against her was that she appealed only to the suburban middle classes of the Home Counties and would be bound to lose the election north of Watford.

It was axiomatic that she stood to lose, because she had vacated the hallowed centre ground of politics where elections were won or lost. Moreover, she stood outside the Disraelian 'One Nation' tradition and would be a divisive force in politics; if she did win, her right-wing zeal would as likely as not open the way to its opposite extreme, Bennite socialism. Here is the not untypical view of one of her critics, a member of the left-wing Tory Reform Group, in 1978:

> Mrs Thatcher's grip on the party may prove short-lived . . . Some on the Tory Left, who dismiss her as an aberration, or a mistake, already regard the period of her leadership, which they expect to be brief, as an unfortunate although possibly necessary interlude: one which allows the party to get the bile out of its system before – regrettably, after another election defeat first – it can settle back into a normal, orthodox pattern once more.

For Ian Gilmour she was the epitome of 'What Conservativism Is Not', a chapter title in his book *Inside Right*, published in 1977:

> British Conservativism then is not an '-ism. It is not an idea. Still less is it a system of ideas. It cannot be formulated in a series of propositions, which can be aggregated into a creed. It is not an ideology or a doctrine. It is too much bound up with British history and with the Conservative Party.[23]

By definition, or at least by Gilmour's definition, 'Thatcher*ism* could not be Conservativism': 'conviction politics' had no place in the Tory tradition. In his speeches and writings at that time Gilmour extolled the virtues of moderation in all things, in terms unmistakably intended to brand Thatcher as an extremist who was defying the centripetal laws of political gravity. 'Others wish to divide the country,' he said in a speech at Amersham in January 1975, at the very moment at which Mrs Thatcher was declaring her candidacy for the leadership. 'Our mission is to unite it. And only moderation can do that. Extremism divides: moderation heals.' Because it relied on winning working class votes, and 'must recruit from the left', as Baldwin had said, extremism was out of the question for the Conservative Party, Gilmour wrote. For this reason, and because it is a 'national party' and not a 'class party', there was no place for ideology in the Conservative scheme of things. For Conservatives, 'talking about what Harold Macmillan calls "the old *laissez-faire* doctrine of classic Liberalism", in the way, say, that Mr Wedgwood Benn or Mr Foot talk about Socialism, is almost as bizarre as the idea that the Labour Party could win an election by threatening to carry Clause 4 of its constitution[24] into full legislative effect in the next Parliament.' Conservatives know that the country can only be well governed from the centre. The fundamental condition for a successful two-party system was that the parties should never be far apart. Conservative goals were not to be achieved by 'waging a holy war': indeed, 'the more Labour moves to the Left, the more relentlessly should the Conservative Party cling to moderation and the Centre.'[25]

When she did win the General Election it was easy for her critics to say that she had done so by default, just as she had won the leadership from Heath by default. Within months the 1979 election looked even less like a watershed than it had on polling night. In office she enjoyed only the briefest of honeymoons. By the autumn of 1981 her economic policies made her the least approved-of Prime Minister since Dr Gallup invented opinion polls.

The government did not recover its lead in the opinion polls until the Falklands war in 1982. In December 1981 the Conservatives stood at 27 per cent compared with 43·9 per cent at the election eighteen months before. This did not seem like the stuff of which permanent revolutions are made. The early failures of her government reinforced the expectations that she would trim, U-turn. The conventional wisdom had been that she would do so before the election, in order to win it; now the conventional wisdom was that she would have to do so in office, in order to govern. This expectation rested, partly, on the assumption that monetarism could not and would not work but, chiefly, on the belief that it was impossible to govern Britain outside the consensus which she had repudiated, indeed was busy smashing.

The conventional wisdom died hard. The country had come to assume that it could only be governed with the consent of the trade unions, which should be appeased not provoked. The social and industrial costs of monetarism were 'politically unacceptable'. The country wouldn't stand for two million unemployed, for cuts laid upon cuts. The conventional wisdom ruled still in most of Whitehall, and in half of the Treasury; it was shared probably by a majority in her own party, certainly by a majority in her first Cabinet. Her policies were viewed with growing dismay as unemployment soared and manufacture was thrown into steep decline. In November 1980 the *Financial Times* commented in an editorial: 'Whatever the monetary aggregates say the economy now is in an unprecedented tailspin.' The high exchange rate was contributing to a deterioration of competitiveness which, said the Bank of England, had 'no parallel in recent history, either in this country or among its major competitors'. Before the end of the year unemployment, at 1·3 million when she came in, had exceeded two million. 'How much responsibility do you feel for unemployment?' Sir Keith Joseph was asked in an interview. Sincere as ever, he replied, 'None. None.' In evidence to a House of Commons Select Committee the Treasury had explained that the object of policy was to reduce inflation 'through a reduction of the rate of monetary growth at reasonable interest rates'; the first effect of this policy was on the exchange rate, costing jobs and output, but in the longer run, prices and wages would adapt; 'it is only to the extent that these wage expectations do not adjust that you get the effect on output and unemployment.' Mrs Thatcher's most influential economic adviser at that time, Professor Alan Walters, later elaborated:

The idea, based on the concept of rational expectations, was that the announcement of these target rates of growth of the money supply etc. would induce entrepreneurs, investors and workers to adjust their behaviour to the new policy as though it were a *new* reality. Much – perhaps all of the pain of adjustment – could be eliminated by a sea change of expectations.[26]

But what was the connection – where was the transmission belt – between monetary targets policy and people's attitudes or expectations? The economist James Tobin told the same Select Committee that the trouble with disinflation was that 'that kind of threat to everybody in general is a threat to nobody in particular'. The conventional wisdom was that collective behaviour had to be influenced through the institutions of collective bargaining, that is by an incomes policy in some form. But the government had no incomes policy in any form. It had disclaimed responsibility for the 'real' economy, the economy of output and jobs. With the Medium Term Financial Strategy announced in the 1980 Budget the economy had been put on automatic pilot. The government had abdicated management of the economy to the forces of the market. That was the profoundest insult to the conventional wisdom. The conventional wisdom indicated that a U-turn was inevitable. When it would happen was the only question. The Cabinet 'wets' were permitted no influence over the conduct of economic policy; they could only await events as the agent of change. The U-turn would come when the Prime Minister was confronted with the full consequences of her policies.

In the run up to the Budget of 1981 she came under intensifying pressure from her colleagues to change course. In the previous autumn she and the Chancellor had been defeated in Cabinet over the spending cuts demanded by the Treasury. They had been allowed only half of what was needed to put the Medium Term Financial Strategy back on its course. In the Budget of March 1981 the Chancellor curbed his borrowing requirement by other means, by taking £4.3 billion out of the economy in raised taxes. He achieved this in large part by failing to raise benefits and allowances in step with inflation, which had peaked at 21·9 per cent the previous June and was still running in double figures. Walters, one of the Budget's chief architects, calls it 'the biggest fiscal squeeze of peacetime' It was probably also the most fiscally regressive Budget of modern times.

The majority in the Cabinet was outraged. In a barely coded speech delivered in Putney, Francis Pym had in February warned: 'Common sense tells us that changed circumstances make adjustments necessary – in both tactics and timing – to meet altered circumstances.' In other words, the government should take account of the recession resulting from events in the oil-producing world and be prepared to borrow in order to sustain demand. The Chancellor had done exactly the opposite, and without consulting any of them. His Budget was the antithesis of Keynesianism: a massive deflation in the middle of a recession. By the Treasury's own projections output would now decline by another percentage point and unemployment rise to above three million the following year. It would remain above three million through the next election. How on earth, Ministers were asking, could the government hope to win a General Election with more than three million unemployed?

The 1981 Budget threw the Cabinet into semi-open revolt. There were leaks and counter leaks. James Prior pondered his resignation. The Prime Minister publicly reprimanded her wayward colleagues in a speech at the Mansion House:

> What really gets me, is that those who are most critical of the extra taxation are those who were most vociferous in demanding the extra expenditure. What gets me even more is that having demanded that extra expenditure they are not prepared to face the consequences. I wish some of them had a bit more guts and courage than they have shown, because I think one of the most immoral things you can do is to pose as the moral politician demanding more for everything, and then say no when you see the bill.

After such a public rebuke the dissidents had no option but to close ranks. Nevertheless, that summer the demands for a U-turn grew still stronger. The riots in Brixton, Toxteth and Moss Side were seized upon by the Prime Minister's opponents in the Cabinet as confirmation of their predictions that monetarism would destroy the social fabric of the nation. Lord Bruce-Gardyne, at the time a junior Treasury minister, says that at this time, 'For once the Prime Minister's nerve seemed momentarily to falter: it seems conceivable that had the critics round the Cabinet table mounted a united campaign for a change of course, their demands might at this moment have prevailed.'[27] But, as he correctly says, they didn't. They were agreed on no clear alternative policy and lacked the will to act.

In September it was she who acted. She purged her Cabinet, sacking Gilmour and banishing Prior to Northern Ireland. For the first time she became the undisputed mistress of her own house, no longer the minority Prime Minister. Gilmour, in a statement accompanying his formal letter of resignation, said, 'Every Prime Minister has to reshuffle from time to time. It does no harm to throw the occasional man overboard, but it does not much good if you are steering full speed ahead for the rocks. That is what the government is now doing.' In that month Gallup reported her the least approved Prime Minister since Neville Chamberlain. The bars and lobbies at the Conservative Party conference in Blackpool that October seethed with sullen revolt. Every reference to Disraeli and his ideal of 'One Nation' was understood as a rebuke to Thatcher for having so divided the nation. As Bruce-Gardyne recalls, 'it would have been hard to find a journalist at Blackpool willing to take bets on a Tory victory in the next election; but easy to find those prepared to speculate on alternative names to lead the party into it. Majority opinion among the commentators was that the party was heading for a defeat of 1945 proportions, or worse.' So much, it seemed, for 1979 as a watershed; so much for the Thatcherite realignment of British politics.

6

Moving Left

The 1979 election results sent the Labour Movement into fierce convulsions. Much the same had happened after the 1959 and 1970 defeats and at first the complacent view of some senior figures in the party was that they were witnessing no more than a display of Labour's endemic disunity in opposition. Nor was it the first time that internecine warfare had broken out against a background of doubt about the party's ability to get itself elected, for a good few premature obituaries had been written after 1959 and, yet, by 1964 a Labour government was back in power. This time, however, events moved swiftly in support of the prophets of doom. By the moment at which Margaret Thatcher became the most unpopular Prime Minister since the invention of public opinion polls, the Labour Party had (a) achieved its first formal split since 1931, (b) adopted a policy of unilateral nuclear disarmament as part of a generally left-wing programme, (c) overthrown the sovereignty of the party in Parliament, and (d) adopted Michael Foot as its leader. These were among the reasons why, in that autumn of 1981, it was not the official Labour Opposition which was benefiting from the government's unpopularity but, rather, the newly-formed breakaway Social Democratic Party in its electoral alliance with the Liberal Party.

There were thus three aspects to the question as to whether – in the cliché of the times – we were witnessing the 'breaking of the mould' of British party politics. One was the possibility that Margaret Thatcher represented a lasting break with the past and would be the agent of a new electoral majority in the land. Another was that the nascent third party might succeed, even within the confines of the British electoral system, in digging the grave of one of its established rivals. A third possibility was that the Labour Party was engaged in digging its own grave as a majority party and, further to that, that the age of socialism was nearing its end. These three hypotheses were far from being mutually exclusive, indeed none could be true without at least one of the others being in some part true. The most crucial of them, however, was the third, for if realignment there was to be, whether of voters or of parties, it was likely to be at the expense of the Labour Party.

Within the Labour Movement itself the inquest had been opened even before the votes were cast and counted in 1979. In the March of the previous year, in a lecture which was to become seminal, the eminent Marxist historian, Eric Hobsbawm, had declared the Labour Movement to be in a state of crisis and listed a whole number of historical factors which, he argued, had made the future of socialism problematical. Although he had appended a question mark to the title of his Marx Memorial lecture – 'The Forward March of Labour Halted?' – his analysis pointed to an affirmative answer. We may think he was saying nothing very new. It was not a new thought that the Labour Party might be locked in a secular, perhaps terminal, decline; Ivor Crewe, as we have seen, had reached this conclusion by psephological analysis and I myself had made a theme of the immobilised condition of the Labour Movement, unable to bring about its version of socialism while, at the same time, unable to abandon socialism in favour of a continental-style social democracy. Quite why Hobsbawm's somewhat muddled essay in nostalgic pessimism should have set off such a debate is not obvious from a re-reading of it today. He has interesting things to say about the extraordinary preponderance of the manual working class during the Victorian–Edwardian heyday of Britain's industrial pre-eminence and the continuing consequences this had for the structure and traditions of the British Labour movement. But it is not exactly clear why the profound changes since that time should have set in motion the political decline of the Labour Party which he 'suspects', although cannot say exactly why, set in at some time in the 1950s. The nostalgic mood of the lecture suggests that socialism is to be seen as a Victorian project which ceased to be practical with the disappearance of the Victorian working class. That may well be the case, but Hobsbawm cannot bring himself to say so. As a Marxist, he insists that he is not a determinist; he deplores the sectionalism of the working class and the narrow 'economism' of trade union militancy[1] of the 1970s, but blames all this on failures of leadership ('the Wilson years') and laments the tragedy of it all, seeing that – or so he asserts – 'we are today in a period of world crisis for capitalism, and, more specifically, of the crisis – one might almost say the breakdown – of the British capitalist society, at a moment when the working class and its movement should be in a position to provide a clear alternative and to lead the British people towards it.'[2]

The importance of Hobsbawm's lecture, given in 1978, lay in the fact that he, no less, should express such gloom about the socialist project, and do so in the Marx Memorial Lecture. The notion that the Labour Movement might be in historic decline took on a new significance after the 1979 defeat and the debate reopened on the Left, conducted chiefly in the pages of *Marxism Today*. It is important to remember that Hobsbawm's pessimism contrasted in 1978, and still more when he came back to the subject in 1981, with a good deal of what – in the Marxist parlance – is called 'triumphalism'. For example, Hobsbawm's critics had taken encouragement from the following points:

1   That in 1979 the working class had at least repudiated the old consensus and indicated that it could no longer be governed in the old Wilson–Callaghan manner.

2   A rising tide of industrial militancy during the 1970s had shown the political muscle of the unions in the destruction of the Heath government in 1974.

3   The leftward shift in the Labour Party and trade union movement had resulted in the virtual abdication of the Jenkinsite right wing.

4   The Bennite Left had emerged, with Benn himself seen as a break with 'the squalid annals of Labour's lost leaders'.[3]

Writing in 1981 Hobsbawm found it necessary to point out that, 'If people don't vote Labour, there can be no Labour government, a fact sometime overlooked by enthusiastic militants.' In the circumstances of the 1970s he had pointed to the great illusion that militant unionism is enough. The even more dangerous illusion of the early 1980s was that '*organization* can replace politics'. Struggling to find a new way forward in the absence of a numerically predominant working class, and in the face of a general decline in class consciousness, Hobsbawm rejected the then-prevailing notion on the Left 'that all that stands between us and the next Labour government is a good left-wing programme for Labour and the proof that the party programme will not be betrayed.' He put it bluntly, to those who took this view, that Labour governments had not been defeated because of secessions of Labour voters disappointed with their records but because of Labour's failures to enlist people who ought to have been Labour voters, but no longer were. The only solution that he could see lay with what he called 'a broad progressive front', which although not specifically including the breakaway SDP – anathema to the Left at

that time – would have to enlist the support of the people it represented who, he thought, ought to support the Labour Party and
without whom the Labour Party would be electorally weakened. It
was these remarks which led some to suppose that Hobsbawm, the
guru of the Marxist left, was advocating some kind of electoral pact
between the Labour Party and the Liberal–SDP Alliance. Hobsbawm denied this. He was unable to tell us how or why a broad
progressive coalition could be expected to form around the flag of
socialism, which he showed no willingness to lower. As his conclusion
was that Labour's long-term decline will not be reversed unless such a
broad coalition comes to accept 'the leadership of the Left' we are
entitled to conclude that Labour's decline was, in his view, unlikely to
be reversed.

I have dwelt on the controversies around Hobsbawm at some
length for two reasons. One is because they convey the intellectual
flavour of the times and help to explain the crisis in the Labour
Movement which accompanied the advent of Thatcherism. The other
is because the theories of Labour's decline tend to be attributed either
to Thatcherites or to Social Democrats and dismissed accordingly,
whereas Hobsbawm puts forward a *socialist* version of the possible
demise of socialism which is essentially similar in its diagnosis. For
we are here dealing with a moment of great political turmoil and
ideological excitement in which reasonable people could variously
suppose that the crisis of capitalism had arrived and that Thatcherism
was the expression of it. Some went so far as to say it was a putative
form of Fascism, or that the Labour Party was in the last throes of a
terminal decline, presaging the ending of the socialist era. Within
these extreme possibilities, realignment was in the air, the political
ground trembling under foot. Perhaps it would turn out to be the most
fundamental realignment since the decline and fall of the Liberal
Party or the coming-of-age of Labour in 1945. And at the heart of it,
for socialists no less than for anti-socialists, the future of the Labour
Party was the fundamental question.

The 1979 defeat produced a rich crop of alibis on the left of the
Labour Party the chief of which, as usual, was that socialism had not
been rejected but betrayed – betrayed by those who had ignored
conference decisions, abandoned the Bennite alternative economic
strategy, and insisted on the 5 per cent pay policy. Although this view
was at gross variance with the evidence of the opinion polls it served
well to support the thesis that accountability was the key to the future
triumph of socialism. If MPs could be made answerable to their

constituency parties, and the parliamentary leadership to the extra-parliamentary movement, then there could be no more betrayals, and when 'Thatcherism' eventually resulted in the return of a Labour government, which it would, it would be a Labour government armed with a socialist programme the implementation of which would be guaranteed.

The long march through the institutions of the Labour Movement had begun in 1973. The story of the organisational advance of the Left between 1973 and 1981 has been well told by David and Maurice Kogan in *The Battle for the Labour Party*. It was in 1973 that Wilson had made it plain that if the Labour Party conference of that year had adopted a resolution calling for the nationalisation of the twenty-five leading companies he would not have had the slightest intention of implementing it in office.[4] 'I see,' he wisecracked at the time, 'they want to bring Marks and Spencer up to the standard of the Co-op.' The next year there were two million votes for the mandatory re-selection of MPs, the Campaign for Labour Party Democracy's first chosen instrument of accountability. Re-selection was carried in 1979 in the wake of Labour's electoral defeat. In 1980 the conference narrowly failed – by only 117,000 votes (with Neil Kinnock, on the NEC, voting against) – to capture control of drawing up the General Election manifesto. However, it voted to remove the election of the leader from the hands of the parliamentary party and at a special conference held at Wembley in January 1981 an Electoral College was established in which the trade unions and the local parties became the dominant forces. The CLPD had achieved a triumph of organisation, tactical manipulation and single-mindedness.

The claim that conference should decide was not a new one. It had been a recurrent cry on the Left which touched on a basic ambiguity in the Labour Party's constitution. Richard Crossman, always preferring *Realpolitik* to constitutional nicety, had described the position exactly:

Since it could not afford, like its opponents, to maintain a large army of paid party workers, the Labour Party required militants – politically conscious socialists to do the work of organising the constituencies. But since these militants tended to be 'extremists', a constitution was needed which maintained their enthusiasm by apparently creating a full party democracy while excluding them from effective power. Hence the concessions in principle of sovereign powers to the delegates at the Annual Conference, and the removal in practice of most of this sovereignty through the

trade union block vote on the one hand, and the complete independence of the Parliamentary Labour Party on the other.[5]

This was the convention now to be overthrown, with the trade union
block votes forming alliance with constituency Labour parties against
the independence of the Parliamentary Labour Party. There was
nothing new, as I have said, in the constituency rank-and-file seeking
to resolve the ambiguity of Labour's constitution in favour of the
conference; what was new was the general fashion for participatory
democracy in which the enterprise could be clothed. The events of
1968 in France had helped to bring participation to the fore. Participation became the major student demand of the late 1960s and early
1970s. It was at once a practical claim to share in decision-making and
a challenge to established authority with revolutionary implications.
At the political level participation was no more than a new word for
the age-old challenge of direct democracy against the forms of
representative democracy, forms which had been made more hollow
by the scale and complexity of modern government. Bureaucracy was
one of the villains of 1968 and all that. The classical liberal model of
representative democracy had long since given way to a system, in all
industrial societies, in which groups of one kind or another were
admitted as valid participants in the decision-making process. As one
commentator put it, 'power sharing . . . was the necessary technique
of government' in modern industrial society.[6] The incorporation of
special interest groups in bureaucratic decision-making, however,
had taken place at the expense of political parties and over the heads,
it could be said, of the people at large.

In industry, participation could mean anything from management's emphasis on improved shopfloor communications, through
co-determination in the German-style (*Mitbestimmung*), to workers'
control which was the new left-wing syndicalism of the day. The
Labour Party had inaugurated a study into industrial democracy
under Jack Jones in 1968 and for the next decade worker participation
was in dispute between corporatists, syndicalists and those who
championed the representative form of democracy. Participation
became an issue also in local democracy, particularly in relation to
planning decisions. The Labour Party launched a campaign called
'Participation '69' with the claim that 'we are a democratic movement, hammering out our policies by argument and debate . . .' but
also with the admission that 'what has been needed is the opportunity
to involve local groups in the working out of our policies.'[7]

In each case what was involved was an opening-up, a 'democratisation', of the decision-making process. Who could be against that? In the process, however, the word democracy took on a new meaning: it applied no longer to the sovereignty of the people, *all* the people, but asserted instead the sovereignty of the members of whatever organisation it was – university, factory, church, political party. In the case of the Labour Party, the claim was that the rank-and-file (conference) should actually make policy and no longer be content to choose leaders, or representatives, to make policy for it. But the claim was entered in the name of the party activists, who were few, and dubiously representative of the party membership at large, which was small, and still less of the electorate as a whole. The claims of inner-party democracy took precedence over the older conventions of representative democracy, the chief of which was that government should be with the consent of the governed. Of course, the argument was not really about democracy in the abstract but about power – who decides. For example, the champions of Labour Party democracy were resolutely opposed to its being exercised on a one-person, one-vote basis. This, it has to be said, was put forward at a late stage in the argument by the defenders of the autonomy of the Parliamentary Labour Party and was intended as an outflanking device. Nevertheless, it exposed the nature of the Left's case for party democracy. Participation could not be extended to people who had not come to the meeting or heard the arguments; that would be to subvent the decision-making process to the manipulations of the media. The same arguments were used against postal ballots in trade unions, in favour of workplace ballots more easily dominated by the activists. Participation, in the Labour Party, meant rule by the party activists.

The Labour Party could scarcely have been more ripe for takeover than at the beginning of the 1970s. The once broad church had become a bare vaulted choir deserted by its congregation. Television and bingo had lured them away; education and greater prosperity had opened better horizons than the party meeting or social. The Welfare State had made Labour largely obsolete as the informal welfare agency it had been. The Labour Movement became a victim of its own success. Individual membership had peaked in 1951 at around 800,000. By 1979 it had declined to probably between 250,000 and 300,000. Hobsbawm was entitled to remark that Labour 'is probably less of a mass party at the moment than the Conservatives'.[8] A spiral of decline had set in: the less Labour was organised on the ground the less it could do for its people; the less it did for them the less it became organised. The planners and architects had played their part in this. The tower blocks of the 1960s were hostile grounds for recruitment and the collection of weekly subscriptions compared with the tight-knit street communities in which the old Labour Party had thrived. Not only was membership in steep decline, it was also ageing rapidly. Here is a description of the Newham North-East Party in 1970:

> Prentice's constituency Party in 1970 was a torpid affair run by a gerontocracy. Its Executive and general Committee were dominated by men, and a few women, in their sixties and seventies. The dominant group was a small knot of old local councillors. Most of the ordinary Party members were old too. Many wards did not bother to hold meetings.[9]

By 1979 it was estimated that less than half the Constituency Labour Parties had more than 500 members on their books and only 13 per cent – fewer than 80 parties – had a thousand or more. Most of these parties could be, and were, run by 30 to 50 people; perhaps there were some 50,000 activists spread across the whole country.[10] As Michels' 'Iron Law of Oligarchy' had recognised: 'It is only a minority which participates in party decisions and sometimes that minority is ludicrously small.'[11]

Labour's 'ludicrously small' minority of activists became, with time, increasingly middle class. They were not necessarily of middle class origin but many were people who had by education, occupational advance or housing location moved on from the working class. The Labour Party in this way became increasingly detached from its traditional working class constituency although, at the same time, the change in its composition did in some part reflect changes which were taking place in society at large. The growth of the middle classes was caused not by any increase in the rate of upward mobility but primarily by the rapid expansion of public sector employment. The salariat grew from 18 per cent of the electorate in 1964 to 27 per cent in 1983.[12]

The 'new class' consisted predominantly of teachers and administrators, lower managerial and professionals or semi-professionals. Its rise was reflected in the burgeoning bureaucracies of local government and the health service authorities in the 1970s and also in the rapid growth of middle class trade unions. In the manner of all new classes the 'new class' which grew up in the 1960s and 1970s was interested in status and in power. It challenged existing authority with a view to gaining better access for itself. Because many of the individuals concerned possessed a status that was lower than that of the professions – their positions were more in the character of being employees – they were not inhibited or squeamish about joining trade unions in large numbers. There was also, between 1964 and 1979, a 10·5 per cent swing to Labour among the professional and managerial classes, a small compensation for the swing away from Labour of from 3·5 to 8 per cent among the more numerous categories of skilled, semi-skilled and unskilled workers.[13]

The archetypal Labour activists of the 1970s were the NUPE organiser, the polytechnic lecturer, and the student agitator. It was they who were interested in constitutional reform, just as it was they who were most interested in Cambodia or unilateral nuclear disarmament; the ageing working class membership of the Labour Party, or what remained of it, was chiefly interested in housing allocations, hospital queues and welfare benefits – it did not much mind who wrote the manifesto or elected the party leader. The new model activist also soon discovered that organisation was fun. The long march through the institutions of the Labour Movement was better than the old trudge around the doorsteps collecting a few shillings a week. Campaigning for Labour Party 'democracy' was more like revolutionary activity; it was conspiratorial, disciplined and occasionally violent. The first stage was to gain control of a local party. This is what happened to the 'gerontocracy' in Newham North-East:

> In 1971 and the first half of 1972 there was a change in the nature of the party caused by an influx of very left-wing newcomers who became active within the party. They were young men and women in their twenties, mostly middle class professionals. Within a short time of joining the local party they became members of the general management committee. At a meeting of that committee on 2 December 1971 there were two very left-wing activists present out of an attendance of twenty-nine. At a meeting on 24 May 1972 there were seven present out of twenty-seven. At a meeting on 27 September 1972 there were eleven present out of thirty-two. Thus, by the summer of 1972, the left-wing activists constituted about one-third of attendants at meetings of the general management committee.[14]

'Entryism' of this kind required dedication and long hours, for an important part of the technique was to keep the meetings going until all good moderate people had gone home to bed. The power of the political activist derives from being unlike other people with normal lives to lead, careers to pursue, families to attend to, other interests to distract. Thus it was, by one little *coup d'état* after another, that the grass roots of the Labour Party were captured in the name of democracy until, in the aftermath of 1979, the sovereignty of the parliamentary party could be overthrown from below.

The civil war which engulfed the Labour Movement after the election of 1979 was conducted as if it were an ideological war, at the centre of which was the battle for democracy, but in truth it was a struggle for power. The struggle was fought between the parliamentary party and the extra-parliamentary party. It was also a struggle for the succession to James Callaghan with Tony Benn now striding to the fore to claim the inheritance of the 1970s.

The Labour Party conference at Brighton in the autumn of 1979 was like a show trial. Members of Parliament, who are entitled to attend *ex officio*, were arraigned like traitors to their class on bleachers at the side of the hall, adjacent to the platform, where they were frequently harangued and abused by fist-shaking delegates from the floor. The party's general secretary, Ron Hayward, although a paid official, played the role of prosecutor-in-chief. To cheers and applause, he said:

> You have got to ask yourself: why was there a Winter of Discontent? The reason was that, for good or ill, the Cabinet, supported by MPs, ignored the Congress and the conference decisions. It is as simple as that.

For many it was just as simple as that. When wars are lost it is of comfort to the troops to believe themselves betrayed by their generals, lions led by donkeys. All of the disillusion and hate, built up since the Wilson years, was now let loose. But the truth was that there was little, if any, evidence to suggest that the policies advocated by the conference would have proved more congenial to the electorate than those put forward in the party Manifesto.

On the eve of the 1979 conference, Austin Mitchell, who had succeeded to Crosland's seat at Grimsby, published a Fabian tract which pointed out that 86 per cent of the electorate had wanted to see bans on secondary picketing, 75 per cent were in favour of the sale of council houses, and 60 per cent wanted to bring back the grammar schools. Labour had opposed these policies. On the other hand, only 24 per cent thought fee-paying schools should be abolished, only 20 per cent wanted to abolish the House of Lords, and only 38 per cent wanted to give trade unionists seats on company boards. All of these were conference policies.[15]

Yet for the Left the abolition of the House of Lords was the test case of parliamentary accountability to the conference. Callaghan was alleged himself to have struck the proposal from the Manifesto. Tom Litterick, a leftist MP who had lost his seat, described how while the NEC had been trying to work the conference's decisions into the Manifesto, Callaghan had turned up.

'That is what he did to your policies,' said Litterick, scattering a handful of papers from the rostrum. '"Jim'll fix it," they said. Aye, he fixed it. He fixed all of us. He fixed me in particular.'

However, the campaign for inner-party 'democracy' fed on the myth of betrayal. In 1979 it came into its own. There were by now three prongs to it. One was the mandatory re-selection of MPs. A second was the election of the leader. The third was control over the Manifesto. Re-selection had been on the agenda since 1974. It would have been carried at the conference of 1978 had not Hugh Scanlon, in typical AUEW-style, mislaid his union's card vote – accidentally-on-purpose it was widely suspected. There was no doubt that re-selection would carry in the atmosphere of the 1979 conference, and it did, by four million to three million votes. The principle that the Manifesto should be written by the NEC, and the NEC alone, was narrowly adopted, but the amendment to the constitution required to give effect to this was postponed, as a result of tactical manoeuvring, to the following year. The question of who should elect the leader of the Party – the parliamentary party or the extra-parliamentary party – had been first raised in 1976. A compromise proposal for an Electoral College, representative of the whole Labour Movement, had been voted down in 1978. In the recriminatory atmosphere of 1979 there was an increased enthusiasm for wresting the election of the leader from the parliamentarians, but no agreement as to how this should be done. Meanwhile, however, the matter would fall within the terms of reference of a Commission of Inquiry and would return to the agenda the following year.

The establishment of the Commission of Inquiry was a crucial development. It was the source of much future disaster for the Labour Party. There would flow from it Michael Foot's accession to the leadership and the breakaway of the SDP. It was the brainchild of senior trade union leaders, chief among them David Basnett, the general secretary of the General and Municipal Workers, shortly (with the addition of boilermakers) to become the inelegant GMBA-TU. We have no need to rehearse in full the saga of the ill-fated, and mishandled, Basnett inquiry.[16] Basnett, like former general secretaries of his union, had lived his life in the shadow of the Transport and General Workers' union. Now he saw it as his chance, with Jack

Jones retired, to become the dominant figure on the trade union scene. He had the ego and the vanity for the job but few of the other qualities required. In Healey's book he was 'as wet as water'. He was a man who needed to be seen coming and going at Number 10 but there the door had now been closed by Margaret Thatcher. The role that remained open to him was to be the saviour of the Movement. But as Alex Kitson, the left-wing leader of the Scottish transport workers, was overheard to say in one of the bars of the Brighton conference centre, 'With Basnett for a foe, we'll n'ae need friends.'

Never for a moment was he in control of the Commission of Inquiry. The party NEC was under complete left-wing tutelage. It was in a position to determine the membership of the Commission and ensured it a built-in left-wing majority. It had 14 members but the parliamentary party, whose autonomy was at stake, was represented only by Callaghan, Foot and Norman Atkinson, who sat on the NEC *ex officio* in their capacities as leader, deputy-leader and treasurer. Atkinson was, in any case, a left-winger.

At various points of the proceedings Callaghan was urged to dissociate the parliamentary party from the Inquiry, insist that the unions withdrew from it, or to stand down from the leadership to make way for Healey while there was yet time. He did none of these things. 'I have as little authority in the PLP as I have in the NEC,' he told one of his aides, who added: 'The Left are the masters now.' 'Let me take the shine off the ball for a bit,' said Callaghan to Healey, who by early 1980 was urging Callaghan 'to fight or go'. Callaghan did not wish to go yet; he was enjoying his new role as international elder statesman, he was looking forward to a visit to China that year.

Moreover, he believed that he could 'work from within' to defend the prerogative of the parliamentary party and that, in the end, as on so many previous occasions in his long, long experience, his union friends would come to the rescue. That was his mistake. It was characteristic of him, endemic in everything he was and stood for and believed. He had been around for too long to be expected to realise that the unions, far from being the upholders of the Labour Movement, had become one of the chief agents of its destruction. Even the experiences of the Winter of Discontent, which had left him feeling deeply betrayed, had not shaken the underlying belief, inculcated in him by history and his whole life experience, that the trade unions and the Labour Party were as one, 'This great Movement of ours'. His view, at bottom, was the trade union leaders' own view. 'It's our

party. It always has been,' said Basnett. This proprietary sense runs
through the history of the Labour Movement, it guided Ernest Bevin
after the débâcle of 1931, Jack Jones after the 'In Place of Strife'
confrontation, and now, after the calamity of the Winter of Discontent, it was the instinct of a lesser breed of men at Congress House.

As the trade union establishment now saw it, the Labour Party was
'on the blink' and needed sorting out. Who else was to do that if not
the unions? They had little if any sense, however, that something
historic or disastrous was in the making. 'A misunderstanding among
gentlemen over *crème de menthe* should not be made into a fundamental division over Marxism,' said one. That was a large part of
the problem. The union leaders felt, instinctively, that they owned
the Labour Party but their proprietorial responsibility tended to be
spasmodic and erratic; their attention span for Labour Party matters
was brief. Trade union general secretaries are, in the first instance,
territorial barons, preoccupied with their own organisations, pursuing their own aggrandisements, and prosecuting their own feuds.
At the TUC they play politics on a larger scale, as statesmen of the
trade union movement, but to the Labour Party executive they send
their deputies, or their deputies' deputies. At the Labour Party
conference once a year it is the great men themselves who brandish
the voting cards before the television cameras, but for the remainder
of the year precious little of their time is devoted to Labour Party
affairs. The way the block votes are cast is determined, in most cases,
by the way their own conferences voted months beforehand; these
conference decisions may themselves be the outcome of intra-union
politicking, the product of deals without very obvious connection
with the interests of the nation or even the Labour Party. In 1980, for
example, the AUEW was in the throes of crucial elections and locked
in power struggles between its various constituent elements. Moreover, the two most powerful natural political allies on the Right, the
AUEW and GMBATU, were engaged in a bitter industrial dispute
concerning laggers on Canvey Island. The autonomy of the PLP was
at stake but, for David Basnett, who should organise the laggers
was a more constant preoccupation.

The union leaders of the Right had no desire to see the conference
being allowed to elect the leader of the Labour Party. For that would
mean, in practice, that the union block votes would elect him or her.
Such an arrangement would invite opprobrium both within the
Movement and in the country at large. In any case the union leaders
preferred power without responsibility. They wanted to be the
king-makers but not the king. The best solution would be to leave

procedures as they were but, unfortunately, the supporters of the status quo had been manoeuvred into a minority position on the Commission. The Commission had been their idea, or at least Basnett's idea, and a failure to agree would be embarrassing. In any case, the trade union way is always to compromise: in a dispute between God and Satan, the instinct would be to split the difference. Another factor was that Basnett, and some of the others, had not forgiven Callaghan for leading them down the garden path to the General Election which never was in the autumn of 1978. Still more bitterly did they blame Healey for the 5 per cent pay policy which, as they saw it, had caused the Winter of Discontent.

It was considerations of this character which, in the summer of 1980, were allowed to determine the fate of the Labour Party. Later, the union leaders' vindictive feelings against Healey played their part in the elevation of Foot to the leadership and, in the following year, in Benn almost capturing the deputy-leadership. But we are anticipating. The Basnett Inquiry was to complete its report at a week-end conference at the ASTMS college in Bishop's Stortford in mid-June. On the eve of the meeting attempts were made in the Shadow Cabinet to ensure that Callaghan and Foot would in no circumstances betray the autonomy of the parliamentary party and make it the poodle of the conference. These moves had led to sharp exchanges. Callaghan was resentful of the mistrust implied. How could he go to a conference with his hands bound, unable to negotiate? How could a leader of the Labour Party refuse to negotiate with union leaders? It was his duty to do all that he could to hold the Movement together and his colleagues would simply have to trust him.

As it turned out, their fears were amply justified. It was agreed at Bishop's Stortford that the election of the leader should be vested in an Electoral College representative of the whole Movement, although no one had been able to agree on the composition of such a college. It was also agreed that the Commission should recommend that responsibility for drawing up the Manifesto be removed from the Shadow Cabinet and vested solely in the National Executive Committee, although the Electoral College should have the final say. In addition, mandatory re-selection of MPs was endorsed by seven votes to six. Callaghan had been outwitted and outvoted. He might hope, as he did, that the party conference at Blackpool in October would reject the Commission's recommendations, but the principle of an Electoral College had been conceded. He and Foot returned from Bishop's Stortford like Chamberlain and Halifax from Munich.

One view at the time was that how the leader was elected did not

matter terribly. Certainly there were those who believed that mandatory re-selection of MPs and control over the Manifesto were more
important battles for the parliamentarians to fight against the extra-
parliamentarians. It was pointed out that in many other countries,
Sweden, Germany, The Netherlands and Denmark among them, all
respectable havens of Social Democracy, the leader was elected by a
franchise wider than that of Parliament alone. Be that as it may, the
merits of the case for or against the Electoral College which had been
agreed in principle within the Commission of Inquiry were no longer
the point: a Holy War had been joined which neither side could afford
to lose. It is not unusual for great contests to come to their head
around issues of secondary importance (take the Reformation for
example). In any case, in retrospect it is by no means clear that the
changes in the Labour Party's constitution made in 1980 were not
every bit as important as their protagonists believed. Neil Kinnock,
for example, according to his biographer, had no doubt that history
was being made when at Blackpool, in that October, the conference
at last voted for the College:

> The conference broke into prolonged applause. Callaghan, who
> had opposed the motion, looked grim. The most remarkable
> platform demonstration was given by Neil Kinnock. 'To this day,'
> recalls one MP, watching from the floor of the hall as the delegates
> cheered, 'I can see Kinnock leaping around with his hands clasped
> above his head. He went crazy. He knew what it meant for him.'[17]

This must be so; for it is hard to imagine Kinnock, no great House of
Commons man, who had held no office of any kind, becoming leader
under the old system whereby the choice rested solely with MPs
voting in secret. It is equally hard to imagine that MPs would have
supposed in 1980 that Michael Foot was the man to lead them into the
next General Election, and into the future, had not the sword of
re-selection dangled over their heads and had not the prospect of the
Electoral College undermined the legitimacy of their proceedings.
For these reasons alone, the turning which the Labour Party took at
Blackpool in 1980 was a fateful one.

The conference took place on the 600th anniversary of the
Peasants' Revolt.[18] By the time the delegates and the attendant
hordes of hangers-on converged upon the Winter Garden in Blackpool, two things were clear. One was that Callaghan was about to go
and that there would be a struggle for the succession. A new priority
had arisen on the Left: it was 'Stop Healey'. The second was that the

[handwritten margin note: Blackpool Labour Conference 1979]

His argument is that the Labor Party gave itself over to party struggles between Benn + Healey + lost touch w/ the people.

launching of a new party, talked about all year, was now a real possibility. The 'Gang of Three' – David Owen, Shirley Williams and William Rodgers – had in August published in the *Guardian* a manifesto which, in effect, set out their terms for remaining in the Labour Party. These plots now unfolded against the background of the Chinese-style Cultural Revolution which raged through Blackpool. The foyer of the once-exclusive Imperial Hotel was like a Soviet permanently in session; the environs of the conference hall were ankle-deep in leaflets and revolutionary newspapers; on the floor of the ornate and gilded ballroom, a fine theatre for politics, the new Labour Party, the product of a decade and more of desuetude and decay, of entryism and militancy, was now on display. Class hatred was rife. Speakers who attempted to stand against the tide were subjected to venomous hissing. Healey, particularly, was denounced as the man 'who led the advance against working people', under the Callaghan government. On the fringe the Left drew huge crowds. Tony Benn moved from meeting to meeting, as if blessed with ubiquity, to be greeted with revolutionary adulation. In a keynote speech to the conference, tumultuously received, he promised that the next Labour government would obtain powers to nationalise industries, control capital and introduce industrial democracy 'within days', would restore all powers from Brussels to Westminster 'within weeks', and – to loudest cheers of all – would abolish the House of Lords, first by the creation of a thousand peers and then by the abolition of the peerage.

Benn = represents a sharp move to the Left

If Benn's speech was triumphal, and shamefully demogogic, Callaghan's speech as leader had the air of a Farewell Address, spoken by a beaten man in sorrow. 'We're all comrades,' he declared plaintively: 'for pity's sake stop arguing,' were his last words of advice. The power struggles in the party had left him powerless to stem the tide of policy. He could not fight on more than one front; scarcely had he been able to fight on one. That summer the Campaign for Nuclear Disarmament had marched unimpeded through the union conferences and now, at Blackpool, Callaghan was obliged to watch the party declare itself for unilateral nuclear disarmament. Whereas Gaitskell in 1960 had pledged himself to 'fight, fight and fight again', Callaghan now was powerless. Moreover, the conference declared itself for Britain to be taken out of the European Community, this time with no nonsense about a referendum.

'There is no doubt at all that the British Labour Party conference is the most democratic body of its kind in the world,' said Benn at the end of the week. In my *Guardian* column I wrote:

> My nightmare of the week is that political liberty is now at threat in Britain, for I cannot feel confident that it would long survive the coming to power of the people who have taken hold of the Labour Party . . . Not many of the lay delegates who spoke this week seemed to be speaking out of working class experience; more often they mouthed the jargon of paperback Marxism. The participatory revolt which has rocked the Labour Movement is the revolt of the *lumpen polytechnic* . . . [The] three tests of a viable democratic socialist party – its commitments to a mixed economy, to internationalism and to representative democracy – were failed at Blackpool this week.

It depended, perhaps, on what you meant by democracy. For many, quite evidently, the 1980 conference in Blackpool was an exhilarating and liberating experience; for others it was deeply appalling and truly frightening. For some it marked the triumph of Bennism, for others the end of the Labour Party they had known and loved. One must be careful, especially from a growing distance in time, not to exaggerate the excesses of popular democracy. Today most would endorse Joseph Chamberlain's response in 1877 to the critics of his own espousal of extra-parliamentary democracy, the *caucus* as it was then called:

> Those who distrust the people and do not share Burke's faith in their sound political instincts – those who reject the principle . . . that the best security for good government is not be found in *ex cathedra* legislation by the upper classes for the lower, but in consulting those chiefly concerned and giving shape to their aspirations wherever they are not manifestly unfair to others – these all view with a natural apprehension a scheme by which the mob, as they are ever ready to term the great bulk of their countrymen, are for the first time invited and enabled to make their influence felt.

Benn might have spoken in very similar terms in Blackpool that week as the 'mob' rampaged through the Winter Garden. But Chamberlain's 'mob' was a pejorative expression for the people, whereas this Blackpool mob represented the people only to the extent that it was the vanguard for the historical march of socialism. The people themselves, asked by Gallup where, for example, they stood on unilateral nuclear disarmament, had on the eve of the conference declared 21 per cent in favour and 67 per cent against. Among Labour's own supporters 26 per cent were in favour, 61 per cent against. Moreover, in its frenzy of democracy the conference had voted for the compulsory repurchase, at below market prices, of the council houses of which their working class tenants had become the owners. Whom did that decision represent? Not the 75 per cent of people who had in 1979 approved of this policy but the 19 per cent who had been against it. The more accountable to its various factions the Labour Party became the less representative it became of the wider public. At Blackpool in October 1980 the Labour Party, in the name of democracy, finally parted company with the people.

All else flowed from that. The way was now open for Michael Foot to become leader when 70 per cent of the public thought Healey was the man for the job. Among Labour voters the preferences were Denis Healey 38 per cent, Tony Benn 17 per cent, Shirley Williams 8 per cent, Michael Foot 7 per cent, and Peter Shore 2 per cent. The choice still lay with the parliamentary party, for at Blackpool the conference had failed again to agree the modalities of the Electoral College and that was to be done at a special conference at Wembley in January. To the Left's great fury Callaghan had stood down all the same, precipitating an election under the old rules. If he still wanted Healey to succeed him he had left it far too late. Benn was ordered by his zealous cohorts not to stand but to await the legitimacy of the College. Foot had decided also not to stand but was prevailed upon by his own vanity, his wife, and the determination of his friends (who included Neil Kinnock) to stop Healey at all costs. Some of the union leaders who had helped matters to reach this pass now put their weight behind Foot as the man who could bring peace in their time to the warring Labour Movement. Fearful now of re-selection, many MPs were reluctant to declare openly for Healey, although for the last time the ballot remained secret. Healey reminded them of the Christian Democratic slogan in the Italian elections of 1948: 'In the secrecy of the polling booth God can see you but Stalin can't.' There was a fear that if Healey were elected the legitimacy of the contest would be challenged and a new contest called in the Electoral College, which Benn might win. Foot was the lesser of two evils. Some, on the hard Left, made no secret of regarding Foot as a suitably ineffectual stop-gap until Benn could mount his challenge. At the age of sixty-seven Michael Foot became leader of the Labour Party.

The spoilt baby of his distinguished family, he had remained an *enfant terrible* until in 1974 at the age of fifty-eight he had condescended for the first time to accept the responsibilities of office as Secretary of State for Employment. Until that time he had preferred the luxuries of opposition, to which his temperament was suited, and studiously avoided acquiring any of the skills of modern government; he was ignorant of economics, unversed in nuclear strategy or the affairs of the European Community, a stranger to Washington. His interests were literary and rhetorical and it is likely that he knew more about the eighteenth century than his own. Loved by his friends, captivating when talking of books and bookmen, he was a House of Commons man although, in my opinion, a somewhat stagey speaker more suited to ranting in Trafalgar Square. A lover of Parliament, he was a great respecter of tradition and opponent of all parliamentary change. He did not bother himself with the detailed drudgery of committee work but, most afternoons, was to be seen in his place below the gangway, the leader of the Tribune Group, heir to the mantle of Aneurin Bevan, whose hagiographer he was. He attributed Bevan's attachment to the expensive Ivy restaurant to the 'good anti-Fascist record' of its Italian proprietor.

During the first Wilson government he had refused all office and railed against all encounters with reality. By then an amiable, and for the most part harmless rebel, he insulated Wilson against the full venom of the Left and in this way was a useful accomplice. In 1974 his first task as Secretary of State for Employment was to buy off the striking miners, which he did by meeting their every demand in full. Thereafter Congress House was treated as if it were a department of government, even having papers circulated. In 1975 he was obliged to bring himself to terms with the need for pay restraint – inflation was at an annual 27 per cent – and this was regarded as a great act of statesmanship on his part. Why growing up at the age of almost sixty should have been thought a matter for special congratulation is not clear. However, Foot's acquiescence in the government's accommodations with the hostile world of the 1970s were important for its stability. For on the backbenches he had been the left-wing conscience of the party.

He contributed to Labour's débâcle in 1979 by his role in talking Callaghan out of going to the country in the autumn of the previous year. But his most profound disservice to his party was reserved for the year 1980 when, having played Halifax to Callaghan's Chamberlain at Bishop's Stortford, he took it upon himself to become its leader. Quite unfitted for the office of Prime Minister and hopelessly ill-equipped to fight an election in the television age, he led his party to catastrophe. The eccentricities which his friends found so endearing in him – the flowing mane, the shabby clothes, the stick – were an image-maker's nightmare. His appearance in a casual duffel coat at the nation's annual Service of Remembrance at the Cenotaph, as if he were attending the CND's Aldermaston March, did him powerful and lasting damage. His invocations of the 1930s and of 1945 stirred old folk memories but meant little to the electorate of the 1980s. Probably few young voters had heard of Aneurin Bevan. Foot appeared to the country as the walking past. It was a shameful betrayal. In the self-indulgence of pure principle, patrician sentimentality and an old man's vanity, the working people of Britain for the first time since 1945 lacked a proper champion.

At Wembley the Labour Party put the finishing touches to the job done at Blackpool. Much energy and cunning was invested in a battle about whether the parliamentary party should have 50 per cent of the votes in the Electoral College, which is what the PLP wanted, or less than half. Foot backed the PLP formula and lost. So much for Foot as the man who could unite the party. The sovereignty of the parliamentary party was ended. The Electoral College was constituted on the basis of 40 per cent of the votes belonging to affiliated unions and 30 per cent each to the parliamentary party and the constituency labour parties. This represented a tactical triumph for the Left although it owed a great deal as well to disunity and incompetence on the Right.

The next day the first public step was taken to launch the new Social Democratic Party. In the words of the declaration issued at Limehouse by the 'Gang of Four' (Roy Jenkins, David Owen, Shirley Williams and William Rodgers):

> The calamitous outcome of the Labour Party Wembley Conference demands a new start in British politics. A handful of trade union leaders can now dictate the choice of a future Prime Minister. The conference disaster is the culmination of a long process by which the Labour Party has moved steadily away from its roots in the people of this country and its commitment to parliamentary government.

There then began the final and most bitter stage in Labour's civil war. This was the symbolic struggle between Denis Healey and Tony Benn, the old guard against the vanguard. Ostensibly they were contesting the deputy leadership of the party but in reality they were engaged in a fight to the finish for possession of the Labour Party.

The deputy leadership itself is an office of no great consequence, more often used as an honourable repository for passed-over leaders than as the last stepping-stone to the top. With it, however, went an *ex officio* seat on the National Executive Committee, a matter of some importance in the context of the power struggle raging within the party. The Left was in complete control of the NEC, with Benn in a powerful position as chairman of the home policy sub-committee. In recent times no right-winger had stood the slightest chance of election by the constituency section, with the bizarre result that, in government, Labour's senior parliamentary figures played little role in party affairs. On the famous occasion, for example, on which Healey as Chancellor of the Exchequer had announced to the 1976 party conference that he would be making application to the IMF for a traditional loan, he had had to make do with four minutes at the rostrum, like any other rank-and-file delegate, much of it lost in boos and catcalls.

Healey had been elected deputy leader without contest after he had lost the leadership to Foot in November. Like Foot he owed his position wholly to the parliamentary party. Now, the leader and deputy leader were to be elected annually by the whole Movement through the Electoral College as constituted at the Wembley conference. So it could be argued that Healey no longer had legitimate title to his office and should be opposed in the name of democracy. But the same could be argued exactly of Foot's position. However, if Benn were to challenge Foot he would lose without doubt. A challenge to Healey therefore was his only next move. This could be rationalised in all manner of ways. One argument was that the new constitutional machinery must be put to use or the Right would soon set about dismantling it. Another was that by forcing the Right to rally around Healey the Left could protect the organisational and policy gains made since 1973. A tactical reason was that the trade unions were now the chosen arena for left-wing advance and a contest in the Electoral College would provide the opportunity for mounting organisational campaigns within the unions. But the overwhelming reason was that Benn by now was the undisputed hero of the Left and that the time had come to show Foot and the parliamentary party who was the true master.

As we have said already, no one – Margaret Thatcher apart – embodied the spirit of the times better than Benn. He was an authentic voice of post-imperial Britain and an exponent of the politics of decline. He was a product of the new age of nationalism and a formidable opponent of Britain's membership of the EEC. He was a mature student of the class of '68, and no one more than he personified the cultural revolution which had swept through the

Labour Movement. An outsider himself, not by birth or origin but through some demonic aspect of his personality, he became the scourge of a failed ruling class and a champion of the aspiring new élites who had been liberated and enthused by the experiences of 1968 and thereafter.

He was never at ease with what he took himself to be. When first elected to Parliament for Bristol in 1950 he announced that he intended to lose the stigma of being an intellectual, to which Crosland (who liked him) rejoined, 'You had better acquire the stigma before worrying about losing it.'[19] Although he could be wildly funny, and occasionally self-deprecating, there was always an earnest, holier-than-thou side to his character. Class guilt was deep in him as in many Englishmen of his generation and background, which was similar to Michael Foot's in that he came from a distinguished, well-off, radical family. Sometimes he would apologise for his privileged circumstances while stressing the 'radical, dissenting and socialist tradition' to which he belonged. At other times he would disown his background, expurgating Westminster School and New College, Oxford from his *Who's Who* entry, as if in an official Soviet biography. Somewhere along the way the Honourable Anthony Wedgwood Benn became plain Tony, and Citizen Benn.

This suggests some personality change but it was not so. 'Wedgie', as his friends called him, was given to enthusiasms no less than the later Tony Benn. One of his earlier ones was public relations. There was the air of a keen public schoolboy about him; he was often to be seen in bicycle clips. In the 1960s Wedgie liked to be 'with it', especially with the gadgetry of the times. There was something in him of Toad, who – you will remember – fell in love with the motor car in the wreckage of his Romany caravan, sitting by the roadside saying, 'Poop, poop. Poop, poop'. One craze gave way to another in Benn's case, and his ideological enthusiasms of the 1970s grew out of the wreckage of the technological enthusiasms of the 1960s. He lost interest in lasers and took up the Levellers. Chartists replaced computers in his affections.

Like Gladstone, he moved leftward as he grew older. He liked the idea of having set out from the House of Lords to finish on the barricades. He could not bear the idea, it was said, of being out-flanked by his own children who were of the 1968 generation. An accomplished dialectician, a brilliant debater from his Oxford Union days, he was never short of arguments in which to clothe his radical progress. But we may suspect that his 'conversion' in the early 1970s was not so much a blinding moral insight into the iniquities of capitalism, or the belated intellectual discovery of its contradictions, as a passionate falling-in-love with the working class.

His romantic attachment to the workers was matched by a growing hatred of his own class and, perhaps – although we can only guess this – of himself. At first his affectations seemed harmless enough, if somewhat foolish – the miners' banner aggressively displayed in his ministerial office, his labourer's tin mug transported around the country with him like a royal chamber pot. But by the mid-1970s he had become increasingly unable to resolve the conflict between the Outsider and the Insider within himself. His outsider role by now made him an impossible colleague but as an insider, to the manner of the Despatch Box born, he lacked the daring, or the confidence, to stake all upon his own Destiny. Had he done so by resigning in 1975, when Wilson vetoed his industrial strategy and banished him to the Siberia of Millbank,[20] his unsullied credentials as the alternative leader would after 1979 have been hard to gainsay.

As it was, he had by then the air of a man of destiny come too late and in too desperate a hurry. He declined to stand in the 'Shadow' Cabinet elections of 1979. But this was a retrospective dissociation of himself from the Wilson–Callaghan governments, the first of many such acts, infuriating to his colleagues, especially those such as Kinnock, who had declined to serve under what Benn now called 'labourist' governments. The decision also enabled him to transfer his energies fully from Westminster to the country and may have represented – although we do not know exactly what was in his mind – a decision to adopt an extra-parliamentary strategy in a more precise sense. A customary first step by a man of destiny is to take his case to the people, over the heads of parliaments, parties and politicians. While he was within the Wilson and Callaghan governments, although increasingly dissident, he had never entirely burnt his boats. At the farewell dinner given for Wilson at Number 10 it was Benn who had provided the wittiest turn of the evening, mocking himself by reading extracts from an obituary of Wilson he had written for *The Times* in the 1950s. While in government he had kept his lines open to the capitalist press and, some of us suspected, his options open too. He was as always courteous, and eager to listen – wherein lies much of the secret of political charm. His ability to distinguish the real from the ideal was at that time unimpaired.

After 1979, however, he increasingly, and in the end entirely, severed his contacts with the orthodox world and moved in an ever-more sectarian world of his own. He aligned himself with various 'hard' Left groups, including the Rank and File Mobilising

Committee (known as the Dank and Vile Mobilising Committee), an umbrella organisation which included the Militant Tendency. The amiable pottiness of his earlier life was beginning now to take a more sinister form, although the old 'Wedgie' in him was occasionally evident, as when he extended his open-house principle to the Posadists, a sect which believes that socialism will be brought to earth from outer space by extra-territorial beings who have achieved a higher level of technological development and, *ergo*, must be socialists.[21]

Like Lenin, he would admit to no enemies on the Left. He happily accepted support in his bid for the deputy leadership from people who had no place in any democratic socialist party. Michael Foot observed sadly how he was to be seen these days intently studying obscure revolutionary newspapers. His vocabulary became more and more extreme, and more strikingly paranoid. Constant vilification goes to the head in much the same way as celebrity; as early as 1975 the *Daily Express* had published a picture of him wearing a Hitler moustache. Now, he was happy to equate Thatcherism with 'Fascism', a word which in semi-private he would throw out in a studiedly casual and matter-of-fact way.

It is easier in retrospect to see how Benn's career became a pilgrimage of self-destruction which led him, like Enoch Powell, whom he in several ways resembles, beyond the fringe and beyond the pale of British politics. Men of destiny seek proof of their greatness by exercising a licence to go too far, and as the fear grows in them that destiny may have played a terrible joke on them, so they double and redouble the stakes on the wheel of their own fortune. In this way they destroy themselves. In Benn's case, at least for the purpose of explaining what happened in the Labour Party after 1979, the task is not to identify his fatal flaw but, rather, to locate the sources of his huge charisma. For he inspired devotion in his followers far greater than the contempt in which his colleagues had learnt to hold him. He packed great halls, the length and breadth of the land, arousing more excitement than any one-man cause since Chamberlain. BENN

He preached mainly to the converted. Or, rather, he converted mainly his own party, transforming it ideologically and organisationally. This was a major feat and a matter of great importance. It was essentially on his programme that the 1983 General Election was fought, and calamitously lost. The constitutional changes which he powerfully helped to bring about registered a substantial leftward shift in the gravity of the Labour Party and opened the way to the succession of Neil Kinnock. In more indirect fashion Benn contributed to the schism of the party in 1981, for it was his maverick scheme for a Common Market referendum which he forced upon the Labour Party in 1972 which provoked the resignation of Roy Jenkins and formalised the split with the old Gaitskellite wing of the party in a way that was never to be healed. In these ways he was, after Thatcher, the most powerful agent of political realignment.

Benn was the apostle to the 'new class', numerous enough to make a revolution within the Labour Party but not numerous enough to constitute a majority in the land. To capture the party and to lose the country was the entire nature of the Bennite phenomenon. It was well illustrated during the by-election at Glasgow, Hillhead in March 1982. Benn arrived during the last few days and packed a large school hall and two overflow rooms with a crowd of some 1,500. He was in cracking inspirational form but his audience, bussed in to working class Scotstoun from all over greater Glasgow, consisted of the new Labour Party, predominantly middle class (in the sense of being educated) people, from the universities and polytechnics, the local authorities and trade union offices throughout the conurbation. The next lunchtime, outside the gates of the Yarrow shipyard, fewer than a hundred workers were gathered to listen in dispirited fashion to the Labour candidate. The seat was lost to the SDP, to Roy Jenkins no less.

The message which Benn brought to his mass audiences was highly congenial to the new classes. He told them that the old system was corrupt and finished, the consensus broken and Keynes dead. They, and the energy in them released by the events of 1968 and thereafter, represented the future. It was they, he told them, who had broken through 'the façade of ritualised parliamentary exchanges about which leadership could run the system best'.[22] He appealed to the resentments of an excluded and aspiring élite; he told them they had been betrayed by an effete and treacherous ruling class which had placed Britain in colonial tutelage to the Pentagon, the Common Market and the IMF. Bennite populism appealed to class resentment and hurt national pride, which were the essence of the politics of decline. And as always with fundamentalist preachers or dema- gogues, the remedy was blindingly simple and consisted in the coming of the socialist light. The Blackpool conference speech, cheered to the gilded roof of the Winter Garden, had come near to saying that Jerusalem could be built in weeks not months.

Benn was obliged to conduct an extra-parliamentary campaign for the deputy leadership, for he could not expect much support from his parliamentary colleagues. That was the more so after the polarisation of the Tribune Group around his personality into 'hard' and 'soft' Left factions and John Silkin had entered the race as the 'soft' Left candidate. An outspoken indictment of Benn's intimidatory style and tactics by Neil Kinnock in Hull had an important influence in the creation of this split on the Left. Kinnock, referring back to the Blackpool speech, accused Benn of 'offering a fantasy that insults adult intelligence, invites derision and guarantees disappointment.'[23]

As the unions commanded 40 per cent of the vote in the Electoral College it was necessary for him to campaign vigorously at their seaside conferences all through the summer. In any case, it was the next tactic of the Rank and File Mobilising Committee, which ran his campaign, to politicise the unions. Some organisational inroads were made as a result but the chief consequence was to split the trade union movement at all levels along the same ideological flaw as the Labour Party. Another consequence was to expose the shortcomings of trade union internal democracy. No thought had been given as to how individual unions would discharge their new responsibility to elect the parliamentary leader of the Labour Party and thereby, in effect, perhaps the Prime Minister of the country. The scandals which arose around the wielding of block votes in the Electoral College gave the Conservative government its opportunity to propose a third trade union Bill, this time to regulate the conduct of inner trade union democracy. The unions had invited this outcome by the casual and half-hearted way in which they had extended their suzerainty over the Labour Party, increasing their power but not their responsibility.

Healey won the election by the narrowest fraction: by 50·426 per cent to Benn's 49·574. Kinnock in the end abstained, together with a number of other Tribunites, and this was enough to deny Benn his victory. From that moment the split on the Left was irrevocable and bitter. The result could be seen as a moral victory for Benn. He had commanded, remarkably, more than 80 per cent support among the constituency rank-and-file and two-fifths of the union block votes. It was a humiliating outcome for Healey and for Foot. Yet at the same time, or so it turned out, the deputy leadership contest marked the turning of the leftist tide. The pre-emption of the Electoral College by Callaghan's resignation before the Wembley conference could take place had denied Benn the chance of contesting the leadership in the only forum in which he could have hoped to win. Thereafter his bid for the deputy leadership was bound to be seen by some, such as Kinnock, who had no use for Healey, as an unnecessary and divisive act. This was especially so after Foot, who commanded affectionate loyalty if not much else, had appealed to Benn either not to run at all or to run against him for the leadership itself. The tactics employed by Benn's supporters, and the ultra-leftist company he seemed happy to keep, gave further offence.

That autumn Foot sought to rehabilitate Benn within the Shadow Cabinet but he behaved in such recalcitrant fashion that no reconciliation was possible. The following year the Right, by then somewhat more organised, regained a tenuous control of the NEC. Benn was purged from his key position as chairman of the home policy sub-committee. He became more and more *outré*, following his Enoch-like path to the very limits of the political wilderness. In 1983, partly as the consequence of the programme he had wished upon the Labour Party, although chiefly due to boundary revisions, he lost his seat in Parliament. This made him ineligible to contest the succession to Foot. The Electoral College which he had played so prominent a part in bringing into being now conferred the leadership on Neil Kinnock, the chief instrument in halting the forward march of Tony Benn. Within two years of his near-triumph Benn was down and out, finished, politically dead.

His legacy remained, however. The Campaign for Labour Party Democracy had achieved most of its goals. The parliamentary leadership had been made more accountable to the extra-parliamentary party. Meanwhile, socialist policies were in place. A broadly Bennite economic and industrial strategy had been adopted. The conference had espoused unilateral nuclear disarmament and had stated its intention to take Britain out of the EEC. The conditions had been created for a victory for socialism. All that was now required was a victory for the Labour Party.

7
The Birth of the Social Democrats

The Labour Party was the victim of economic decline and social change. The Social Democrats were their offspring. The crisis which engulfed Labour after the General Election of 1979 was the midwife which brought the new party into being in the spring of 1981 but the SDP was a child of the times in more fundamental ways. During the 1970s British politics may be described as consisting of a two-party system from inside which a third party was trying to get out. There had been a Liberal revival in 1962 with the advent of Orpington Man[1] but the return of a reforming Labour government in 1964 had put a damper on it. The Liberal revival resumed with the Heath government of 1970 and in the General Election of February 1974 the Liberals, who in 1950 had scored only 2·5 per cent of the votes, won 19·3 per cent (21 per cent in England), although this brought only a meagre harvest of 14 seats. Through the 1960s and 1970s the Liberal vote tended to move up, ratchet-like, although somewhat erratically, rising under Conservative governments and falling under Labour governments. From 11·2 per cent in 1964 it had increased to the dizzy 19·3 per cent in February 1974, from 7·5 per cent in 1970 to 13·8 per cent in 1979.

The recovery of the Liberal Party was only one aspect of a general malaise of the two-party system in the 1970s. In Scotland the Scottish National Party experienced a meteoric ascent. From a sensational by-election victory in Hamilton in 1967 the nationalists won 11·5 per cent of the votes in Scotland in 1970 (giving them one seat), 21·9 per cent in February 1974 (7 seats) and 30·4 per cent in October (11 seats). In Wales nationalism was less rampant but it had been on the increase since 1966 when Plaid Cymru won the Carmarthen by-election. In the 1966 General Election it took 4·3 per cent of the votes in Wales, in 1970 it scored 11·5 per cent and more than 10 per cent in both 1974 elections.

Nationalism was a phenomenon with its own roots, chiefly linguistic in Wales, but in Scotland with the wealth of the North Sea ('Scottish oil') stirring historic memories of nationhood. Essentially it was a form of protest, by the periphery against the centre, and a part of a pattern of protest in which the Liberals had a share. While the by-election successes of the Liberals implied a rejection of the two-party choice nationally, the nationalists in Scotland and Wales were rejecting it locally. A revulsion against the two largest parties was an aspect of the ungovernability of the 1970s.

In the 1951 election the two main parties had between them monopolised 96·8 per cent of the votes cast. In 1970 they still had the support of 91·5 per cent. In the two elections of 1974 their share had fallen to just over 75 per cent. From 1945 to 1974 there were on average 13 minor party MPs; the two elections of 1974 returned 37 and 39.[2]

The volatility of the electorate was another sign that allegiance to the two-party system was breaking down and in the two elections of 1974 nearly a third of the electorate voted for parties other than Conservative or Labour. By-elections in the 1960s and 1970s frequently resulted in huge swings against the government, which had not happened in the 1950s. Opinion polls in the 1960s and 1970s discovered around three times as many 'don't knows' as in the 1950s. There was the marked decline, noted by Ivor Crewe, in voter identification with both established parties.

The hankering by the electorate for a third party was not new but it grew stronger in the 1970s. Over the post-war period opinion polls had consistently discovered some 40 per cent of the electorate to be sympathetic to the idea of coalition (in 1967 Gallup put it at 52 per cent) but this may represent not much more than vague desire to escape from party politics. Voters were also telling the pollsters how they would be ready, in considerably greater numbers, to vote Liberal if only they could believe that the Liberals had some real chance of winning. This was the 'wasted vote' syndrome, a heavy handicap on a third party in a two-party electoral system.

In September 1972 an ORC poll commissioned by *The Times* reported that 35 per cent of respondents claimed that they would vote for a 'left-of-centre' party composed of an alliance between the Liberals and Labour moderates such as Roy Jenkins and Shirley Williams, who were at that time at war with their own party over the Common Market. Some 40 per cent said they would vote for an alternative, centrist alliance between the Liberals and Tory moderates. When similar questions were put by ORC in January 1980, after Roy Jenkins had mooted the notion of a new party of the 'radical centre' in his televised Dimbleby Lecture, 55 per cent favoured such a party. However, only 23 per cent professed themselves ready to vote for the left-of-centre alliance of Liberals and moderate Labour, and only 16 per cent for a simple breakaway party. While both these polls cast doubt on how much 'cashable' electoral support there would be for a realignment in the centre they clearly revealed a high level of disaffection with the existing party system and a wide sense of disenfranchisement through the choice on offer.

The notion of realignment had been around for a long while. The maverick voice of Woodrow Wyatt had proposed a Lib–Lab pact after 1959 as a means of dislodging the Conservatives from what at that time had begun to look like a permanent ascendancy. In 1965, when the Wilson government had an overall majority of only three (later to be reduced to one), the then leader of the Liberal Party, Jo Grimond, proposed a coalition the purpose of which, he insisted, could not be simply to maintain Labour in power but, rather, to bring about a radical realignment:

> We must mobilise the great central body of opinion for a long campaign of reform. I am more than ever certain that what Britain needs is a vehicle for Liberal or radical progress, not for a year or two, but for a decade at least.[3]

The *Guardian* took up the cause and went so far as to urge a merger of the two parties into 'a single reforming movement on the Left'. In offering this advice, however impractical, the *Guardian* was reverting to an old tradition, for its most famous editor, C. P. Scott, had from 1912 consistently championed a progressive alliance between Liberals and Labour. Scott could not believe that the British worker, individualistic and acquisitive in spirit, would ever embrace socialism. In one of his very last editorials he wrote:

> The time may not be very far distant when real political affinities may assert themselves and a great middle party be formed out of the existing progressive forces of the country.[4]

Wilson's landslide victory in 1966 dished Grimond's dream of what he called a 'non-socialist radical party'. The realignment he had hoped to see was postponed for another fifteen years. He wrote later in his autobiography:

Our strategy depended upon the Labour Party or some part of it being convinced that, as a socialist party committed to public ownership of all the means of production, distribution and exchange, it had a poor future. The state of public opinion pointed to a realignment. There was a hope that the full-blooded socialists would split off to the left leaving a radical party on the left of centre of British politics but free of socialist dogma.[5]

Realignments in party politics of the kind that Grimond had in mind are rare phenomena and usually associated either with war, which hastened the demise of the historic Liberal Party after 1914 and ushered Labour to majority power in 1945, or an extension of the franchise, as after 1867,[6] or with the rise of a new class or interest in the land, the Peelite middle classes of the 1840s and the trade unions in the 1880s and 1890s. Was there any comparable development in the 1960s and 1970s which would be capable of sustaining a realignment less ephemeral than the politics of by-election protest? Not unless the new 'post-materialist' middle class proved adequate to the task. This phenomenon had been identified in the late 1960s with the help of elaborate multinational surveys by the American political scientist, Ronald Inglehart. His thesis was that the 'formative affluence' of the post-war period, combined with an unusual absence of war, had resulted in a generational change in attitudes to give higher priority to post-material, or 'post-bourgeois' values and a lower priority to material needs or aspirations. These values did not fit easily into the conventional spectrum of Left–Right issues.

> The strongest indicators of whether one is on the Left or the Right are the new political issues, such as support for liberalising abortion and support for the peace movement, at the leftist pole; or support for nuclear power plants, belief in God and patriotism at the other pole. In short, the *issues* that define Left and Right for Western publics today are not class conflict, so much as the polarisation between the goals emphasised by post-materialists, and the traditional social and religious values emphasised by materialists.[7]

In part post-material politics were a revolt against parental affluence, which at its extreme took the form of middle class terrorism as practised by the Baader-Meinhof gang and its successors. In this respect it was likely to be temporary and may already have been superseded by what we might call *post*-post-material politics as here described by Peter York:

Today's teenager has discovered something a little more pleasant than poring over the garbled philosophy of third-rate continental novelists, than trying to look gaunt and angst-ridden. And what is it, that glorious land over the adolescent rainbow? Is it the Land of Oz, the yellow brick road, Dorothy and Toto? No, it's dinner for two at the Chelsea Wharf, a Porsche and an American Express card, even if we can only gaze at them in the pages of *Harpers* and *Queen*. It is having money, the money our babyland parents would not give us . . .[8]

However, post-materialism could be seen as something more than reaction against too-comfortable affluence; it could be seen as the ideological expression of the emerging 'post-industrial society'. That phrase, originally coined by the American sociologist Daniel Bell, referred to a society in which knowledge played the central role in determining power and wealth, a society which therefore placed a premium on higher education and advanced technical skills. It was characterised by the decline of manual work and the predominance of the service sector. In such a society the middle classes became more radical, the working classes more conservative. The theory, if true, would help to explain a number of related phenomena which stretched right across the spectrum of Western politics – enthusiasm for participation and freedom of information, the growth of the peace movements, the emergence of 'Green' politics, the new importance of sexual politics, the anti-statism of the Right and of the Left. It is part of the other side of the coin of the decline of class-based politics, the polarisation of politics around issues which cut across class and party lines.

Inglehart and his colleagues found post-materialist values to be less prevalent or, at least, less relevant to the political process in Britain than in many European countries. The reasons are not surprising. Britain's politics in the late 1960s and in the 1970s were the politics of decline. If the post-industrial society was characterised by its educational attainment then Britain was not a post-industrial society. One American commentator has suggested that one mark of the post-industrial society is that at least 40 per cent of its school leavers should enter college education. The United States achieved that level in about 1963. Even by 1984 only 15 per cent of British school leavers entered higher education. Nevertheless, there does seem to have been some kind of generational change after 1968 or thereabouts, a change which contributed to a different mood and a different political style. Inglehart's thesis helps to explain middle class protest in all its forms – the march of the Bennites through the Labour Party, the anti-collectivism of the New Right, the resurgence of the Liberal Party and the birth of the SDP. In Britain's case these developments were constrained largely within the two-party system but in the multi-party societies on the Continent the most striking phenomenon of the 1970s was the rise of Green politics at the expense of the New Left. In Britain, a similar though less pronounced realignment may have been taking place within the new middle classes, at the expense of the Labour Party and to the benefit of what was to become the Liberal–SDP Alliance.[9]

At the same time, the imposition of middle class values and priorities on the Labour Party helped to alienate still more its traditional working class supporters. This had happened to the Democratic Party in the United States when it became the party of peace and pot in 1972, when George McGovern was its presidential candidate. It happened to the German Social Democratic Party (SPD) as it became increasingly involved in ecological, libertarian and peace campaigns. The process reinforces the tendency of the middle classes to move left and the working classes to move right in the context of post-industrial society.

However, we shall not make too much of this as a factor contributing to a realignment in the centre of British party politics. When Roy Jenkins delivered his Dimbleby Lecture in November 1979 he could point to no new block of voters entering the electorate, nor to any new class or interest arisen in the land, but only to a widespread dissatisfaction with party politics as presently organised and conducted. As president of the Commission of the European Economic Community in Brussels, Jenkins was at that time in political exile, the king across the water or – as the joke was – Le Roi Jean Quinze. He called his lecture 'Home Thoughts from Abroad'. It addressed not merely the shortcomings of the political parties and the politicians but what he took to be a crisis of the system. The party system had worked well enough for a while after the war but as Britain fell progressively behind the countries which had participated in the formation of the EEC the politicians had made more and more extravagant promises of faster economic growth. Their failure to achieve this had bred disillusion with the system for which his remedies – scarcely exceptional – were greater continuity of policy and moderation of language. But turning then to the institutional framework of party politics he declared that the case for proportional representation had become 'overwhelming'. This was important for, although the prospects of proportional representation being introduced were virtually nil, it signalled to the Liberals – by pre-arrangement with David Steel – that there was a basis on which they and the Jenkinsite elements in the Labour Party could form common cause. His remedy for decline was in essence the adoption of continental-style Social Democracy, a goal which had eluded the right wing of the Labour party since Hugh Gaitskell's ill-fated attempt to emulate the German SPD and repudiate doctrinaire, Clause 4 socialism. 'We need,' he said, 'the innovating stimulus of the free market economy without either the unacceptable brutality of its untrammelled distribution of rewards or its indifference to unemployment.' This, he went on to say, somewhat cautiously and modestly, could be 'assisted by a strengthening of the radical centre'. That was it, apart from the inevitable quote from Yeats about how, otherwise,

> The best lack all conviction, while the worst
> Are full of passionate intensity

and thus:

> Things fall apart; the centre cannot hold.[10]

A 'radical centre', was this not a contradiction in terms? In the then atmosphere of British politics, so it seemed to many, Margaret Thatcher had expropriated radicalism for her 'conviction politics', Tony Benn for his campaigns for inner-party democracy and left-wing socialism. To be sure, a great many people disliked this intense partisanship and ideological polarisation. The people were consistently more moderate than the parties.[11] But that did not mean that they would vote for a moderate centre party. There was a paradox here. The centre was simultaneously sought after and despised. 'All centre and no circumference,' said Harcourt of Randolph Churchill's plan to form a new party.[12] His was a typical attitude. Similar jokes were made about Jenkins's project. 'Thought of joining myself,' said Lord Thorneycroft, then the chairman of the Conservative Party. 'After all it isn't a party; it hasn't a programme and I'm told the claret is very good.'[13] It was discovered that Jenkins himself had said in Oxford in 1973:

There has been a lot of talk about the formation of a new Centre Party. Some have even been kind enough to suggest that I might lead it. I find this idea profoundly unattractive. I do not believe that such a group would have any coherent philosophical base.

People might not like a great deal of what the two major parties stood for but that did not stop them complaining perennially that the third party did not seem to stand for anything either. The more policies it published, the more they would complain. A party in the centre was 'neither fish nor flesh, nor good red herring.' Moderation was a bit like a health food, good for you but rather dull: when it came to it, people preferred meat to muesli. Who went to moderate plays or looked at moderate paintings? Even moderates seemed to prefer immoderate newspapers. It is striking too how moderation in politics is frequently championed by immoderate men. Cicero is the best example. Danton is another. It is the usual fate of the heroic moderate to become caught in the crossfire of revolution and reaction.

It is, perhaps, an endemic feature of class-based, two-party politics that voters have great difficulty in recognising any other kind of party as being a real political party at all. In British politics the centre was not an idea but simply a place, the no-man's-land between the trenches of the class war. One reason why third parties had failed to prosper was that the two major parties, for all their Manichaean rhetoric, had remained singularly adept at contesting the centre ground between the trenches. That, according to the conventional wisdom, was where elections were won or lost. Now perhaps the conventional wisdom had been cast aside with Thatcher and Benn. Jenkins plainly thought so.

A passionate man beneath his fastidious surface, he had always been of the moderate tendency. His father, Arthur Jenkins, was a miner who had risen within the South Wales Miners' Federation to a safe seat at Westminster, where he had become Attlee's Parliamentary Private Secretary. Arthur Jenkins had been sent to prison for nine months for an incident during the General Strike. This had been kept from the young Roy, who was five at the time, and he learnt about it only by accident years afterwards. Great pleasure was taken in the Labour Party at the thought that the Jenkins family regarded the matter as a social disgrace rather than a noble martyrdom in the workers' cause. It is true that Roy's background was more lower middle class than working class. He saw little of the inside of the chapel and had little of a Welsh accent to lose by the time he reached Oxford, although it was said that even the slight impediment to his speech was an upper class affectation. The union had sent his father up to Ruskin College where he had become a linguist, continuing his education in Paris; the young Roy's early gastronomic experiences were in Paris. At home in Wales his mother kept a maid. The family could afford to send Roy to Balliol as a fee-paying commoner. He took to Oxford with effortless superiority. He was, he said later, 'a great believer in not working excessively long hours.'

His friendship with Hugh Gaitskell was more personal than political but he became one of the group dubbed by Aneurin Bevan as 'revisionists'. He was welcome in the salons of New York and Washington and admitted to the Kennedy circle. Like Gaitskell, he had a talent for friendship but, in general, preferred the company of women to that of men. When in London he seldom dined alone. He wrote an elegant life of Asquith with whom, perhaps, he identified as a latter-day Whig. He was a social and literary success before he became a political one.

Europe was his first cause. It resulted in a painful, although temporary, estrangement with Gaitskell and more lasting estrangement with his own party. Under Wilson he became a reforming Home Secretary and then a successful Chancellor, although he was blamed for losing the 1970 General Election through fiscal probity. As heir to Gaitskell he was regarded by Wilson with the utmost suspicion. He invited some suspicion by his liking for cabal and he was invariably surrounded by a group of devoted acolytes and protégés – Roy's boys.

His position became somewhat more comfortable when in 1967 Wilson, with a show of great enthusiasm, espoused the Common Market. The enthusiasm lasted only until the election. Jenkins, for his part said, 'I believe that what was right in 1967 is at least as right in 1971.' He found himself now the leader of the pro-European faction of the Labour Party and felt obliged, on 28 October 1971, to lead 68 MPs against a three-line whip into the lobby in support of a motion approving Britain's belated entry into the European Economic Community. Later, he resigned the deputy leadership of the party in protest against the referendum on continuing membership of the Community to which a future Labour government became committed, at the instigation of Tony Benn.

These were fateful events. The 1971 split over Europe prefigured the schism of 1981. One result was that the pros and antis broke party ranks to fight the referendum in 1975. Jenkins quickly learnt to prefer the company he kept in the 'Britain in Europe' campaign to the company he was obliged to keep in the Labour Party. His dedication to the European cause made him increasingly isolated within his own party. When Wilson resigned the leadership in 1976 Jenkins could muster only 56 votes on the first ballot against 90 for Michael Foot and 84 for Callaghan. In the deputy leadership contest in 1970 he had

beaten Foot by 133 to 67. This was a measure of the party's leftward
shift. From time to time he complained. In 1975 he said: 'Unions are
and should be an important part in our national life. But they should
not usurp the functions of the government. They should certainly not
be asked to tell the government what to do.' The next year he said: 'I
do not think you can push public expenditure significantly above 60
per cent and maintain the values of a plural society with adequate
freedom of choice. We are close to one of the frontiers of social
democracy.'

The former Gaitskellites now commonly described themselves as
social democrats. It was a long while since Jenkins had thought of
himself as a socialist. His European enthusiasm had made him
increasingly aware of the virtues of Social Democracy in the German
style. That is where Gaitskell had hoped to go with his campaign in
1960 to expunge Clause 4 from the party constitution. In 1959 at their
Bad Godesberg conference German social democrats had come to
terms with the market economy and had abandoned statist socialism.
Gaitskell had tried to follow suit after the 1959 defeat but had failed.
Now prospects of making the transition to Bad Godesberg from
inside the Labour Party were even more forlorn. Beleaguered on the
European front, the Jenkinsites were discredited and inhibited from
fighting on the ideological front. It was during this time that the social
democratic cause within the Labour Party was lost.

Ironically his European convictions debarred Jenkins from the
Foreign Office in the eyes of the Labour Party. When Callaghan
refused it to him, he accepted the presidency of the European
Commission in Brussels and retired from British politics. The President of the Commission is an office not without honour but largely
without power. It is a job more suitable for a Permanent Under-
Secretary than a Cabinet Minister. Jenkins's skills were not of the
bureaucratic kind, his style was to rise laconically to the great
occasion. The influence which a President can exercise on member
governments is not commensurate with the salary they afford him or
the pomp which goes with the job, the white-gloved butler and
the large black limousine. Roy Jenkins lived well but not happily in
Brussels.

He had left England believing himself a political failure. That was one
reason why he was now eager to return. 'My adrenalin is flowing
again,' he said. 'The sap is rising in my old bones.' Perhaps what had
been lost from within the Labour Party could be regained from
without. What had now to be done, he said in his Dimbleby Lecture

of 1979, was 'not to slog through an unending war of attrition, stubbornly and conventionally defending as much of the old citadel as you can hold, but to break out and mount a battle of movement on new and higher ground.'

The invitation was plain enough. It was by no means welcome to all who heard it. Most of Jenkins's friends had tried to dissuade him from saying what he said. The timing was premature, the game not yet lost in the Labour Party, or so they thought. But Jenkins had told them, 'You don't get asked every year to give the Dimbleby Lecture.' The leading Social Democrats in the Labour Party fell over each other to disassociate themselves from the notion of a centre party. Shirley Williams declared that such a party would have 'no roots, no principles, no philosophy and no values'. David Owen described Jenkins's initiative as 'a dastardly act' and told his friends, 'It is important for people to realise that some of us who are staying to fight are doing so not simply because we think that Roy's party won't take off.' Owen, in fact, believed that it might well take off. William Rodgers, although the closest of them to Jenkins, also believed the best hope still lay with fighting to save the Labour Party from inside although he did, in a speech on 30 November, warn that the Labour Party had only one year in which to save itself.

These statements are of some importance because they remind us of people's intentions at the time. Following Jenkins's lecture, and as the crisis in the Labour Party deepened, talk of a new party became incessant; slowly the assumption built up that, in the end, something would happen. But what? Jenkins had not committed himself to a new party, he had spoken of 'strengthening the radical centre'. It was not ruled out that he and his political friends, who were mostly now out of Parliament, might join the Liberal Party. This was not David Steel's wish. Since becoming leader of the Liberal Party in 1976 his aim had been to lead it out of protest into power. To the first Liberal Assembly which he addressed as party leader he said:

> We must not give the impression of being afraid to soil our hands with the responsibilities of sharing power. If people want more broadly based government they must vote Liberal to get it. And if they vote Liberal we must be ready to help provide it.

Power-sharing became his consistent theme; patiently Steel set about educating his unruly and recalcitrant party in the virtues of governmental responsibility and the tactical necessity of coalition. The Lib–Lab pact, which between March 1977 and August 1978 sustained the Callaghan government, was a one-sided arrangement but it enabled the Liberals to brush shoulders with power. With the Conservatives now back in office Steel could rely on the cycle of protest resuming; the Liberals could hope to harvest a few more seats but there was no hope of a breakthrough into power. His life would be wasted in the futility of permanent opposition. If the mould was to be broken a new departure was required, something capable of firing the imagination of the electorate, a force more credible than the Liberal Party which he led, the limitations of which he knew too well. The best hope that he could see lay with a social democratic break-out from the Labour Party; in electoral alliance with the Liberals that might stand a real chance of cracking the system; the total, he reckoned, would be greater than the sum of its parts. Jenkins's commitment to proportional representation would help Steel to sell this project to his party. Meanwhile, he urged Jenkins – with whom he was in frequent touch – to stay his hand and await events in the Labour Party which, Steel hoped, would drive the social democrats into his arms.

The timing of the Dimbleby Lecture had been unwelcome to the Labour Party dissidents because there was nothing they could say or do until the battles inside the Labour Party had been fought to the end and lost. That outcome was not yet certain. At least they would have to wait until the conference at Blackpool and for Callaghan to step down. Much therefore depended on Healey. He was their last best hope. The trouble was that his own best hope was of succeeding Callaghan quietly. His chances of becoming leader rested entirely with the parliamentary party. If the election was thrown open to the Movement he would be bound to lose. The trade union leaders had not forgiven him for the 5 per cent pay policy and Basnett, in particular, was ready to wage vendetta against him even at the cost of making Foot the leader; he was the *bête noire* of the constituency parties to the same degree that Benn was their darling. The sooner Callaghan stepped down, the greater Healey's chance of inheriting the leadership and digging in; but if he played it rough with the Bennites, or put public pressure on Callaghan to fight or go, he risked opening the way to Foot as the man who might least split the party. So, through most of 1980, Healey complained in private and in public kept his head down and his mouth shut.

The Bishop's Stortford meeting was his downfall. His fatal error was to allow himself to be compromised by Callaghan and Foot. He took no stand on the principle of the autonomy of the parliamentary party or, at very least, the election of the leader according to one person, one vote. He clung still to the hope that by attaching himself to Callaghan he could succeed him. When members of the Gang of Three (Owen, Williams and Rodgers) inquired of his position before the Blackpool conference he admitted that his attitude was that he would accept an Electoral College if it could be constituted on a basis which would endorse his leadership. So much for principle, they thought. Now no one trusted him: the Left believed that he would split the party, the Right that he would flinch from doing so. The Footites now could argue that for the PLP to choose Healey would be to invite a challenge to him in the Electoral College and open the way to Benn. The Bennites calculated that they could make Foot their prisoner while Healey might somehow contrive to overthrow or defy the organisational advances they had made. The social democrats believed they could no longer rely on Healey as their champion although, had he won, and in spite of his take-it-or-leave-it attitude towards them, the schism would at least have been postponed.

After the Wembley conference, and the subsequent breakaway to form the SDP had occurred, Healey considered very seriously putting himself at the head of it. He had no doubts as to where the future of the Labour Party must lie if it was to have one. The transition to Bad Godesberg could no longer be delayed. The Thatcher government's liberal economic approach made it all the more urgent for Labour to abandon its old-style socialist dogmas and adopt the social market approach. Gaitskell had been right, but he had taken a hammer to the party tablets; Healey had hoped to succeed where Gaitskell had failed. Austria was his favourite model. In a lecture delivered shortly before Jenkins's Dimbleby Lecture, but scarcely noticed, he had said:

> Austria came to terms with its political and economic disadvantages after the war, jettisoned those parts of its Marxist ideological inheritance which were obviously no longer relevant, and turned a country which in the inter-war years had been suffering from an ex-imperial hangover into a model welfare state, without sacrificing any of its cultural attractions in the process.

He was offering no New Jerusalem, he went on to say, 'simply a country with stable prices, jobs for those who want them and help for those who need it.' If he was to offer more who would believe him? To achieve his Austrian dream would be to achieve more than any post-war British government had managed.[14]

In the same lecture Healey quoted some words of the émigré Polish philosopher, and the historian of Marxism, Lesjek Kolakowski. I want to requote them at some length not only because they are noble words but because, eighteen months later, at the launch of the SDP they were used by David Owen to convey what he took to be the quintessence of social democracy:

> The trouble with the social democratic idea is that it does not stock and does not sell any of the exciting ideological commodities which various totalitarian movements – Communist, Fascist or Leftist – offer dream-hungry youth. It is no ultimate solution for all human misery and misfortunes. It has no prescription for the total salvation of mankind, it cannot promise the fireworks of the last revolution to settle definitely all conflicts and struggles. It has invented no miraculous devices to bring about the perfect unity of man and universal brotherhood. It believes in no final easy victory over evil.
>
> It requires, in addition to commitment to a number of basic values, hard knowledge and rational calculation, since we need to be aware of and investigate as exactly as possible the historical and economic conditions in which these values are to be implemented. It is an obstinate will to erode by inches the conditions which produce avoidable suffering, oppression, hunger, wars, racial and national hatred, insatiable greed and vindictive envy.

These were Healey's values. With Roy Jenkins out of Parliament he would have made the obvious and natural leader of a party which, unlike the Labour Party, might hold them dear. Ancestral loyalty held him back. So did his knowledge of international politics, for wherever the Left was divided on sectarian or religious lines the hegemony of the Right prevailed, while wherever the Right was divided between Catholics and Protestants, Conservatives and Liberals, or farmers and industrialists, a united Left became the natural majority. Healey could see no future for a social democratic party cut away from its trade union base.

Holding him back also was an indomitable optimism, the vast resilience of his spirit and the huge stamina of his frame. He was frequently accused of being a politician of no fixed belief – ideas yes, plenty of them, but no settled convictions. This was neither fair nor true, for he was a cultured man imbued with civilised values, who trod his way undaunted through a wicked world armed with the incrementalist creed described by Kolakowski. An ounce of such values is worth a pound of ideological belief. However, Healey was a true believer in one respect: he had an unshakable faith in the proposition that it would all be all right on the night.

Partly this was born of an immense confidence in his own abilities, a confidence which was well justified. A powerful brain, agile intelligence, combined with a good memory and a driving energy, had made him into a political polymath. He was an expert in international relations who could hold his own in the dismal sciences of strategic theory and economic practice. He could sing German drinking songs and tell dirty jokes in his Eighth Army Italian, he could give interviews in French on monetarism or nuclear strategy. At home the cloakroom in his hall housed an eclectic collection of gramophone records numbering thousands; his library included shelves of poetry and the *avant garde* novels he had read at Oxford. He claimed to have introduced Iris Murdoch to Beckett's *Molloy*. He was a great name-dropper, usually of international statesmen – Robert McNamara and Helmut Schmidt were among his favourites – but if it was not them it would be 'Claudio' (Abbado) or, if he was trying to fix something with the unions, Charlie Kelly of ACATT. He liked to be one up. He was the most enjoyable politician of his day.

In his own party he was regarded as an intellectual bully. True, he would often begin a remark with the words 'With respect' and then proceed to flatten the recipient without the slightest respect. However, he could take as good as he would give, was of thick skin and cheerful disposition and bore no grudges. Fastidiousness is usually the inhibiting vice of the intellectual in politics but not in Healey's case. Rather he believed himself to possess a special understanding of power and its uses. This made him a bit of a thug. Like Machiavelli, he was neither surprised nor shocked when he found principle to be at variance with practice and he regarded the truth as no more than one good to be set against another as necessity required. He may have acquired these habits of mind as a youthful recruiter for the Communist Party and, later, as an apparatchik at Transport House.

Yet when the time came for him to bid for power he had no cabal of political friends to call upon. He did not even possess an indexed book of their home telephone numbers. Denis Healey had always walked alone. His mother has recounted how as a boy, out walking with his family on the moors above Leeds, he would walk ten paces or so ahead of everyone else. Now he was the despair of his campaign managers. Many of the MPs whose votes he now sought were numbered among the fools he had failed to suffer gladly down the years.

In the first Wilson government he had been Secretary of State for

Defence throughout and presided, though reluctantly, over Britain's withdrawal from east of Suez. That was when he had learnt to think about the unthinkable and he had played a part in equipping NATO with a new strategic doctrine, that of Flexible Response. In the second Wilson administration and in Callaghan's he had been Chancellor of the Exchequer throughout and, as we have already said, equipped the Treasury with its new strategic doctrine: monetarism – a doctrine some would say of inflexible response. In truth his mix of monetarist and fiscal policy struck a good balance between curbing inflation and not curbing production but his own party would not soon forgive him for having compromised with what, in economic terms, was to them the equivalent of Satanism. In terms of experience, knowledge and intellect he towered high above his rivals. He was a big man in every sense. He was the only man equipped to become Labour's next Prime Minister. But his party no longer required these qualifications in a leader.

Healey was effectively one of the founding fathers of the SDP. Had he become leader of the Labour Party there would have been no breakaway, or at least not until he had been given a chance to restore the position of the parliamentary party, reverse the policy decisions on nuclear weapons and the Common Market, and abandon the Bennite economic strategy. Had Healey stood and fought when he could, Callaghan and Foot might never have sold the pass at Bishop's Stortford and then, too, the political map might have been different. But what happened happened. In their Open Letter to the *Guardian* on 1 August 1980 the Gang of Three in effect set out the terms on which they could remain in the Labour Party. These could be interpreted as, first, the leader of the party must continue to be elected by the parliamentary party or, failing that, on a one-person, one-vote basis; second, Britain must not disarm unilaterally and must remain a member of the European Economic Community; and third, the next leader of the party must uphold these positions. 'We are not prepared', they said, 'to abandon Britain to divisive and often cruel policies, because the electors do not have an opportunity to vote for an acceptable socialist alternative to a Conservative government.'

Their experiences at the Blackpool conference made up their minds for them. By the end of that horrendous week in which the Labour Party appeared to have succumbed to what Shirley Williams had called 'the Fascism of the Left', they were prepared to go. Only if Healey won might they have been deterred. Essentially what had happened was that the broad church of the Labour Party, into which the broad Left had moved, would no longer serve as a sanctuary for moderates. The social democratic project had ceased to be realistic within the Labour Party. As one of the Gang of Three saw the prospect: 'An endless succession of Kinnocks and Hattersleys and never again a Gaitskell.'

It happened that during the conference I dined with the three of them together in a small Italian restaurant. Neil Kinnock and some friends were at another table and there were shouts of 'Claret, claret' as we came in. I was asked my advice on what they should do next. I said that for some while I had seen no prospect of the Labour Party becoming an effective social democratic force but that I was a journalist, with nothing to lose or gain, while they were politicians in the prime of their promising careers and it was no use their supposing they would be back in their Rover cars with their red despatch boxes at the next election. The last realignment in British politics had taken from 1918 to 1945 and what they were envisaging would take at the very least ten years to come about. I added that there must have been a good few rising politicians in the last Asquith administration whose names were now lost to us. I was told that I was unduly pessimistic.

Between Blackpool and Wembley there were doubts and hesitations, second and third thoughts, backsliding and slipped disks, but on the day after the Wembley fiasco the Gang of Four, as they had become with Roy Jenkins's arrival at Dover, issued the Limehouse Declaration which said, *inter alia*:

> We do not believe in the politics of an inert centre merely representing the lowest common denominator between two extremes. We want more, not less radical, change in our society, but with a greater stability of direction.

The three who were leaving the Labour Party, tearing up the roots of a lifetime, were not interested in 'a strengthening of the radical centre' as proposed by Roy Jenkins, already deracinated, in his Dimbleby Lecture. Their project was to replace, and eventually to bury, the Labour Party. We must make allowances for emotional attachments, for the rationalisation of life-long convictions, for the horrors of apostasy. When men and women make dramatic departure they do so usually in the name of consistency, believing that it is not they but the world around them which has changed. Those who broke with the Labour Party in the charged atmosphere of early 1981 did so in the name of such consistency of purpose. It was their values which would march on. Shirley Williams, for example, wanted an 'absolute commitment to equality and classlessness'. It was not democratic socialism they were abandoning but the Labour Party which had abandoned democracy. Owen, who from being the most opposed to a break had become the driving force behind it, had had no doubt that if a new party was to be created it was to be a *social democratic* party. Even at that time he was cool towards the Liberals. He saw no role at all for David Steel in what was being projected; eventually there would have to be some kind of electoral arrangement but the first task and absolute priority was to get the SDP off the ground.[15] (Shirley Williams's attitude at that time was 'to hell with the Liberals'.) Like her, Owen continued to speak the language of socialism. The first chapter of the book he published to coincide with the official launch of the SDP was headed, 'The Values of Socialism'. For Owen at that time the terms socialism and social democracy were inter-changeable:

> For all socialists, whether they use the label social democrat, democratic socialist, or whatever position they may occupy in the political spectrum of socialism, there is common ground in one particular set of beliefs, the need to redress poverty and to reduce inequality.[16]

There were many such statements at the time. In part they reflected old habits of mind, in part perhaps an emotional need to reaffirm old commitments, but they leave no doubt that the SDP was originally conceived – although not by Jenkins – to stand within the socialist tradition. Furthermore, although an alliance with the Liberals might be a necessary electoral convenience, there was no thought of any marriage of minds. The Liberals were amateurs, the SDP was a party being launched by professional politicians; the Liberals were all things to all voters, the SDP was emphatically to be a party of the Left.

But what did these refugees from the Labour Party mean by social democracy? Essentially they still meant what Gaitskell and Crosland had meant: equality and the redistribution of wealth created by economic growth. But equality had its price in liberty and the joining together of the words socialism and democracy had always begged one of the fundamental questions of political philosophy. For a while Crosland, with the powerful assistance of Keynes, appeared to have solved it: socialism could be, as Gaitskell had said, 'about equality' provided there was growth. But socialism had never really been about wealth creation. It had been about wealth distribution. Of course, the

old revisionist approach could be made to seem eminently reasonable
when set beside the Bennite socialism adopted by the Labour Party.
By 1981 to call for the reinstatement of Keynes and Crosland was to
beg some large questions. As Ralf Dahrendorf joked, they seemed to
be 'promising a better yesterday'. We have seen how the recessions
of the 1970s, Britain's accelerating decline, trade union militancy and
the increasingly onerous burden of public expenditure had conspired
to undermine the post-war order. Keynes and Crosland had both in
their ways endeavoured to increase the role of the State without the
need for the coercive statism required by socialism. Keynes had
attempted to cure the disease of unemployment 'whilst preserving
efficiency and freedom' and by this means he had hoped to side-step
the class war, changing behaviour without having to change the
political and social system. Crosland had, in effect, declared the class
war over and hoped that in future economic growth would enable the
redistribution of income without the need for State ownership. As
Keynes's biographer puts it:

> Keynesian management became generally acceptable because it
> was manipulative, not coercive. If Keynesianism moves to coer-
> cion it loses its basic political function, its ability to provide
> consensus; or, more precisely, to obviate the need for consensus.[17]

The same could be said of Croslandism.

However, conversely, in each case, successful performance depended on the efficacy of the technique – deficit financing to correct
recession and prevent high unemployment, economic growth to
enable equality without tears. Neither appeared any longer to do the
trick. Keynes and Crosland had armed social democrats with a
political theory but not with an economic strategy. The social democrats had no new recipes of their own for curing unemployment or for
creating the wealth with which to gratify their passion for equality.
What is more their attitude towards the State, which was instinctively
Fabian, required rethinking. David Marquand, an academic politician turned politico-academic, was the one who saw most clearly the
necessity for revising revisionism. He now believed that:

> the policies through which post-war Social Democracy has sought
> to realise its fourfold commitment to personal freedom, social
> justice, resource redistribution and economic growth have rested,
> in practice, on a number of over-optimistic assumptions about the
> nature of the State, about the possibility of changing society by

acting through the State, and about the risks involved in trying to act through the State.[18]

If the State was no longer able to serve as the agent for Croslandite redistribution, or even to perform its Keynesian managerial functions, then not only was socialism dead but so was social democracy, or at least social democracy in its British revisionist form. The mould had been broken more thoroughly than the mould-breakers realised. Keynes and Crosland were among the pieces.

The post-war success of continental social democracy was owed in large part to the pursuit of liberal-market economic policies. In Germany it was called social market policy and under Adenauer and Erhard it had been the elixir of the German 'economic miracle'; it was this approach to which the SPD became reconciled at Bad Godesberg, jettisoning much of socialism in the process. It is true that the Bad Godesberg declaration speaks of socialist values, asserts a role for planning within the social market regime and reserves a residual, last-resort role for public ownership. But, to all intents and purposes, it turned the SPD into a non-socialist progressive party. Moreover, ideological intent was effectively subordinated to electoral necessity and the SPD came to power, first, through a Grand Coalition with its right-wing opponents and, subsequently, in alliance with the liberal Free Democrats. Planning and public ownership were soon forgotten. In 1979, as new radical pressures were building up within the SPD, Willy Brandt was to deny that Bad Godesberg had implied a renunciation of socialism[19] but for twenty years that was how it had seemed: social democracy in Germany had successfully combined broadly liberal economics with social reform. Free of the Labour Party, the British social democrats were now to move in this same direction. Some more rapidly than others, they shed their socialist impedimenta. The notion that the SDP could or should become a Labour Party Mark II receded, not least because of the failure of the new party to gain much of a foothold in the Labour strongholds. The logic of its position, ideologically and electorally, pushed the new party towards becoming an explicitly non-socialist party of the Left-centre. The word socialism was dropped from the SDP vocabulary, as Roy Jenkins some while since had dropped it from his. When the second edition of Owen's *Face The Future* appeared, the chapter head 'The Values of Socialism' had become 'The Values of Social Democracy'.[20] After the 1983 election Owen was to embrace explicitly the 'social market' economy and was accused of embracing

Margaret Thatcher at the same time. In truth there was little difference between her approach to wealth creation and that of the continental social democrats and, in a speech at Chicago, the Mecca of monetarism, she had held up Helmut Schmidt as a paragon of economic virtue. We were, it seemed, all social marketeers now – all, that is, except the Labour Party.

8

The Thatcher Factor

In the autumn of 1981 Margaret Thatcher's fortunes reached their lowest ebb. The newly formed SDP–Liberal Alliance was riding on the crest of its wave. Labour, in the aftermath of the Benn–Healey struggle, was floundering in the polls. The MORI poll, averaged over the last quarter of the year which had seen the great schism in the Labour Party and the launching of the SDP, put the Alliance at 38 per cent, Labour barely in second place at 28 per cent, with the Conservatives, as unemployment rose inexorably towards three million, one point behind. Following Shirley Williams's sensational victory in the Crosby by-election,[1] the Gallup poll for December reported the Alliance set to win a General Election, 'if held tomorrow', in a landslide with 50 per cent of the vote against 23 per cent each for Labour and Conservative.

In moments of euphoria Alliance politicians began constructing their first Cabinet. A leading psephologist said on television that he would be 'very surprised' if the Alliance did not take at least 30 per cent of the vote at the next General Election. With 60–80 seats in Parliament – which was pretty much what the Alliance's own strategists had in mind – a significant breakthrough would have been achieved. At Buckingham Palace and in the Cabinet Office contingency studies were conducted into the constitutional and political implications of a Parliament in which no party had a clear majority. Coalition became the gossip of the day.

With the Warrington by-election in the previous July Labour Party's strategists had begun to wake up to the threat posed by the SDP. In public at least, they had purported to pooh-pooh it as a serious electoral force; 'fluff' was what Callaghan had called it. At Warrington, the 60th safest Labour seat in the country, Roy Jenkins came close to winning with 42·4 per cent of the vote. The Labour candidate, a supporter of Tony Benn, scraped in with his majority humiliatingly reduced from over 10,000 to 1,759 – 14 per cent down on 1979. Had Shirley Williams put up the seat could have gone. As it was Jenkins could describe the result as 'my first defeat in thirty years in politics, and it is by far the greatest victory that I have ever participated in.' It was an exciting moment. The Alliance went on to scoop up the Tory marginal Croydon and then the ultra-safe Crosby. Local election returns meanwhile supported the impression that the Alliance phenomenon differed from previous Liberal revivals in that it was winning over large numbers of Labour voters.

They had, at that time, ample cause to desert. Benn, having so nearly captured the deputy leadership, had spurned an olive branch proffered by Foot and was continuing on his defiant wrecking course. His defeat in the Shadow Cabinet elections was among a series of setbacks for the Left which, it was becoming clear, had achieved the pinnacle of its fortunes at the Wembley conference. From now on its advance was impaired by the deepening split between the 'hard', or Bennite, and the 'soft', or Footite, Left. But for the public, and the voters, this was not the impression: Benn was still in the news and Foot was manifestly feeble; moreover, the spectacle of disunity did little to inspire confidence in Labour as an alternative government. Foot was further embarrassed by the selection of Pat Wall, a leading supporter of the Militant Tendency, for the constituency of Bradford North, and doubly so when Wall preached the overthrow of the State at a rally organised by the revolutionary Socialist Workers' Party. His embarrassment was compounded when Peter Tatchell was selected for the ultra-safe Labour seat of Bermondsey. Tatchell was on record with the opinion that:

> Debates and parliamentary divisions are fruitless cosmetic exercises, given the Tories' present Commons majority. And if we recognise this we are either forced to accept Tory edicts as a *fait accompli*, or we must look to new, more militant forms of extra-parliamentary opposition which involve mass popular participation and challenge the Government's right to rule.

January 1982 was the point of no return for the first Thatcher government. Her reshuffle of the previous September had made her the mistress of her Cabinet to an extent that her colleagues, and the governmental machine, were slow to grasp. But now she was in the position to decree that there was to be no going back. She hoped to be able to say, 'I held firm and things are getting better,' but, as a senior official put it at the time, 'they all know things can't get very much better.' For the question now facing the government was: could it hope to win an election with more than three million unemployed?

The official projections accompanying the 1981 Budget had shown production falling by a further 1 per cent (2 per cent below 1980 levels) and unemployment rising inexorably to above three million and, most alarming of all, remaining there for the duration of the Parliament. The history of the first Thatcher administration could in large part be written around the 1981 Budget. Confronted by the wage explosion of 1979–80 it was an article of monetarist faith that this would not, and could not, cause inflation unless it was accommodated by a government ready to print money. The monetary posture which the government had taken necessitated high interest rates which helped to force up the exchange rate, as did the oil wealth of the North Sea. The high exchange rate weakened industry, especially manufacturing industry, and industrial decline forced unemployment up. In 1981 it had to be admitted that this devastating exchange rate was neither God-given nor decreed by the market but was the consequence of a too-tight monetarist policy. In order to bring down interest rates, and thereby devalue the pound, the 1981 Budget combined a relaxation of monetary policy with a fierce fiscal squeeze. As the Cabinet had refused to impose the expenditure cuts demanded by the Treasury the previous autumn, the Public Sector Borrowing Requirement (PSBR) would be reduced by other means – by a sharp increase in taxation; meanwhile, interest rates would be cut, causing the pound to depreciate and – it was hoped – output to revive. However, the immediate effect of the Budget was to pile deflation upon deflation. Keynes was now stood on his head. The Prime Minister's economic adviser, Alan Walters, arch-monetarist and a chief author of the new strategy, takes much pride in the fact that: 'In spite of rapidly increasing unemployment and output the government introduced the toughest peacetime budget in memory.'[2]

When the monetary squeeze was relaxed, and a narrower target substituted for the broader M3, some saw this as a U-turn by the monetarists but for Walters the 1981 Budget marked the serious implementation of the Medium Term Financial Strategy to which he attributes chiefly what he calls 'Britain's Economic Renaissance'. By another way of looking at it, the monetarists in 1981 resorted to good – or, rather, bad – old-fashioned, 1920s' style deflation. In a letter to *The Times*, 364 economists, previous economic advisers to previous governments among them, warned that: 'Present policies will deepen the depression, erode the industrial base of our economy and threaten its social and political stability.' Already manufacturing output was down by more than 15 per cent. Activity in the 'metal-bashing' industries of the West Midlands, once the workshop of Britain, was down by more than a quarter. The CBI had proclaimed a slump and its president, Sir Terence Becket, rashly promised the Prime Minister 'a bare-knuckle fight'. At the July meeting of the Cabinet when the Prime Minister and the Chancellor stood alone, demanding yet more cuts, there were accusations of monetary madness and political suicide.

According to the Keynesians, whose beliefs were neatly set out in their round robin to *The Times*, there was:

> no basis in economic theory or supporting evidence that by deflating demand they will bring inflation permanently under control and thereby induce an automatic recovery in output and employment.

But the economy did begin to grow again and to grow while inflation continued to fall, although unemployment continued to rise. Was the recovery of output due to the policy adopted in 1981, as Walters is pleased to believe, or due simply to the revival of world trade? The question is fiercely disputed between rival schools of economists and, in any case, is incapable of final resolution until we see whether Britain's severely reduced manufacturing base proves sufficient for the day when the North Sea oil runs dry.

Whatever its economic consequences, the 1981 Budget was for Mrs Thatcher the triumph of her will. She had defied the conventional wisdom. There were riots in the cities that summer to add further to the alarm of those who believed that she was pressing beyond the limits of social and political tolerance. That autumn, as we have seen, she broke all records of unpopularity. Odds were being laid against her survival in office. Yet by the end of the year the polls were recording a recovery in the government's fortunes and, eighteen months later, she was to sweep back into office in defiance of the three million unemployed. The war to recover the Falklands had intervened and the 'Falklands Factor' contributed to the remarkable victory of 1983. So did the 1981 schism on the Left and the 'Foot Factor'. Yet these are insufficient explanations for the 1983 triumph and obscure its meaning. For in the meanwhile something more extraordinary had happened: the country had lowered its expectations and consented once more to be governed.

The success of the government in this respect is not to be measured by the achievement, or non-achievement, of arcane money targets. It is more likely that inflation was brought down in spite of monetarism than because of it, chiefly by general deflation and falling commodity prices. But monetarism, perhaps, was important as a cover for what had to be done. The mumbo-jumbo of M3, M1, M0, and NIBM1[3] gave a scientific air to a policy which was wanting in simple humanity towards its victims, enabling ministers to attribute what were, in reality, political decisions to the sovereignty of the market. Or, as a senior Bank of England official put it:

> [overt deflation] would have meant disclosing objectives for, *inter alia*, output and employment. This would have been a very hazardous exercise and the objectives would have either been unacceptable to public opinion or else inadequate to secure a substantial decrease in the rate of inflation, or both.[4]

Moreover, setting targets and sticking to them had the smack of Thatcherism about it. It was like living within the housekeeping money. The Chicago school and the Grantham school had much in common. Indeed, for the public, monetarism, whatever it was, became synonymous with Thatcherism. Moreover, it symbolised a break with the past. By 1983 many were ready to blame unemployment on the international situation, not on the government of the day. Moreover, they were ready to blame it on the prodigalities of the past, on prolix over-manning, on trade union militancy and bloody-mindedness. Their daily experience told people that a great deal of what Margaret Thatcher was saying was true. Blaming unemployment on external factors, or on forces beyond the government's control, was a stage in the process of blaming unemployment on nobody. The appeal of market economics lies in precisely this: it is a means of avoiding social responsibility. There is no economic logic, no logic of any kind, in saying that because Keynesianism no longer achieves its purpose, the 'laws of the market', whose deficiencies Keynes had addressed, have miraculously been restored. 'Thatcherism' was a way of filling an intellectual and a moral vacuum.

However, a high price had been paid for the conquest of inflation. Calculations have been made which attribute up to half of the rise in unemployment after 1979 to the deflationary policies of the government, although we may suppose that if the recession bit deeper in Britain than elsewhere it was also because the economy had been progressively enfeebled by decline. By 1983 there was not much to show for the pain endured. There was little evidence that the lower rate of inflation would of itself result in the faster growth which might arrest and reverse Britain's relative decline. Taxation, which the government had promised to cut, had increased. True, the basic rate had come down from 33 to 30 per cent but all but the rich were paying more of their incomes to the State: nearly 40 per cent of the national wealth was being collected in taxes compared with under 34 per cent when Margaret Thatcher came to power. The increased tax burden was one measure of the government's failure to cut public expenditure overall, another of its central pledges. Partly this was due to the high cost of the recession in terms of unemployment benefit and partly to planned increased spending in the fields of defence and law and order. Other social spending, indeed, had been cut in real terms, chiefly in education and housing. The result was a litany of protest about 'the cuts' without commensurate benefit in rolling back the frontiers of the State.[5]

At best roll-back had given way to containment. In the autumn of 1982 the government ran up against the political limits of Thatcherism. Projections made by the Treasury showed that the performance of the economy would be unlikely to prove adequate for sustaining the Welfare State in the face of demographic pressures upon it. The 'Think Tank' then confronted Ministers with the kind of measures which would be required to bring spending into line with performance. They included decoupling social benefits from inflation, private health insurance in place of the National Health Service, an end to State funding for higher education. A great furore resulted when these measures were leaked to *The Economist*. The Welfare State was an aspect of the old order which voters had shown no sign of rejecting in 1979. It continued to be supported across the classes. Moreover, the Prime Minister had made a specific pledge to maintain the real value of social security benefits and NHS spending. At the Conservative Party conference later that autumn Mrs Thatcher felt obliged to declare, 'The National Health Service is safe with us.' The price, it was turning out, of getting the government off the backs of the people in the field of welfare was to set the people at the throats of the government.

The frontiers of the State had not been pushed back far in other directions either. For the Thatcherite 'enterprise society' to be brought about in Britain required, paradoxically, a State strong enough to roll itself back and open the space for free markets. But apart from the sale of council houses there had been little in the way of privatisation by 1983. That arch-non-interventionist, Sir Keith Joseph, in his capacity as Secretary for Trade and Industry, had become the agent of massive cash injections into loss-making nationalised industries, British Leyland and the British Steel Corporation. The Prime Minister herself had become an enthusiast for the encouragement by the State of new technology, although this willingness was combined incoherently with an aversion to the public sector and a refusal to develop an industrial policy to shape the restructuring of basic manufacturing industries such as chemicals and engineering.

The most important change achieved on the supply side was the curbing of trade union power. The government had pledged to redress the balance of industrial power between union and employer and this it had done. The Trades Union Act of 1980, piloted through by James Prior, had outlawed secondary picketing and removed immunity for most secondary actions (sympathy strikes, blacking). Norman Tebbit's Act of 1982 exposed union funds to claims for damages resulting from unlawful acts and removed immunity from political strikes. Both Acts had placed restrictions on closed shops. As important as these laws themselves, however, seems to have been the government's demonstration that the trade unions were no longer running the country. Trade union leaders, to their great chagrin, were no longer to be seen coming in and out of Number 10. Kept at arms-distance by the government, they came to be in less demand by television producers. The days when Jack Jones's opinion was sought on almost everything were gone; there was little interest in David Basnett's opinion on anything. This was one reason why trade union leaders came to invest so heavily in the return of a Labour government and became increasingly embroiled in the internal power struggles of the Movement. On one of the rare occasions on which the Prime Minister condescended to receive a delegation from the General Council, the TUC general-secretary, Len Murray, emerged to complain, 'we're in two different worlds'.

It was true. The union ethos no longer pervaded the country. The curve of militancy was now sharply downwards. As the Left advanced within the Labour Party it was in retreat across the land. Partly, of course, this was due to the recession and rising unemployment but there does seem also to have been some kind of change in attitudes, a sense of release perhaps from the prisons of the past. Erstwhile militants, the British Leyland car workers for example, were refusing their shop stewards' calls to strike. The TUC's Day of Action against the trade union laws was a flop, a day of inaction. By 1983 the number of days lost in industrial disputes was the lowest since the war. The great confrontation which many had predicted never came about, although Thatcher in 1981 – haunted as always by what had happened to Heath in 1974 – beat a tactical retreat in face of a threat from the miners. That battle was to await another day.

The country she governed was a more divided place: the rich had got richer but the poor had got poorer and the gap had grown wider between north and south, city and suburb, town and country. But what was remarkable was how she was able to win re-election in 1983 in the absence of a general improvement in the condition of the people. Real living standards had begun to improve again in 1983, with the rate of inflation down to below 5 per cent, but the expectation of a significant annual increment to real wealth which had prevailed since the 1950s had been scarcely gratified since 1979. Real disposable income in 1983 was about the same as it had been when Mrs Thatcher came to power in May 1979. Production was still more than 3 per cent down, manufacturing production by more than 15 per cent. Unemployment, at well over three millions, had almost tripled since the government had come to power.

This was not the sort of record on which governments could expect to be returned to office. Moreover, the Thatcher government could not claim with much plausibility that discipline and self-sacrifice had arrested or reversed the relative decline of the British economy. Britain's share of world trade had continued to diminish and 1983 was the first year since the Industrial Revolution in which the one-time workshop of the world had run a deficit on trade in manufactured goods. It is true that since 1981 the rate of growth was above the average of the industrialised world, but that was most likely due to Britain's being first into and first out of the recession. More hopeful was the trend in productivity, which had increased at a faster rate than in competitor countries, and at a considerably faster rate than the underlying post-war trend; but it was not clear whether this represented some real and lasting change or was merely the temporary concomitant of lower output, of drastic labour-shedding and the closure of inefficient plant. There was little sign of improvement in that other symptom of the British disease, which was the propensity of wages to run ahead of prices and at the expense of unit costs. In spite of some devaluation of the pound since 1981 the British economy was substantially less competitive than it had been in 1979.

How then was it that the government could be re-elected in 1983? Certainly no one could any longer say with plausibility that the country was ungovernable. The power of the unions had been curbed. It was no longer true to say as Norman St John Stevas had done in 1976: 'No Government in Britain can hope to succeed today without the goodwill of the unions.'

The country had suffered a tripling of unemployment and a more than decimation of its manufacturing industry, but the authority of the government was under no serious challenge. For left-wing writers, such as Hobsbawm and Hall, Britain was experiencing a crisis of capitalism, no less, something comparable to the 1930s; and yet the militancy of the 1970s seemed largely spent and there was no sign to be seen that the forward march of labour would be resumed.

What had been a crisis for government in the 1970s had become a crisis for those in opposition. The schism of 1981 in the Labour ranks had meant that in so far as there could be said to exist an anti-Thatcher majority in the land its forces were divided between the Labour Party and the SDP–Liberal Alliance. The Alliance might be incapable of forming a government in the foreseeable future but its flash in the pan in 1981 had been bright enough to signal to the electorate that Labour's days of power were over. Labour, meanwhile, seemed determined to disqualify itself from office. Michael Foot, whose approval-rating was to slump to rock bottom, had been put where he was, into a position for which he was wholly unfitted, by the people who had known him best. They had put him there for sentimental reasons mitigated only by inner party expediency, and he personified in every way both Labour's unfitness to govern and the extent to which it had lost touch even with its natural constituency. For its part the Alliance, after the heady moments of its birth, had confirmed many of the forebodings about the fate of centre parties. It suffered special disabilities in that it consisted not of one but of two pigs in the middle. Due to the defections from the Labour Party the SDP was, pending the election, the larger party in the Commons while the Liberals were the stronger on the ground, with a base in local government. The SDP was the senior member of the partnership in the special sense that its leaders had sat in Cabinets while no Liberal politician alive had ever done so; but the Liberal Party was the senior historically and in being the more experienced in campaigns and in the specialised, and sometimes dubious, arts of third-party politicking. The device of anointing Roy Jenkins as 'Prime Minister designate' and David Steel as 'campaign leader' neither capitalised on this division of labour nor resolved the bemusement of the public's mind. It served to blur further the already blurred image which is the occupational hazard of centre parties.

The old adage about oppositions not winning elections but governments losing them was stood on its head: in 1983, or so it seemed, the opposition lost. But in what sense did the government win? In an interview with the *Sunday Times* in 1981 Margaret Thatcher had said:

> What's irritated me about the whole direction of politics in the last thirty years is that it's always been towards the collectivist society. People have forgotten about the personal society. And they say: do I count, do I matter? To which the short answer is, Yes. And therefore, it isn't that I set out on economic policies; it's that I set out really to change the approach, and changing the economics is the means of changing that approach. If you change the approach you really are after the heart and soul of the nation. Economics are the method; the object is to change the heart and soul.[6]

This statement contains the essence of what we might call 'religious Thatcherism'; her project was the conversion of the British no less. To what extent she had begun, by 1983, to bring about a cultural change, or ideological counter-revolution, it is hard to say. The statistics of economic performance did not suggest that the 'enterprise society', which was her equivalent of the American dream, was struggling to be born. Perhaps, in a limited sense and for the time being only, she had won the argument about the economy, won it negatively in that the electorate was largely persuaded that there was, truly, 'no alternative'. Of course, the alternative consisted in rejecting false alternatives and lay somewhere between the extremes of Thatcherite deflation and Labour's exorbitantly inflationary spending plans. Nevertheless, the public was correct in its conclusion that a return to the ways of the past offered no alternative if Britain's problems were ever to be solved. A return to full employment, as promised by Labour – within the lifetime of a Parliament! – was no longer seen to be a feasible goal.

Essentially, however, the Conservative victory of 1983 marked the political triumph of Thatcherism, not its economic or ideological triumph. The earthquake which had cracked the surface and sent tremors through the system in 1979 now transformed the political landscape of Britain.

What of the Falklands Factor? One may doubt its salience in any literal sense by the time voters came to enter the polling booths, one year after Port Stanley was retaken from the Argentinians. At least that is what they would have had the pollsters believe. The Falkland Islands were of no concern to the electorate before the war and it would not be surprising if they became of little concern once more

he downplays
VIPce of
Falklands

soon after it was over. Indeed, an important cause of the war was that a small but single-minded pro-Falklands lobby had been able to take advantage of governmental timidity and huge public indifference to prevent some negotiated arrangement with Argentina which would guarantee the status of the islanders while ending a territorial dispute which had been going on for longer than anyone could remember. It had been the policy goal of successive governments to liquidate a post-imperial commitment which Britain, at a distance of 8,000 miles, no longer had the means of honouring except by expensive distortion of her other defence requirements.

For some months before the Falkland Islands were thrust upon the national consciousness the government had been regaining popularity, chiefly at the expense of the SDP–Liberal Alliance, whose bubble had reached bursting point at the time of the Crosby by-election in December 1981. In that month the standing of the parties (according to Gallup) was: Conservatives 23; Labour 23; Alliance 50. By March the parties were running virtually neck and neck. The figures were 31: 33: 33.[7] Nevertheless, the war did transform the political scene. In July, with the war won, the government had a 19 point lead: Cons. 46: Lab. 27: All. 24. On the eve of the 1983 General Election the figures were 49: 31: 16. The actual result was 43·5: 28·3: 26. The mould was thus set by the Falklands War but that does not mean that it might not have been set in the same way for other reasons. That we can never know.

The Argentinian invasion of those remote and unimportant islands threw the nation into a patriotic fit. Parliament set the lead. When news of the invasion was first rumoured this commentator failed totally to grasp the significance of the matter. The Falkland Islands were a post-imperial leftover of no strategic or economic value and far removed from the real problems facing the country, at home and abroad. I left London that Friday for the country and the next day, annoyed at the disturbance of my Saturday, listened to the emergency debate in the Commons on the radio. Had I been in my place in the Press Gallery perhaps I, too, might have been carried away by the excitement of the moment but as it was, listening at my kitchen table, I could scarcely believe my ears. That the Commons was sitting for the first time on a Saturday since the Suez crisis of 1956 was an invitation to exaggerate the importance of the occasion. One speaker went further and solemnly compared the invasion of the Falklands with the fiasco of the Norwegian campaign in 1940, one of the darkest moments of the war which led to the fall of the Chamberlain government. The most jingoistic speech of the morning came from

Michael Foot, who having proclaimed Britain's role as 'defender of people's freedom throughout the world' and asserted the 'absolute right' of the Falklanders to British protection, called upon the government to 'prove by deeds – they will never be able to do it by words – that they are not responsible for the betrayal and cannot be faced with that charge.'

It seemed to me then, and it seems to me now, extraordinary that it should be supposed that Britain could be responsible for 1,800 people and their 600,000 sheep in the remoteness of the South Atlantic. That we should hold ourselves responsible was honourable, noble in the extreme, but foolhardy. It had been irresponsible to continue with such a commitment without the capability of discharging it. The defence of the Falklands had for some time rested on bluff. Now that that bluff had been called the proper course was to seek to discharge our responsibility to the islanders as best we could through negotiations to guarantee their status as British citizens or to repatriate and compensate them as need be. It was preposterous, it seemed to me, to assert their absolute right to self-determination. Rights could not exist without the means of upholding them and it was quite unrealistic to expect Britannia to rule the South Atlantic in the year 1982.

Karl Marx had said that history repeated itself as farce but then had gone on to say that when it repeated itself for a second time it did so as tragedy. In 1956 the folk-guilt of the ruling class had led an out-of-touch generation to mistake the nationalisation of the Suez Canal by Gamal Abdul Nasser for another Munich. Suez had been a post-imperial farce, a tilting at windmills; but now, it seemed, young lives were to be sacrificed tragically in the Quixotic cause of making a world safe for South Atlantic sheep-shearers. For it was questionable to claim – as Mrs Thatcher did throughout the affair – that liberty was indivisible to the extent that if aggression were allowed to succeed in this case licence would be given to aggressors everywhere, in Afghanistan and Cambodia or wherever. We were deluding ourselves if we supposed that the rest of the world, even our American allies and Common Market partners, would regard a dispute over an insignificant outpost of a lost Empire as an event on the same footing as the Nazi invasion of Poland. Thus:

> At the State Department, in the early hours of the crisis, most of the staff shared the amusement of the press and public over what was perceived as a Gilbert and Sullivan battle over a sheep pasture between a choleric old John Bull and a comic dictator in a gaudy uniform.[8]

In his memoirs General Haig, then the Secretary of State, disassociated himself from this mockingly contemptuous view of the matter but when shown maps he was alleged to have said at the time: 'Gee, it's only a pimple on their arse.'

Indeed, there seemed to me, and here I consulted theologians, something disproportionate about the British response to the Argentinian invasion, reprehensible though it was. St Thomas Aquinas had laid down three conditions for a 'just war' – it must be authorised by the sovereign, the cause must be just, and the belligerents of valid moral intention. Recent Catholic moralists have stressed a fourth condition, most relevant to modern times: a war, to be just, must be waged by proper means (*debito modo*). Could this be said of the despatch of a large naval Task Force (which on its way would sink a cruiser and drown 308 young men) to avenge an act which, if the truth were admitted, was more costly of national pride than of true national interest? The Falklands, as we know, were recaptured in glorious fashion and the Union Flag flies once more over Government House, Port Stanley. The death toll all round was about a thousand, plus some 1,700 wounded – for 1,800 islanders and 600,000 sheep. *Debito modo*?

There were two flaws to this analysis, more apparent in hindsight than at the time perhaps. The first was that it pointed to no clear alternative course of action. It would have been disproportionate equally to have done nothing. The Junta in Buenos Aires were a nasty lot ('a gang of thugs' Haig told the Cabinet) and their aggression could in no way be condoned; even the Security Council of the United Nations had condemned it. Resolution 502 required Argentina to withdraw but, if she did not, Britain had the right under Article 51 of the Charter to repossess her territory by the use of reasonable force. Diplomacy backed up by the threat of force, it seemed to me, was the appropriate and proportionate strategy.

The Prime Minister's intention from the beginning was to get the islands back and undo the humiliation which had been done. The Foreign Office was in such disrepute as a result of the invasion that it was, literally, *hors de combat*; a peace strategy never really received a hearing. Nevertheless, the Cabinet was from the outset united on the total war objective. The services had many options but no clear plan. The Americans stepped into the diplomatic action. The 'war cabinet' in London in fact went a long way in co-operating with the Haig mission but it was his reports on the character of the Junta in Buenos Aires, anecdotes of drunkenness and imbecility, which convinced the doubting members of the inner group that the 'Argies' would be neither willing to make peace nor capable of it. And, as it turned out, it was the Junta which rejected, first, terms to which Mrs Thatcher had reluctantly agreed, and subsequently – to her huge relief – terms which she would herself have declined to put to Parliament had Galtieri had the wit to accept them. Meanwhile, as the Task Force approached its destination, the options narrowed until the only choice was between all or nothing. Her military strategy achieved its goal; looking back, it is hard to see how a diplomatic approach could have succeeded.

Be that as it may, we are concerned here with the politics of the matter, with the contribution of the 'Falklands Factor' to the realignment in British politics brought about by, or under, Mrs Thatcher. The second flaw in the position of those of us who at the time were critics of the war is that we underestimated, perhaps, the psychological needs of the nation. I do not mean by that a need for crude chauvinistic distraction, for one thing which was striking about those ten weeks was how rare it was to hear of the spirit of high patriotism degenerating into hatred or crude 'Argie' bashing. It might have been otherwise if the horrendous sinking of HMS *Sheffield* had preceded the tragic sinking of the *Belgrano*. Nor do I mean simply that the country was willing to have its attention diverted by an external adventure, the oldest trick in the book, from three million unemployed at home, although diverted it was for a while as the places of public entertainment emptied and all eyes became riveted to the nightly television news bulletins. No, the psychological need was for a success, a success of some kind, an end to failure and humiliation, to do something well, to win. Nostalgic knee-jerk reaction it may have been, vainglorious posturing in a post-imperial world of Super Powers, but it made people feel better not worse.

Moreover, it aroused genuine admiration around the world and, where not that, reluctant respect. There is a slight note of astonishment in Haig's account of how:

> In a reawakening of the spirit of the Blitz that exhilarated Britain, warships were withdrawn from NATO, civilian ships, including the liner *Queen Elizabeth II*, were requisitioned and refitted, troops were embarked, and in an astonishingly short time a task force of over 100 ships and 28,000 men was steaming under the British ensign toward the Falklands.[9]

Perhaps no people were more surprised than the British, accustomed to being told they did not know how to run a motor car factory. By jingo they knew how to launch a Task Force. The point was not lost upon the Prime Minister in her heady hour of victory. On 3 July a great throng assembled on the race course at Cheltenham – where better? – and she said:

> It took the battle in the South Atlantic for the shipyards to adapt ships way ahead of time; for dockyards to refit merchantmen and cruise liners, to fix helicopter platforms, to convert hospital ships – all faster than was thought possible; it took the demands of war for every stop to be pulled out and every man and woman to do their best.

On she went, dishing out the medals to British industry, the British people – the British worker! Of course, Churchill had to be quoted at such a moment – he had said something somewhere about the need to work together in peacetime as in war, a banal enough sentiment, and now – thirty-six years on – the truth of it at last was dawning on the British people, or so she said.

> We saw the signs when, this week, the NUR came to understand that its strike on the railways and on the Underground just didn't fit [we can hear the voice] – didn't match the spirit of these times.

And on she went. Printing money was no more.

> Rightly this Government has abjured it. Increasingly this nation won't have it . . . That too is part of the Falklands Factor.

Not only was the Falklands Factor making the trains run on time, it was – it seems – rallying the nation behind the Medium Term Financial Strategy. And as the climax is approached, the sentences grow shorter:

> What has indeed happened is that now once again Britain is not prepared to be pushed around.

> We have ceased to be a nation in retreat.

> We have instead a new-found confidence – born in the economic battles at home and tested and found true 8,000 miles away.

> That confidence comes from the rediscovery of ourselves, and grows with the recovery of our self-respect.

Britain found herself again in the South Atlantic and will not look
back from the victory she has won.

Such oratory is not to be taken too literally; it is indicative of a state of
mind, not of the state of the nation. War is a celebrated midwife but it
is improbable that the loss and recapture of the Falkland Islands in
1982 will prove to have been the rebirth of Britain, or the apotheosis
of Thatcherism. What it may have done, however, is to help link in
people's minds their images of her with this powerful image of
success. She was a winner. Luck was on her side. What she said she
would do she would do. She was a sticker whose determination paid
off. What had worked so brilliantly abroad, would work at home.
And she was quick to reinforce these thoughts in people's minds: 'I
think people like decisiveness, I think they like strong leadership,'
she told an interviewer. In this way the Falklands Factor became the
Thatcher Factor.[10]

The schism on the Left gave the Conservatives their parliamentary
landslide in 1983. A 42·4 per cent share of the vote, fractionally down
on 1979, yielded them 61 per cent of the seats, a majority overall of
144 compared with 43 in 1979. There are two interpretations of this
result: it can be noted that this share of the vote is smaller than the
share with which Churchill lost in 1950 and Lord Home in 1964; or it
can be remarked how support for the government had held almost
steady in the face of the challenge from the SDP–Liberal Alliance and
in spite of three million unemployed. I prefer the second view; the
first, it seems to me, is an observation about changes in the party
system and not about the relative showing of the parties. Another
way of looking at the 1983 result is to say that with more than three
million unemployed Labour should have won and that it lost only
because of its defence policy and its spectacular disunity, or that the
Tories won only because of the Falklands Factor. Alternatively, it can
be said that the continuance of the social and political trends which
had contributed to Labour's loss in 1979 virtually doomed it to lose
again in 1983 and, probably, thereafter. Of these I strongly prefer the
second view.

That is not to suggest that Labour's defeat was inevitable, although
there is no doubt that most of the changes taking place in society were
making it more difficult for it to win. Between 1979 and 1983 the
working class, itself further diminished in size, swung 3 per cent to the
Conservatives – in spite of 'Thatcherism', in spite of the unemployed, the welfare spending cuts, the union laws – or, perhaps, not

in spite of but because of some of these things. Only 38 per cent of manual workers and 39 per cent of trade unionists voted Labour while 32 per cent of trade unionists voted Conservative. The Tories led Labour by 12 per cent among the skilled working class, but trailed 15 per cent among the unskilled. In 1983, still more than in 1979, Labour became not 'the party of the working class' but rather the party of the underclass.

In part this was due to continuing demographic change. The trend of a quarter of a century or more towards polarisation between north and south, city and suburb, town and country, had continued. Outside London, Labour in 1983 held only three of 186 southern seats while the Tories had only five remaining strongholds in the Metropolitan County conurbations in the north.[11] Not only was Labour becoming the party of the underclass but in 1983 it became, more than ever before, the party of declining Britain, geographically driven back into the decaying inner cities and the depressed industrial regions of the north.

However, there were new or special factors at work. In 1979 Labour appears, roughly speaking, to have punched its class weight. In 1983 it did a good deal worse than socio-economic or demographic changes can explain. By one calculation Labour's 'natural' constituency is now around 35 per cent of the electorate. In 1983 Labour's share of the vote was only 27·6 per cent, compared with 37 per cent in 1979. In 1983 Labour presented an unelectable face to the electorate, in terms of its leaders, many of its policies and in its general demeanour as a party aspiring to government, and this must explain a good deal of its unnaturally poor showing. Yet at the same time there would appear to have continued, and perhaps accelerated, the ideological shift which had been a part of the reason for Labour's defeat in 1979, indeed for its decline over two-and-a-half decades. The Oxford study of the General Election for 1983 endeavours to make some measure of this shift but its general conclusion is that what damaged Labour more than the specifics of its policies was the unattractiveness of its image as a party. 'It is the fit between the general character of the party and the voter's own general ideology which, we believe, best accounts for electoral choice.'[12]

Just so, Labour and the electorate in 1983 made a poor 'fit'. Labour had moved Left and the electorate Right; or, as I would rather put it, the spectrum of Labour's preoccupations and the electorate's had grown increasingly apart. For the first time since the war, in 1983 more voters identified with the Conservatives than with the Labour

Party, although identification with any party at all had continued to grow weaker.

These were not haphazard developments to be cited in support of an argument that, even in 1983, Margaret Thatcher's victory was some kind of aberration to be explained by special or temporary factors. For the ideological gap between Labour and the voters, including a great many of its own erstwhile supporters, was not an accidental matter but, as I have tried to show, in part an endemic consequence of the structure, composition and character of the Labour Movement. And even if we regard the Party as having been hi-jacked by predominantly middle-class ideologists and activists, the reasons why this could happen, and was allowed to happen, themselves weigh against Labour's claims to have remained a representative party of the masses. That it could put forward Michael Foot as its prospective Prime Minister in the year 1983 says nearly all. But hi-jacking is too facile; the 'Cultural Revolution' which engulfed the Labour Party, as I have tried to show, was a consequence of disillusionment with socialism, of the shortcomings of social democracy, of the rise of a new class and, above all, one of the responses to the painful experience of decline which was reshaping British politics during the 1970s and 1980s.

Neither was the schism of 1981, which ensured Margaret Thatcher her parliamentary landslide in 1983, an accidental occurrence. The split was rooted in the ideological division of the Labour Party which had grown increasingly acute after the ending of the 'long boom' in 1973 and with the intellectual collapse of Croslandite socialism. Moreover, the new self-assertion of the political centre was another expression of the growth of the middle class, and the rise within it of a 'new class' of educated professionals and technicians, or, perhaps we should say, the rise not of a new class but of *a new classlessness*. It was an expression also of that ideological shift which, with the changing composition of the classes, was rendering obsolete many of the old preoccupations of Labour as a working class party with ostensibly a socialist programme. The Alliance is a child of the 'Cultural Revolution' in the Labour Party. It is also an aspect of the politics of decline.

Hence, in so far as these events and trends are seen as among the explanations for Margaret Thatcher's victory in 1983, they reinforce, rather than qualify, the thesis of realignment. A process that had begun some time after 1966, and had manifested itself in 1979, was taken a big step further in 1983. To be sure, the elections of 1979 and 1983 did not give Mrs Thatcher a 'new' or 'natural' majority in the land, or any kind of majority at all. But that is hardly surprising if she too is seen as a feature of a shifting political landscape. As class politics break down, whether due to the decline of class itself or the weakening of class allegiances, so the electorate by definition becomes more volatile, more fickle, more open to argument, more suggestible by the media. Voters come to be increasingly of no fixed ideological abode.

The Conservative victories in 1979 and 1983 were not socially determined, they were brought about partly because Margaret Thatcher was the most successful player of the new game. She seized advantage of Labour's decline by making populist appeal to working class or erstwhile working class voters. It was she who was most attuned to the changing spirit of the times. The Thatcher style of politics – and I have suggested that 'Thatcherism' is more a style than it is an ideology – may not have commanded majority support in the country in 1983 but it was more applauded by Labour voters than by Conservative voters![13]

It was her purpose to bury socialism which she saw as chief perpetrator of the decline which she was pledged to arrest and reverse. Hers was the first Conservative administration since 1945 which saw its task not to postpone or mitigate the advance of collectivism but to reverse it. This she set about by means which were as political as they may have been ideologically inspired. She aimed her attack at the bastions of Labour's power – the trade unions, the council estates, the Socialist local authorities, and the nationalised industries. She curbed the unions at law but, more important, banished them from centre stage until, by 1983, it was no longer held to be axiomatic that the country was ungovernable without their consent. She sold council houses to their tenants, contributing to the increase in owner-occupation from 55 per cent of households in 1979 to 60 per cent. And she won 47 per cent of their votes. Labour won 49 per cent of the votes of council tenants – but these constituted only 29 per cent of the electorate. According to some commentators tenure had some while since replaced class as the prime determinant of voting behaviour and if the Thatcherite Conservative Party can be said to have a core majority it consists, perhaps, of the 40 per cent of the electorate who are non-trade-unionist houseowners. Of them 60 per cent voted for her in 1983.[14]

The assault on municipal socialism was yet to come. It was promised in the Manifesto, a target for the second term. Nor had privatisation yet more than dented the public sector. Shares were sold in British Aerospace, Britoil, and Cable and Wireless. However, support for privatisation among the voters had increased from 22 per cent to 42 per cent in 1983. That was beginning also to show populist potential as a vote-winner.

One view of the 1983 General Election is that the Thatcher government was re-elected in the face of an anti-Thatcher majority. Another view is that she and the Labour Party between them had conspired to create an anti-socialist majority in the land. The SDP–Liberal Alliance was a part of that majority willy-nilly. But its support was spread thinly and evenly across the land. In this regard the new Alliance had not progressed significantly beyond the position of the Liberal Party. The authors of the Oxford study identify the makings of an Alliance 'heartland' in the form of the more educated and liberal wing of the salariat, or what I have more loosely called the 'new class'. Potentially this is an important constituency, for on the Oxford reckoning the salariat as a whole is almost as large as the working class and continuing to grow. It is a constituency that the Labour Party cannot do without if it is to become once more a broad progressive force.

The Alliance's putative socio-ideological base, however, was no match for the huge disadvantages imposed by geography. The concentrations of Conservative and Labour strength in their regional bastions made it more difficult than ever for a third party to win seats. None of the Tory targets in the south was toppled by the Alliance, no gains were registered in the Labour heartland. The Alliance cut across the two political nations, cut across its class divides and demographic boundaries. In Tory Britain the Alliance became the second party in two-thirds of its seats; across the country more than one-third of Labour's 1979 supporters defected to it; but nowhere save in tiny pockets or at the very fringe of the nation did the Alliance possess territory of its own.

Geography saved the Labour Party in 1983. With 28 per cent of the votes it obtained 209 seats. In 1931 Labour won 31 per cent of the votes and only 52 seats. The geographic polarisation of Britain was the product of many factors. Labour Britain, the urban north, was where the working classes were most concentrated; Tory Britain, the south outside London, was where the middle classes lived in greater numbers. The spread of owner-occupation had been greater in Tory Britain; in Labour Britain more families lived in council houses. Where the working classes were congregated together, as in the north or London, they were more likely to vote Labour than where they had become dispersed into more mixed communities, as in the south and the countryside. The manufacturing industries of the north were in decline, the new service industries were growing chiefly in the south.

Tory Britain had more of everything – more people, more jobs, better schools, more cars, telephones and dishwashers. Nearly twice as many working class people voted Tory in Tory Britain than did in Labour Britain.[15]

The anti-socialist majority was very largely the south against the north. The 1983 General Election established a hegemony whereby a Conservative government could govern, or at least hope to be re-elected, without much deference to the other and less prosperous half of the nation. Tory Britain ruled. Margaret Thatcher was its ruler.

3
PICKING UP THE PIECES

9
Prime Ministerial Government

The tasks facing Margaret Thatcher at the beginning of her second administration were those left unfinished from her first. She had yet to arrest and reverse the nation's decline, yet to confine socialism to the attic of history. To achieve these goals there would need to be, she believed, a profound change in national attitudes, some kind of moral regeneration which would replace the collectivist mentality which had ruled since the War with a thrusting spirit of enterprise. She had frequently insisted that the task she had set herself would take ten years or more – at the very least two full terms of office. Here she was embarking upon her second term, the first Prime Minister in this century to win a second after a full first term in office, in her case by a landslide, and yet she had no strategy for completing her revolution, scarcely a programme enough to keep Parliament busy. The General Election of June 1983 had been called in a hurry while the going was good. She had been urged by campaign advisers, notably the Conservative Party chairman, Cecil Parkinson, to strike while the 'Falklands Factor' was still hot. There was insufficient time, and insufficient thought, to compile a radical Manifesto. Said one disgruntled colleague, 'She thinks that her own re-election is all that is necessary to save the country.'

The 1983 Manifesto prescribed more of the same but in bland and reassuring terms. It had been launched in the blue womb of the conference hall at Conservative Central Office to the accompaniment of musak. Inflation would be brought lower, public expenditure and borrowing firmly controlled, the taxes cut. This time there was a list of industries to be privatised but nothing to indicate the role which

Program for 2nd Term

privatisation would come to play in the second phase of Thatcherism. Union members were to be given the right to secret ballots – 'giving the unions back to their members', this was called – but nothing was proposed for curbing the right to strike in essential industries. Mrs Thatcher herself, it was said, had insisted upon the inclusion of a pledge to abolish the Greater London Council and six other Metropolitan Authorities. She had described these as 'the last vestiges of feudal power'. She had also insisted on a renewed commitment to rate reform, having herself promised to abolish them in 1974 when she had been the Shadow spokesman on the matter.

These reforms of local government – which were to occupy an inordinate amount of parliamentary time – were scarcely the most urgent problems facing the country, although they were relevant to her goal of destroying the remaining bastions of socialism. The reform of the Welfare State, from which she had flinched during the expenditure review of 1982, was not at the top of the agenda. (As always, however, there were allegations that a 'secret agenda' existed.) The published manifesto pledged the government to maintain the real value of the retirement pension and other benefits. It turned out that getting on for two-thirds of the vast cost of social security was protected by election pledges. All in all, the manifesto did not read like a prospectus for permanent revolution.

However, manifestoes are as nothing to the authority which electoral victory confers upon a government and a Prime Minister. Mrs Thatcher had gone to the country as herself, her style of doing things and her ideological intentions as clear as could be. Her victory had been overwhelming, at least in terms of seats. If it was argued – and, of course, it was – that 57 per cent of the votes cast had been against her, she could riposte that 72 per cent had been cast against the Labour Party and socialism. She had all the authority she needed to do what she would, if she knew how.

Her first move was to sack her Foreign Secretary. Had she fallen as a consequence of the Falklands expedition, Francis Pym very likely would have succeeded her. Now he was out. He had annoyed her during the campaign by observing – correctly, it soon was to seem – that 'Landslides on the whole don't produce successful governments.' But, in any case, she had never liked him, simply couldn't get on with him – nor he with her. Pym was an officer and a gentleman from Cambridgeshire stock going back to the Civil War. She disliked his gloomy disposition, even the way he sat at Cabinet table, shoulders hunched in despondency. To her he represented the defeatism which had for too long pervaded the natural ruling class.

She was the mistress now. With two of her protégés, Nigel Lawson and Leon Brittan, promoted to the Treasury and the Home Office and the ever-obedient Geoffrey Howe transferred to the Foreign Office, the Cabinet now became the complete instrument of her will. James Prior remained banished to the Irish bog while Peter Walker was transferred to the Department of Energy – our nearest equivalent to a Siberian power station – where he occupied the very same room in which Tony Benn had languished under Wilson and Callaghan. Her most adored favourite, Cecil Parkinson, the architect of her victory, was promoted from the Central Office to her least favourite spending department, Trade and Industry. This was to the great chagrin of Norman Tebbit, Parkinson's chief rival for her favours. Indeed, he had believed the job to be his and had his bags packed at the Department of Employment.

The reason for Tebbit's last-minute disappointment was not to transpire until some months later when the Parkinson Affair, or rather Parkinson's affair with Sarah Keays, became a public scandal. His mistress had become pregnant in April and on the night of the great Conservative triumph at the polls he had been obliged to inform the Prime Minister of the tangle in his personal life. For all her public moralising Margaret Thatcher was no prude; she herself was married to a divorcé. Her advice to Parkinson was to stay with his wife; she saw no need for him to resign from the government. However, she did now abandon her plan to reward her campaign manager with the Foreign Secretaryship no less. That would have left no doubt about his status as her heir apparent. Instead she accommodated Parkinson at the DTI, at the expense of Norman Tebbit's ambition. Miss Keays revealed her highly-damaging side of the story to *The Times* on the eve of Mrs Thatcher's keynote speech to the Conservative Party conference in Blackpool that October. Parkinson was obliged to resign. Norman Tebbit moved in to the Department of Trade and Industry.

The Parkinson Affair was the first of many mishaps which plagued Mrs Thatcher's second administration from its earliest days. Prime Ministers in their second term seem to become accident prone. In 1959 Harold Macmillan had led his party to a spectacular victory, its third in a row, within three years of the Suez débâcle which had destroyed Eden and brought him to power. Yet within three years everything had gone wrong for Macmillan and after sacking half of his Cabinet in 1961 – the wrong half was Wilson's joke – his administration ended in the Profumo scandal. John Profumo, the Minister of War, had an affair with a pretty call girl, Christine Keeler. Profumo lied to the Commons and was forced to resign. In June 1966 Harold Wilson turned the tiny majority he had scraped together in October 1964 into a near landslide. Yet it was then that his real troubles began. Gripped for a while by a strange lassitude, perhaps exhausted by the tactical exertions of his earlier survival trick, he lost his grip on events and his government stumbled from crisis to crisis until, in November 1967, there was no escaping a devaluation of the pound. Unlike Wilson in 1966 Margaret Thatcher had had four grinding years in what has increasingly become a destroying job. Like Wilson, perhaps, she had expended more emotional energy than she knew and suffered something resembling a post-electoral depression.

The government backbenches were crowded with new faces, men – and a sprinkling of women – many of whom had not expected to be there. Very quickly they grew to like the House of Commons – proverbially the best club in London – and had no wish to lose their marginal seats at the next election. Pym had been right. With a majority of 144 the Parliament was much more difficult to manage than with the 1979 majority of 45, which had seen her comfortably through the previous one. A smallish working majority keeps a party, and a government, on its toes; a landslide is bad for party discipline, enabling rebellion with impunity. Radical Thatcherites by conviction, instinct or in tone of voice as many of the new intake were, they were conservative enough – conservative, that is, with a small c – about anything which might lose them votes in their constituencies. They were more frightened of their postbags than of the Whips. Through 1984 and 1985 a series of backbench revolts occurred on such matters as university fees, which it was suggested the middle classes might in part pay for themselves, and the proposal to withdraw tax subsidies from private pension schemes. These revolts culminated in early 1986, following the Westland Affair, in the prevention of the break-up and sale of British Leyland and the defeat of a government Bill to permit trading on Sundays. Ironically, the size of her majority became one of the brakes on radical Thatcherism.

In the early sessions of the Parliament she was also in trouble on her own backbenches over the choice of the new Speaker, on banning trade unions at the GCHQ, housing benefits, rate support grants and the reform of local government. The dispute over the future of the Westland helicopter company provoked a major Cabinet crisis which shook the government to its foundations. In some cases these were revolts of the faithful in fear of their seats and inspired by middle class protest, in others they were rearguard actions by the High Tory wing of the party against what it took to be the excesses of Thatcherism. At one point, briefly, the flag of rebellion was hoisted by Pym himself. He announced the formation of a new inner party grouping to be called Conservative Centre Forward which, it was said, might on occasions defy the party Whip en bloc in favour of its own. The move contained the hint of a split in the Conservative Party. Pym had no intention of putting up against Thatcher for the leadership, if only because he knew that such a bid would be forlorn, but he was in effect declaring himself as a candidate for the succession. Some 32 Tory backbenchers, a good few from the old squirearchy of the party, had originally signed up for Conservative Centre Forward but some quickly backed out under pressure from the Whips or the big-wigs of their local parties. Pym himself was in trouble down in Cambridgeshire.

'Pym's rebellion' may have sounded like a Peasants' Revolt but in fact it was more of a patricians' reaction. Like most rebels, the supporters of Centre Forward regarded themselves as the defenders of true tradition; it was Thatcher, as they saw it, who had departed from the central stream of the Tory Party which they took to be the Disraelian tradition of 'one nation'. In part they were motivated in this by the fear that David Owen, who was making his mark as new leader of the SDP, would appropriate the Disraelian banner. In a recently published book, *The Politics of Consent*, Pym had written: 'my concern is that the flag of traditional Conservatism is kept flying, and that people are reminded of its values and worth, so that one day a standard bearer can pick it up and put it back at the centre of our affairs where it belongs.'[1]

By this time, which was May 1985, the miners' strike was over and the Falklands War had faded in the public's memory; there was no 'Scargill Factor' or 'Falklands Factor' to buoy up the Prime Minister's popularity. MP's were beginning to wonder whether, without such special factors, Thatcher and Thatcherism provided a winning combination for the future. The party had done badly in the recent local elections in the English shires. The grandee wing of the Tory Party disliked Mrs Thatcher for a number of reasons. Partly it was snobbish disdain for the politics of a shop-keeper's daughter; partly it was aversion to ideology, an 'ism, which lay uneasily upon what John Stuart Mill had named 'the stupid party'; and partly it stemmed from patrician concern for the 'condition of the people'. This last was the product in part of social conscience and in part of *noblesse oblige* and sheer prudence, their response to Joseph Chamberlain's rhetorical question: 'what ransom will property pay for the security it enjoys?' With three million unemployed in the land and the cities recently in riot, that question seemed real enough to some.

Thatcher, however, was having no nonsense about Disraeli. 'I am much nearer to creating one nation than Labour will ever be,' she declared. 'Socialism is two nations. The privileged rulers, and everyone else. And it always gets to that. What I am desperately trying to do is create one nation, with everyone being a man of property, or having the opportunity to be a man of property.'[2] That went for the 'wets' in her own party as well. There was much in what she said. Disraeli's famous remark – it comes in his novel *Sybil* – was: 'I was told that the Privileged and the People formed Two Nations'; but in 1985 it was the people who were, for the most part, the privileged, while the poor, the other nation, consisted chiefly of an underclass of the unemployed, underpaid, uneducated. That underclass had grown during the Thatcher years but so had the prosperity of the people. One of the profound changes underlying the Thatcher Revolution was the coming of age of the majority of the 'haves' over the minority of the 'have nots'. It had been the Labour Party which had claimed to speak for 'the people', while the Tory Party had – in Labour eyes – been the party of the ruling class, of landed interest and property. But now property was spreading among the people. The old model was no longer valid and Mrs Thatcher, the first wholly to grasp and exploit the change which was occurring in society, had converted the majority of the 'haves' into a political majority cutting across old party lines. That she had achieved this, and had – as Disraeli would have put it – 'dished the socialists', was not yet understood either by the Labour Party or by the old patrician guard of her own party.

Disraeli had had something to say also on the subject of local government, which was at this time a cause of trouble in the Tory Party. 'Centralisation is the death-blow of public freedom,' he had said.[3] Here again traditional roles had been reversed. It was the Conservatives who were now the centralisers, Labour the decentralisers. Indeed it was one of the ironies of Thatcherism, another way in which it departed from the mainstream tradition of the Conservative Party, that the power of central government needed to be invoked on an unprecedented scale in order economically to 'set the nation free'. As the Marxist commentator, Andrew Gamble, had well put it: 'The state is to be rolled back in some areas and rolled forward in others

. . . The real innovation of Thatcherism is the way it has linked traditional Conservative concern with the basis of authority in social institutions and the importance of internal order and external security, with a new emphasis upon free market exchange and the principles of the market order.'[4]

Local government reform divided the Conservative Party between those – Pym was one – who adhered to the traditional view of local democracy rooted in the shires and the boroughs, sustained by local squires and burgesses (Alderman Roberts of Grantham, for example), while others were of the opinion that reversing Britain's decline was too serious a business to be left to the sort of people who these days got themselves elected to the town and county halls.

The government had embarked upon reform for three reasons. One was that Mrs Thatcher had rashly pledged to abolish the rates as long ago as 1974 and even more rashly renewed it in the 1983 manifesto. A second was that she had been provoked by the left-wing antics of the Greater London Council under Ken Livingstone and decided to close it down, together with six other second-tier Metropolitan Authorities which had arisen out of the Heathite bureaucratisation of the early 1970s. The third was that the spending of the local authorities was inconsistent with the government's borrowing targets which were a part of the mumbo jumbo of monetarism.

Local authorities accounted for about a quarter of all public spending. Central government provided more than half of their income but had no control over their expenditures. Successive governments, Labour as well as Conservative, had found this highly unsatisfactory. Rates absorbed between 2 to 3 per cent of personal incomes, compared with 14 per cent in expenditure taxes and 12·5 per cent in income taxes, but were more painful to pay because they had to be handed over as a lump sum.[5] For both these reasons, it was widely agreed that the rating system was in need of reform. But nobody had been able to come up with an acceptable solution to the problem. The rapid inflation of the early 1970s had sparked off rates revolts and had led to Mrs Thatcher's promise of abolition. Labour in 1974 had appointed the Layfield Committee, which reported in 1976. It recommended a reduction in the government's share of local government finance from the then 67 per cent to nearer 50 per cent. Otherwise, it warned, local democracy would continue to be undermined by the unsatisfactory division of responsibility between central and local government.[6] But Labour did nothing.

After 1979 it was not ratepayers in revolt but zealous monetarists who kept the issue to the fore. 'Two very legitimate concerns of

central government', Nigel Lawson had said, were 'the overall burden of taxation and the total of public expenditure.' Another problem
was that many voters did not pay rates. In an electorate of 35 millions,
there were 18 million ratepayers compared with 21 million income-
tax payers. Moreover, some 6 million people received full or partial
rate rebates under the social security system. In Sheffield, for example, as many as 26 per cent did not pay, in London's Tower Hamlets
28 per cent. Thus the rate burden fell heavily on business. During the
government's first term rates had risen on average 91 per cent, other
prices 55 per cent. In consequence business was fleeing from the
cities, or so it was claimed. Heseltine had attempted to deal with the
problem by cutting the funds from the central government but instead
of cutting their spending accordingly many authorities had simply
pushed their rates still higher. Twenty local authorities had overspent
to the tune of £750 million in the four years since 1979. The government argued that since it was Parliament which had delegated
democratic power to local authorities they had breached the conventions of the Constitution by such overspending. This was true in
a strict constitutional sense, although it had been a purpose of the
Local Government Act of 1888 to diminish the power of the central
government.

The government now proposed to bring the big spenders to book
by capping their rates, that is, making it illegal for them to levy rates
above a certain prescribed level and thereby forcing them to reduce
their expenditures. This was the issue which posed the question of
whether the power of central government was growing too great
and ought to be diminished. A former Tory Minister, and a former
mayor, Geoffrey Rippon, told the Commons that rate-capping
would confer upon the central government, 'wide, sweeping general
powers of a kind that have not hitherto been regarded in this country
as being in accordance with the rule of law. We stand for the Town
Hall not Whitehall,' he declared, echoing the traditional Tory
view.

Similar doubts were felt about the proposal to abolish the GLC and
the other Metropolitan Authorities. They had never been popular in
the Conservative Party and were regarded as of doubtful utility.
Nevertheless, they were democratically elected bodies. The only
legitimate way to remove them was through the ballot box, argued
Pym. Edward Heath warned that to close them down would invite
reprisals of a similar nature if Labour returned to power. 'It seems to
me,' said Gilmour, the Highest Tory of them all, 'that the lack of
political scruple being shown is, at least, stupid.' All Tories wished to

spare the country from socialism but some believed that this would best be achieved by governing in a spirit of moderation and generosity. The Prime Minister believed that the best way to destroy socialism was to eradicate it in its strongholds. She was not in the business of putting off the evil day, her aim was to prevent it from ever happening. As Norman Tebbit put it, 'The Labour Party is the party of division. In its present form it represents a threat to the democratic values and institutions on which our parliamentary system is based. The GLC is typical of this new modern, divisive version of socialism. It must be defeated. So we shall abolish the GLC.'

On both Bills the government lost the argument but won the day. As Edward Heath pointed out, 'The fact that the Government have lost the argument has not been due in large measure to the efforts of the Opposition.' The more effective opposition to the march of Thatcherism was coming not from the Labour benches but from the government's own backbenches.

Thatcherism had some unpleasant implications for the middle classes which espoused it or, at least, espoused Mrs Thatcher. The middle classes gained considerable benefit from state subsidies, in the form of tax breaks, and made extensive use of the Welfare State, both of free education and the National Health Service. Although already by the autumn of 1984 ministers were alert to the danger of 'banana skins' – the favourite cliché of the time – Sir Keith Joseph managed to elude their grasp. In the course of that summer's public expenditure review in which, as a means of extracting money from the Treasury, spending ministers customarily make lavish bids in the hope of being scaled down only to their true requirements, Sir Keith – characteristically – volunteered cuts in his own budget. Too pure for politics, he deemed it immoral to ask for more when the logic of doing so was in conflict with the strategy he supported.

In consequence he now proposed to levy charges to recoup a portion of the cost of tuition at universities and other institutions of higher education. This would have saved the Treasury some £39 millions a year, £24 millions of which would be re-allocated to scientific research which had been badly impaired by government cuts and was the subject of an articulate and vocal lobby. What he proposed would have involved some 50,000 families with incomes of around £22,000 a year paying £725 a year towards their children's university fees while 180,000 would be worse off in some lesser degree. Families with higher incomes would have to pay more, up to a limit of £4,000 a year, and the scheme would be particularly severe for those on around £25,000 a year. In the previous year there had already been a tightening up on the housing benefits which students were entitled to claim.

Students' maintenance grants had long been means-tested but it had been a principle that tuition fees should be paid in full by the State on a universal basis. The Thatcher government was no respecter of such principles. Joseph queried the justice of the predominantly better-off minority whose children attended university being subsidised by the less-privileged majority of taxpayers, for that is what it amounted to. Moreover, he did not allow that education was solely a public good for it was also a highly desirable form of private consumption. In addition he pleaded 'the desperate plight of scientists' in support of his scheme, although their desperate plight was the result of government parsimony and many considered that cutting scientific research was hardly the best way to go about reversing Britain's industrial decline. However, the fees proposal was vigorously protested against by Conservatives in the constituencies who were not interested in such theorising. One complained to *The Times* in typical terms: 'Life assurance premium relief abolished, VAT imposed on home building improvements, and now punitive charges for higher education, all aimed squarely at those who hold to the principles of self-help and family betterment.' Cascaded with mail from their constituents, besieged at Westminster by students, 180 backbench Tories signed motions of protest. It was the largest backbench rebellion yet to occur. It was also the broadest. It brought together High Tory and Thatcherite, united those who cared about learning and the advancement of science and those who cared chiefly for the pockets of their £25,000-a-year constituents.

Although ill-judged, Joseph's plan had been consistent with the general thrust of Treasury policy. The Chancellor, Lawson, was eager wherever possible to save money on tax subsidies to enable him the more to reduce the basic rates of taxation. For example, in his Budget – as the correspondent to *The Times* complained – he had withdrawn tax relief from private life insurance policies. He now wished to do the same on the private pension schemes of companies, which would have yielded him a huge saving. He would also have liked to end the payment of child allowances regardless of means. The trouble was that the logic of the government's financial strategy was leading it once again into the no-go areas of the Welfare State, the areas from which it had flinched in 1982. Moreover, it was severely constricted by pledges made at election times. It had variously promised not to introduce hotel charges in hospitals, not to charge for GP services or make changes in the exceptions to prescription charging, and not to abolish mortgage tax relief. That was another reason why the privileged tax position of occupational pension funds was of such interest to the Chancellor. Later this too had to be abandoned. So did a move to decontrol rents. So did the plan to abolish the State Earnings-Related Pension Scheme (SERPS). The imperious style of the Thatcher prime ministership was in sharp contrast with her ability to push through reforms unpopular with her middle class supporters.

She saw herself as activist, not as arbiter of disputes. She had said on taking office, 'It must be a conviction government. As Prime Minister I could not waste time with any internal arguments.'[7] Her style in Cabinet was a tendency to lead rather than to take the voices. In any case, hers was the most insistent voice. Her Cabinet proceeded by argument rather than by discussion.[8] 'I take your point about frankness,' she wrote in reply to James Prior's letter of resignation. 'That's what Cabinets are for, and lively discussions usually lead to good decisions.' Francis Pym saw her as embodying the 'absolutist spirit of the age'.

Her dominance of the government was achieved partly through the force of her personality and partly by the technique of side-stepping the Cabinet whenever she could. 'I am the Cabinet rebel,' she once said. The number of Cabinet meetings a year was reduced to about half the post-war norm.[9] Ministers were mostly scared of her. To request an interview was to invite a detailed grilling on departmental policy. Only Sir Keith Joseph was masochist enough to enjoy that sort of thing. 'My eyes light up at the sight of her even though she's hitting me about the head, so to speak.'[10] Keeping the head down was the wiser course. She ruled through a web of ad hoc committees manned by trusties. For example, Prior and Pym were kept off the key economic policy committee and John Biffen, when he fell from her favour, was virtually excluded from the government although still occupying the important position of Leader of the House of Commons. When the decision was taken to ban trade unions from the intelligence headquarters (GCHQ) the first most Cabinet Ministers knew was when Sir Geoffrey Howe announced the decision in the Commons. It was a style well-suited to crisis management – the Falklands War, the miners' strike – but less so to crisis prevention.

Myths surround the subject of Cabinet government. In retrospect the previous age seems always a golden age of collective responsibility while the present is invariably taken to be the apotheosis of prime ministerial or presidential government. But according to the former Permanent Under-Secretary to the Treasury, Douglas Wass, 'The extent to which prime ministers behave like presidents and the extent to which they behave like chairmen of committees, varies almost randomly.'[11] Wilson was both in his time, Callaghan perhaps the best chairman since Attlee. The notion of 'first among equals' has long been a fiction. The prime minister of the day controls the agenda of the Cabinet and it is the prime minister who sums up. 'A majority of us think,' Mrs Thatcher would say, meaning, 'I think,' or, perhaps, 'Geoffrey and I think'. In addition the prime minister has the last word concerning the minutes. One reason why prime ministers keep business out of Cabinet is that nothing brought before Cabinet stays secret for long. Some 200 people see the most restricted Cabinet papers. But the power of a prime minister resides not in the institutions of the system but rather in the political standing of the incumbent. When prime ministers are up they are very, very up but when they are down they can be virtually powerless. Moreover, Mrs Thatcher's imperious style cut two ways: when matters did reach Cabinet she was defeated on more numerous occasions than any other post-war prime minister.

Her outsider mentality led her to regard government as a personal conspiracy against her. Her technique was to conspire against it. This she did by bringing in outsiders, by dealing directly with officials who took her fancy, by operating a network of trusties strategically placed in the departments. 'I think she instinctively dislikes anybody who is not helping in the wealth creation process,' said Sir Frank Cooper, then PUS at the Ministry of Defence. 'I'm not sure she dislikes civil servants in their own right. I don't believe she does. But I don't think that she regards them as a group of people who are contributing to the wealth of the nation.'[12] Hers was a highly personal and frequently arbitrary style of governing. Her private office at Number 10 hectored and bullied the private offices of her departmental Ministers. 'I was quite amazed at the rudeness of the letters that came round,' said one. The leak was also an instrument of her personal power. Pym first learnt he was for the chop from the newspapers, actually during the 1983 General Election campaign. The word was out against him. It happened to others. When Prior was endeavouring to establish a new assembly in Northern Ireland her own parliamentary secretary, Ian Gow, lobbied against it among backbenchers.

The outsiders she brought in or the officials she promoted were by no means invariably 'yes' men. Anthony Parsons, whom she installed at Number 10 as her foreign policy adviser (to Pym's annoyance) on one occasion dared even to tell her once to shut up. That had been at

Chequers during the Falklands War. 'Excuse me, Prime Minister, but would you mind allowing me to finish,' he had said. Often the people she took a fancy to came from similar backgrounds to her own and were not of the Establishment. They were grammar school not public school, men like Peter Middleton, an irreverent monetarist whom she made PUS at the Treasury in succession to the unreconstructed Keynesian Wass.

But she did not transform the role of prime minister in any institutionalised sense.[13] Richard Crossman had argued many years before that the tendency towards presidential or 'prime ministerial government' could not be resisted and would better be institutionalised. Wilson for a while had talked vaguely of making 'a power house' at Number 10. But as Douglas Hurd had discovered while serving as Heath's political secretary, Number 10 remained more of a private house than an office. Thatcher was an imperial Prime Minister in style but, like her predecessors, did little to increase the power of her office. Her attitude was that it was better to get on with the job than to waste time worrying about the tools. Her staff at Number 10 consisted of half-a-dozen senior officials. One of them on arrival reported, 'Any idea that you have a power house running things from Number 10 is entirely misplaced. I soon discovered that it was done with brown paper tied up with string.' Only the most trusted cronies or advisers were admitted to the flat upstairs. There she would kick off her shoes and cook bacon and eggs for her officials. Lloyd George is not known to have cooked. Hers was the first literal 'kitchen cabinet'.

The style in which she governed became an issue in the Westland Affair, which was by far and away the most serious of the difficulties of her second term. It was the nearest she came to nemesis. In a television interview during the 1987 General Election David Frost challenged her gently with the suggestion that on 27 January 1986, she had said, 'I may not be Prime Minister by six o'clock tonight.' She could easily have denied it. Instead she said, 'You suddenly come out with these things. I would not necessarily take them as if they had any very great deep significance.'

Exactly how close to the brink she did come has never been properly established and perhaps never will. Some say she did, some say she didn't, but some know or saw more than others and no one was witness to the whole story. It is said that by the end of the affair she was reduced to tears and it may have been in a moment of misery or depression that she made that desperate remark on the day she was to face the emergency debate in the House of Commons which was tantamount to a motion of censure against her.

The Westland Affair destabilised the government and left it profoundly demoralised. Yet, as one Cabinet Minister said afterwards, 'It was about nothing, absolutely nothing.' Ostensibly it had been about helicopters. Westland was Britain's only helicopter manufacturer and it had been in financial difficulties for some while. By 1985 it was facing bankruptcy and unless a solution was found for its difficulties would by mid-December become insolvent. The American company Sikorsky was prepared to take a minority stake in Westland sufficient to save it. But this would mean Britain becoming dependent on the United States for helicopters, which had come to play an increasingly important role in modern warfare, as in Vietnam for example. An alternative would be some form of European association or consortium.

It was suspected that Sikorski was interested in Westland only because it wished to secure a foothold within the common market of the European Community and because it wanted to sell its Black Hawk helicopter to the British government. The defence chiefs didn't want it. The European manufacturers had an interest in keeping Sikorski out of their markets if they could. Collaboration might enable them better to compete in American markets.

As the problems of the company became more urgent the government looked increasingly to the quickest available solution, which was Sikorski. Its market philosophy prejudiced it in this direction. Leon Brittan, who was the Secretary of State for Trade and Industry, had begun with an open mind about the European alternative – if such there was – but at an early meeting of the committee of the Cabinet which was handling the issue he had said: 'I don't give a toss if Westland goes to the wall and I'm not going to spend a penny of DTI money.'

The Secretary of State for Defence, Michael Heseltine, was an ardent European and as a junior Minister in the Edward Heath government had championed European aero-space collaboration. He came to see the government's growing partisanship for Sikorski as a mark of its anti-Europeanism. Later in the affair he was to tell a friend that he had been sickened by the poison which poured from the Prime Minister's lips concerning Europe.

These were the familiar tensions of the Thatcher government, between free marketeers and interventionists, between enthusiasts and unenthusiasts for Europe, and there was no reason why they should now produce a major Cabinet crisis. But they did. The problems faced by Westland provided Margaret Thatcher and Michael Heseltine with their opportunity to lock horns, something they had been waiting to do for some time.

She regarded him with suspicion, as she did all potential rivals. When his name was mentioned, 'Michael,' she used to say, 'he is not one of us.' Back in February, long before a helicopter had appeared on the horizon, she had suspected him of looking for a resignation issue which would enable him to set up against her from the back-benches. Paranoia is one of the many occupational hazards of a prime minister. However, she was not far wrong in this case. Heseltine was becoming increasingly disaffected by her style of governing. He believed that if she continued as she went she would lose the next General Election. He hoped that the Conservative Party might look instead to his own more traditional, more paternalistic brand of radical Conservativism. By the time of the Conservative Party conference at Blackpool that autumn he certainly had resignation in mind – although not over helicopters.[14]

The argument within the government over Westland came to a head in December 1986. On 9 December Sir John Cuckney, the chairman of the company, was invited to attend a meeting of a Cabinet committee under the chairmanship of the Prime Minister. For the chairman of a commercial company to attend such a meeting was in itself unusual. He urged the government to leave the decision to the Westland board, which was what Brittan and Thatcher wished to do. Heseltine once more pressed the European suit. He succeeded in winning time. He was allowed a week in which to put together convincingly the European consortium he had been talking about.

The Prime Minister later saw this as her big mistake. She should there and then have slapped him into line. She should have insisted on collective responsibility for a Cabinet decision to allow Westland to decide its own future. She should have accepted his resignation if necessary. But she did none of these things. She was too afraid of him.

Heseltine's understanding following the 9 December meeting was that there would be a further meeting of the committee the following Friday. The Prime Minister's understanding was that it had been decided in any case that the decision was for the Westland board not for the government. When the full Cabinet met the following Thursday Heseltine discovered to his rage that there was to be no meeting the following day, no further meeting at all. He claimed that the meeting had been cancelled. The Prime Minister claimed that none had been arranged. The reason it had been cancelled, he believed, was that his European initiative had succeeded. He had been permitted to go ahead with it, he was now convinced, only because his opponents were sure that he would fail. Now it was plain that the Prime Minister and Leon Brittan were wedded to the Sikorski deal come what may. He demanded that his protest about the cancelling of the meeting be recorded in the Cabinet minutes. It was not.[15]

The following day the Westland board, as was to be expected, rejected the European proposal. Heseltine from that point set out to campaign for his solution to the problem. What ensued now was an increasingly open inter-departmental row between the MOD and the DTI. It was an unscrupulous affair on both sides. When such civil wars break out in Whitehall a standard weapon is the press leak. There is nothing particularly reprehensible about leaking to the press. In the relatively closed British system of government it enables a policy argument to be conducted in public or semi-public. In more open systems bureaucratic battles are fought in semi-public. There would have been nothing in the least remarkable about the way Heseltine set about trying to reverse the government's policy had London been Washington. He waged a war of leaks.

But London was not Washington. His activities increasingly became an embarrassment to the government and an annoyance to the Prime Minister. In the last week before Christmas she did consider sacking him. Some told her she should, some told her she shouldn't. John Wakeham, the Chief Whip, was one who favoured keeping him on board.

The name Heseltine was not far from her mind during the family festivities at Chequers that year. No sooner was Christmas over – what a relief to be back at her desk – than she launched a new move to bring Heseltine to heel. It was arranged that Sir John Cuckney should write to the Prime Minister requesting clarification of the European consequences of going ahead with the Sikorski tie-up. Heseltine had been alleging it would mean the virtual exclusion of British helicopters from the European market. Thatcher's draft reply to Sir John reached Heseltine on New Year's Eve. He considered the letter to be tendentious and inaccurate. He consulted the Solicitor General, Sir Patrick Mayhew, who advised that the government ought to warn Westland that there had been some indications of anxiety from Europe about the arrangement with Sikorski. Heseltine wanted to specify these threats in some detail. Eventually Downing Street added a vague health warning to its original letter and sent it off.

Heseltine then contrived an opportunity to put his own version on record. He inserted all of the language the Prime Minister had